ALL ABOUT EXCHANGE-TRADED FUNDS

ALL ABOUT EXCHANGE-TRADED FUNDS

ARCHIE M. RICHARDS, JR., CFP

McGraw-Hill

New York Chicago San Francisco Lisbon London
Madrid Mexico City Milan New Delhi San Juan
Seoul Singapore Sydney Toronto

The **McGraw·Hill** Companies

1 2 3 4 5 6 7 8 9 0   DOC/DOC   0 9 8 7 6 5 4 3 2

ISBN 0-07-139302-1

McGraw-Hill books are available at special discounts to use as premiums and sales promotions, or for use in corporate training programs. For more information, please write to the Director of Special Sales, Professional Publishing, McGraw-Hill, Two Penn Plaza, New York, NY 10011. Or contact your local bookstore.

This publication is designed to provide accurate and authoritative information in regard to the subject matter covered. It is sold with the understanding that the publisher is not engaged in rendering legal, accounting or other professional service. If legal advice or other expert assistance is required, the services of a competent professional person should be sought.
—*From a Declaration of Principles Jointly Adopted by a Committee of the American Bar Association and a Committed of Publishers and Associations.*

This book is printed on recycled, acid-free paper containing a minimum of 50% recycled de-inked paper.

Library of Congress Cataloging-in-Publication Data

Richards, Archie M.
    All about exchange-traded funds / by Archie M. Richards, Jr.
      p. cm.
    Includes bibliographical references and index.
    ISBN 0-07-139302-1 (pbk.: alk. paper)
    1. Exchange traded funds. I. Title.
  HG6043.R53 2002
  332.63'27—dc21   2002011406

*This book is dedicated with thanks and love to my wife
Carolyn Younglove Richards*

CONTENTS

ACKNOWLEDGMENTS

Many thanks to Dianne Fezza, of the American Stock Exchange, and Jay Baker, of Spear, Leeds, and Kellogg, for the fascinating and enlightening visit they hosted for me at the American Stock Exchange.

It was indeed a pleasure to talk with Nate Most, the father of exchange-traded funds.

I appreciate the patience of J. Parsons and Lana Ariue at Barclays Global Investors for their responses to my pesky questions. I am grateful also to Mitch Cox, of Merrill Lynch, Bryan Reilly, of State Street Global Advisors, Maureen O'Shea, of Standard & Poor's, and Michael Babel and Clifford Weber, both of the American Stock Exchange, for their conscientious responses to my questions. Many thanks to Gene Kunda, of the Chicago Board of Trade, for teaching me so patiently about the niceties of warehouse receipts, to Margaret Starner, of Raymond James Financial, for her explanation of zero-cost collars, and to Ken Fincher and Kathleen Cardoza for enlightening me about Nuveen Investments offerings.

Thanks to Ron Ryan, of Ryan Labs, for explaining his intriguing offerings. Derek Sasveld, of Brinson Partners, and Mike Gmitter, of Securities Research Company, were most helpful in furnishing information for charts.

I do appreciate the assistance of Whitman Miller and Melissa Hagan on technical matters.

Thanks to Neville Golvala, of ChoiceTrade for reviewing the chapter on trading.

Many thanks to Jack Treynor for opening windows of opportunity.

CHAPTER 1

What Are ETFs?

June's father was as certain as he'd ever been that the fledgling technology company he talked about so excitedly would become a huge success. Every penny he had in the world he dumped into the stock.

Oh, he had plans. A second home on the Gulf, near Sarasota, Florida. A Caddy out front. A sleep-in boat, parked in the canal out back. He had it all down—what he was going to do with the money when that little company became a big success.

But just three years later, all those plans floated out the window when the company went down the tubes into bankruptcy. At least her father hadn't mortgaged his little house in Detroit. There he would remain for the rest of his life. No Cadillac. No boat. Not much going for him, frankly. It was sad.

June had a pretty good job. She'd accumulated some money. No way was she going to rely on just a single enterprise. But she did have the feeling that America as a whole would continue to thrive. More than 100 million people, some of them fabulously inventive, working and creating. If only there were some way she could buy into that wholesome economy—a single stock that would capture that marvelous productivity. She found it. An exchange-traded fund.

She could buy it through a brokerage firm just as easily as her father had acquired that dumb venture. Even easier, in fact. Instead of talking with a real-live broker, she chose to acquire the exchange-traded fund online. For a commission of only $8.00, she could buy into the whole of the U.S. economy.

The investment seemed so insignificant, but it tracked 3000 U.S. companies. Three thousand, including big ones and a whole lot of little ones. Unless some disaster knocked everyone to kingdom come, June knew that those businesses couldn't all fail. As the United States goes, her one little investment would go. She didn't intend to sell, but if she had to, the stock could be sold just as easily as it was acquired. How did they come up with such an investment?

In 1993, a remarkable new financial vehicle, called an exchange-traded fund, came into being. This one didn't track 3000 stocks; that came later. But it did track 500, which is a lot. It opened up new vistas for traders and investors alike. Each exchange-traded fund (ETF) can be bought and sold as readily as shares of IBM stock, yet each represents an entire aggregation of companies.

The growth of equity exchange-traded funds all over the world has been extraordinary. As of this writing in December 2001, they number 199, plus 17 quasi-ETFs. They trade in the United States, numerous European exchanges, South Africa, Israel, Singapore, Hong Kong, Japan, and Australia. Other ETFs are being prepared for Indonesia, Thailand, and Turkey, not to mention the United States. The values of all exchange-traded funds so far total $103 billion. During the week prior to Thanksgiving, 2001, the most popular exchange-traded fund, the Nasdaq 100 Fund, traded an average of $3.3 billion per day. During the same week, the original ETF, called "Spiders," traded $2.8 billion daily.

Some exchange-traded funds track the U.S. stock market in its entirety. Others track foreign markets or individual industries. But all can be traded quickly and easily, as if they were single stocks.

If you're an experienced investor, you may have discovered that trading—at least rapid trading—is a marvelously efficient way to lose money. If you're a novice investor, plan, right from the start, on doing the job right. Use exchange-traded funds, by all means. But use them for their convenience, simplicity, and their ability to defer capital gains taxes. Do not trade ETFs. Be a long-term investor.

HAVING A LOT LATER ON

The goal of financial planning and investing is to maximize how much you'll have when you need the money. Since you're thinking about investing now, presumably some of your money doesn't need to be spent at this time. We're talking about having a lot later on.

Oh sure, the investments you select and the rates of return are important. But they're not the most important aspect of investing. The essential ingredient is to invest as much as possible now. You're continually faced with trade-offs between the present and the future. If you think hard, any number of things might come to your mind, for example, that you'd like to buy. A three-month trip to the Andes for example. If you're under the control of a foot fetish, 1000 pairs of shoes wouldn't be half enough. But the more you spend now, the less you'll have later to educate children or provide a long and fulfilling retirement. To illustrate how to have a lot later on, let's say you're a lousy saver and a good investor. You put aside $50 a month. The money appreciates at 12 percent a year for 25 years. The ending value is $93,900.

Alternatively, assume you're a good saver and a lousy investor. You set aside $200 a month. But the money appreciates at only 6 percent a year for 25 years (not 12 percent). The ending value is a respectable $138,600. We quadrupled the amount saved and halved the rate of return. The final result is considerably more than $93,900.

Being a good saver is harder than being a good investor. In Chapter 11, I suggest investments you need to review only every 13 months. But why not be a good saver and a good investor too? You set aside $200 a month. The money appreciates at 12 percent a year for 25 years. You end up with $375,700. Now we're really getting somewhere.

Shoot for at least 10 percent. I'm going to show you how to accomplish this—or something like 10 percent—using mostly exchange-traded funds and without your having to watch the darn things every other minute. Since 1946, U.S. stocks have appreciated at a little more than 12 percent a year. During this time, the United States went through thick and thin.

Just equal the market, and you'll come out fine. But remember this: The rate at which the money grows is less important than the rate at which you set money aside. The key is to start now. The sooner, the better. We've already seen that if you invest $200 a month at 12 percent a year for 25 years, you end up with $375,700. Let's assume instead that the starting time is a year from now. You begin then, in 12 months, to invest $200 a month at 12 percent a year, this time for 24 years. The ending value is $331,200.

You cut down the investment time by 1 year out of 25. That's a 4-percent reduction in the number of years. But the ending value falls by a whopping 12 percent ($331,200 is 12 percent less than $375,700). The one lousy year missed at the beginning has a disproportionate effect. You reduce the number of years by 4 percent but end up with 12 percent less.

Instead of missing a year of savings at the beginning, this time you miss a year of savings at the end. You start now, setting aside $200 a month. The funds grow at 12 percent a year for 24 years, resulting in $331,200. You then knock off the investing, but the money already invested continues growing for one more year at 12 percent. The ending value is $370,900.

When you put in $200 a month for the entire 25 years, the ending value is $375,700. When you discontinue investing during the final year and the money continues to appreciate at the same 12-percent rate, the ending value is $370,900.

A missed year at the beginning causes the final balance to decline by 12 percent. A missed year at the end causes the final balance to decline by only 1.3 percent. You might call this the magic of compounding. There are two ingredients: time and the rate of appreciation. Most people concentrate on the rate of appreciation and forget about the time. This is understandable. We live in the now, one moment at a time. Oh sure, we know that things change. But our thoughts and feelings at any one moment have far more meaning and impact than what came before or what will come in the future. Therefore, we forget about the importance of time.

In your investment life, I don't want you to forget about time. I want you to shoot for an attainable rate of appreciation, and I want you to achieve this over as long a time as you can, starting as soon as you can.

CREDIT CARDS

Let's say you're paying 19-percent interest on credit cards. Instead of paying off the cards as rapidly as possible, you're wondering whether you should instead place some of your money into investments.

Let's assume that the last dollar you earn in salary is federally taxed at 27 percent. Interest or dividends earned from your investments are taxed at 27 percent also, piling on top of your salary. But if you acquire an investment and hold it for at least a year and a day, any profit is taxed at a maximum of only 20 percent, regardless of how high a tax bracket your salary carries you.

We'll forget about dividends for now and assume you earn nothing on your investments except capital gains taxed at 20 percent. If you want to invest before the credit cards are paid off, you want the returns to at least equal the 19 percent you're paying on the credit cards. To end up with 19 percent appreciation after tax, the investment must grow at 23.75 percent, pretax. This rate of return, reduced by 20-percent capital gains tax, equals 19 percent.

At 23.75 percent, you're at nearly twice the 12-percent rate I want you to shoot for. But even 23.75 percent isn't enough. Unless you can earn *more* than 19 percent after tax, why bother with diverting the money from the credit cards to invest at all? No, you'd have to shoot for something like 30 percent a year, every year. After all, the 19 percent is charged to you consistently. You'd have to earn 30 percent consistently.

Believe me, you won't. Nobody consistently invests money at 30 percent—nobody. Until the high interest debt on your credit cards is repaid, forget about investing. The best way for you to save is to get rid of that debt as soon as you can.

THE HOUSE

Exchange-traded funds are remarkably sophisticated investment vehicles. You'll get the feel for them as we go along. But any kind of complete description can't be attempted until we nail down a number of other things. We're going to visit a four-story house. In the basement is finance, which lies at the foundation of any investment program. You probably don't spend much time in the basement of your house, and we won't spend much time with finance either. Then, in successive floors, come the following:

- Stocks and bonds
- Indexes
- Mutual funds
- Index funds
- In the penthouse, exchange-traded funds

THE BASEMENT: FINANCE

The entire world of investments arises because the people who make the goods we use have to keep eating. But the goods they make must be designed, manufactured, sold, shipped, and paid for. There's a delay, often a long delay, before the revenues come in. If new technology is involved and the goods are newly developed, payment doesn't arrive until years after the job is first undertaken. If you're one of the extraordinary Silicon Valley people who are exploring new ways of manipulating electrons and photons of light, the payoff probably won't arrive for a good long time. Meanwhile, you and the people who work for you want a building to work in. You want to turn the lights on when you're working late. You have to develop ways of bringing your product to the public's attention. (With so much claiming the public's attention, this takes money, too.) To obtain the funds for these and many other purposes, either you have to borrow money from people who have some to spare or you have to offer them partial ownership of your business. To the members of the public who lend you money, you provide bonds (IOUs). To those who become partial owners, you give stock in your corporation.

Even companies that have been around for a while offer additional bonds or stock when they need more financing. Let's say that, 100 years ago, General Electric (founded by the remarkable Thomas Edison) sold stock to the public to finance the development and sale of electric motors. In current parlance, this is called an initial public offering, or IPO. Those primitive motors no longer exist, except in museums, and the investors who bought the original General Electric stock are dead. But the stock isn't dead. The shares continue to be passed around from investor to investor today.

Let's say that General Electric later needed to finance the building of factories to make refrigerators. It sold new stock to the public (called a secondary offering). Some of those investors are dead, too. But that additional stock, combined with the original GE stock, continues to be passed from one investor to another. If you buy General Electric stock today, you're not doing so because of GE's past. You don't care which of the company's shares you're buying; they're all the same anyway. You're buying a small portion of ownership because of what you expect the company to accomplish in the future.

So much for finance. That's it for the basement. Now let's walk up to the first floor.

THE FIRST FLOOR: STOCKS

Stocks represent shares of ownership of corporations. Here are aspects of stocks that pertain to exchange-traded funds.

Dividends: The profits you enjoy from stocks come from two sources. (Pssst, if you buy and sell too much, there won't be any profits.) Some companies pay out a portion of their earnings to shareholders in the form of dividends. The dividends are cash in hand, usually paid every quarter. You can spend them, if you like, but they're part of your investment package. If you can arrange it, reinvest the dividends back into one or more of your investments. Dividends are taxed to the recipient at high rates, as if they were salaries.

The other portion of your profit stems from buying the stock low and selling high. This is called appreciation. If you've held the stock for at least a year and a day, the tax on such a long-term capital gain is capped at only 20 percent maximum. Note that I said at least a year *and a day*. If you buy a stock on April 1 and sell it a year later on April 1, sorry, that's a short-term profit, taxable at your highest tax rate, as if the money were earned in salary. Maybe this is the IRS's idea of an April Fool's joke. In any month, the joke's on you. You must hold for at least a year and a day. To generate long-term gains, you'd have to sell on April 2 or later.

If your top tax bracket on ordinary income is only 15 percent, rather than 28 percent, the tax rate on long-term capital gains is reduced to 10 percent.

More good news. The tax reduction act of 2001 provides that if you hold an investment for five years (and a day), the long-term capital gains rate is only 18 percent, not 20 percent. And if your top tax on ordinary income is only 15 percent, the capital gains tax on securities held for at least five years is reduced to 9 percent. These are no small matters. I want you to hold exchange-traded funds indefinitely. Not only are the tax rates lower, you also give yourself the opportunity to gain appreciation on money you didn't pay out in taxes. Yes, you'll probably have to pay taxes eventually, but because of the favorable compounding effect, you end up reducing your taxes overall.

The portion of earnings that is paid out to shareholders as dividends is not deductible to the corporation. But the portion of earnings that is reinvested by the corporation in its own growth is indeed deductible to the corporation. Companies don't like to pay taxes any more than anyone else. They do like to reinvest for growth. Therefore, U.S. corporations are generally paying a relatively small portion of their earnings in dividends and reinvesting a relatively large portion of earnings into the company's growth. More rapid growth makes the stock price rise faster, which enables the shareholders to enjoy the low tax rates of long-term capital gains. By suppressing dividends and expanding the reinvestment of earnings, corporations reduce their taxes and enable shareholders to cut theirs as well. Dividend yields (the annual dividend per share divided by the price per share) have gone down, sure, but this doesn't mean that you're the loser. More of your total return should stem from price appreciation, taxed at lower rates. Corporations lower their taxes, and you lower yours. Everyone wins except the IRS.

There's a little problem, however. Dividends are pretty much cash in hand. Appreciation, on the other hand, is indefinite. In the long-term, say, 10 years, prices almost always go up. But in the next year or two, who knows? A lot of people think they know what's going to happen to stock prices in the next year or two. But they don't, not consistently. I mean *any* year or two, you understand, not just the two years after you happen to read this book. Relying more on appreciation and less on dividends does save taxes, but it requires more patience.

Splits: When a corporation increases its earnings rapidly, the price of its stock usually rises. But when the price rises too high, investors tend to shy away. How high is too high varies from one stock to another. IBM usually favors its stock price remaining above 100. Others consider 60 to be too high. To bring the price down to where investors feel comfortable buying, corporations arrange for stock splits.

Let's say you own 200 shares of XYZ, and the current price is $60 a share. The company undertakes a 3-for-2 stock split. For every two shares you owned before, the company wants you to own three shares. Having owned 200 shares before, you now hold 300. The price was $60 before; now it's $40. The stock split does not change the value of your holding. Three hundred shares at $40 ($1200) have exactly the same value as two hundred shares at $60 (also $1200). The sole purpose of stock splits is to bring the price down to where investors feel more comfortable buying it. If IBM had never arranged any stock splits, each share would cost millions of dollars a share. Hardly anyone could afford to buy shares at such exalted levels, and IBM would be less of a company than it is today. Stock splits can also be 2-for-1, 3-for-1, 10-for-1—whatever the company's board of directors chooses.

Price-earnings ratios: When you buy a suit for, say, $200, you acquire something whose usage is worth $200 to you. But when you buy 10 shares of a stock at $20 a share, how can you evaluate whether the purchase is cheap or expensive?

Here's how: The stock is valued in terms of the company's earnings per share. If the earnings are $2 a share and you're paying $20 a share, you're buying the stock at a price that's 10 times the earnings per share. These days, that's cheap. The price is 10 times larger than the annual earnings. If the earnings do not increase, you'd have to wait 10 years for the cumulative earnings to equal the price you're paying. The earnings of such a company are probably expected to grow slowly.

Alternatively, let's say that the current year's earnings of the corporation are only $.50 a share. If the price is $20, the price-earnings ratio is 40, which is on the high side. (The average PE ratio for the stocks included in the Dow Jones Industrial Average at the time of this writing is 28.) The earnings of such a corporation are probably expected to grow rapidly, and the stock would be referred to as a growth stock.

Another way to evaluate the worth of a stock is to compare the price with the company's book value per share. Book value is a record of the company's historic costs and liabilities. If a company buys a truck for $50,000, that $50,000 is the truck's book value. As time goes on, this value is reduced by assumed usage, or depreciation. But no income is recorded until the truck is sold or salvaged. Until then, the truck's current market value is not taken into account on the company's books at all.

The book value of a corporation contains no estimate of the firm's current value; it's an historic record. The books show the total assets, reduced by the total liabilities. The net book value is then divided by the number of shares outstanding of the company's stock to arrive at the book value per share.

The term "book value per share" will come up again in the connection with the exchange-traded funds that are differentiated by "growth" and "value."

Capitalization: The market value of an entire company is the current price multiplied by the total number of shares outstanding.

The outstanding shares include those owned by employees, investment institutions, and the public. For example, Microsoft's price is $68. It has 5.39 billion shares outstanding, and its capitalization is therefore $366.5 billion. If Microsoft split its stock 2-for-1, the number of outstanding shares would double, but the capitalization would remain the same because the price would fall by half.

BONDS

Bonds are IOUs. Each bond pays $1000 at maturity. Some may mature tomorrow, others 30 years from now. Most bonds pay a specified, level amount of interest every half year.

Many investors confuse the interest *payments* of a particular bond, which remain constant, with the interest *rates*, which change continually for bonds. Assume that on August 15, 2003, you acquire 10 U.S. Treasury bonds due in 30 years on August 15, 2033. You buy the bonds at par, meaning that for the 10 bonds you pay $10,000. Thirty years later, the bonds will pay off at $10,000.

While you own the bonds, you'll receive $550 per year ($275 semiannually). At the time you buy them, the interest rate for Treasury bonds of 30-years maturity is 5.5 percent—hence the $550 interest payments per year.

The interest *payments* of the bonds remain constant throughout the 30 years. The date of maturity, August 15, 2033, remains unchanged. The value at maturity also remains unchanged at $10,000. But as Treasury bonds are bought and sold throughout the trading day, the interest *rates* for those Treasuries change constantly.

Let's see now. The interest payments, maturity date, and maturity value remain fixed. But the interest rates for bonds of a particular maturity change. Something has to give. What changes is the price of your bonds. As Treasury bonds are traded from one party to another, the prices fluctuate. You happened to have paid $10,000. A few seconds later, you might have paid a little more or a little less, depending on the then-current rate for 30-year Treasury bonds.

Ten years later, your bonds are no longer 30-year bonds. They will mature in 20 years. Assume that new 20-year bonds offered by the U.S. Treasury at that time are priced so that they yield only 4.5 percent. Ten bonds that pay $450 interest a year are priced at par, that is, at $10,000.

You then decide to sell your bonds. The buyer, note, can buy new bonds at par that pay $450 a year. But your bond pays $550 a year. You won't sell your bonds at the $10,000 par. No way. You'll insist that the buyer pay you more than par. Not counting commissions, the price would be $11,300.

The buyer pays $11,300. She receives $550 a year for 20 years. At maturity, 20 years later, she receives $10,000. The loss of $1300 on the principal value of the bonds pulls the net annualized yield down from 5.5 percent to 4.5 percent. For her, the "yield to maturity" on the bonds is 4.5 percent.

As interest rates fall from 5.5 percent to 4.5 percent, the price of the bonds rises from $10,000 to $11,300. Bond prices move opposite to the changes in interest rate. When interest rates go down, bond prices rise.

Alternatively, let's say that, during the 10 years you own the bonds, interest rates *rise* from 5.5 percent to 6.5 percent. New Treasury bonds of 20-year maturity paying $650 a year are selling at par. The buyer of your bonds won't pay par ($10,000) for your bonds because your bonds pay only $550 interest a year. The buyer insists that the price be less than $10,000. Not counting commissions, the price would be $8900.

Having paid $8900, the new owner receives $550 a year. Twenty years later, the bonds mature for $10,000. The profit from $8900 to $10,000, plus the annual interest payments, causes the net, annualized yield to maturity to be 6.5 percent a year. When interest rates rise, bond prices fall. Bond prices move opposite to the changes in interest rates.

CHAPTER 2

Spreading Risks

SPECIFIC RISK VERSUS MARKET RISK

Let's say you buy the stock of a company that builds houses in the Southeastern United States. Over the next couple of years, the nation's home-building industry performs well, and so does the stock market in general. But the company whose shares you bought is devastated by a severe hurricane in the region, and its stock price falls.

By acquiring the stock of a specific company, you take what is referred to as a specific risk. This is a considerable risk because, as the saying goes, you have all your eggs in one basket. Alternatively, by buying shares of all the stocks in the whole U.S. home-building industry, for example, the poor performance of those in the southeast are offset by the better performance in other regions. In the latter case, you still take a risk, of course. The industry as a whole might falter. This is called industry risk. But the danger of loss is reduced because your money is invested among many companies.

When you buy a fund that owns hundreds of stocks from all different industries in the United States, you take the risk that the entire U.S. market will falter. The danger of loss is further reduced.

About 15,000 U.S. stocks are publicly traded. (Hundreds of thousands more are owned privately and not available for public ownership.) You cannot acquire a single investment vehicle that enables you to participate in all 15,000 stocks. But you can acquire an investment vehicle that participates in over 3000 of them. Since these include all of the biggest companies, such an investment incorporates about 98 percent of the value of all publicly traded U.S. stocks. For the U.S. market, that's a low enough risk for me.

When you diversify still further and buy an investment that owns thousands of stocks from throughout the world, you take a worldwide market risk. This reduces your risk still further.

Some say, "The risks are greater in many foreign nations than they are in the U.S."

Maybe so. But wherever the risks are greater, the price-earnings ratios are lower, equalizing the risks for all nations.

Diversification increases safety. It makes the value of your portfolio less volatile. While one stock does poorly, another performs well. When the entire market falls to a significant extent, most stocks fall with it. Such risk is unavoidable. But you're better off spreading your money as widely as possible.

Exchange-traded funds (ETFs) provide marvelous opportunities to spread your risk among a multitude of stocks. Some ETFs track specific industries. Others track entire markets, both domestic and foreign. Yet despite the underlying complexity, each exchange-traded fund can be bought and sold like a single stock. Costs are minimized, except for brokerage commissions, which can be modest. Even though an exchange-traded fund tracks the performance of many stocks, the ETF shares appear as a single item on your brokerage statement. If you hold several ETFs representing different types of investments, spotting the value of each one is easy.

In the basement of our "house," we covered financing. On the first floor, stocks and bonds. Now let's walk up to the second floor and look at indexes.

AVERAGES AND INDEXES

The Dow Jones Industrial Average: Back in 1896, Charles H. Dow, Editor of the fledgling newspaper, *The Wall Street Journal,* had a problem. The readers were Wall Street investors, brokers, and market makers. The New York Stock Exchange closed each day at 3:00 p.m. (It closed earlier than it does now.) Mr. Dow wanted to provide some idea of how "the market" had performed by the time the readers went home.

Computers wouldn't be invented for another half century. Including printing and distribution, the editors had only an hour or so to calculate an average by hand. Out of the many stocks traded on the New York Stock Exchange, Mr. Dow selected 12 that seemed to have promise and represented the entire market as closely as possible. The number was later increased to 30. (For simplicity, we'll assume that 30 stocks were chosen from the beginning.)

Dow simply added up the prices of the 30 stocks and divided by 30. Presto—the Dow Jones Industrial Average. As the individual prices fluctuated, so did the average. Dow also prepared averages for railroad stocks and utilities.

Assume that every one of the 30 stocks included in the Dow Jones Average is priced at $60 a share. The average would be 60 (1800 divided by 30). What to do about stock splits, which change the stock's price but not the company's market value?

Let's see; we have 30 stocks, each priced at $60. The Dow average is also 60. On a single day, each of the stocks splits 2-for-1. The price of each one falls to $30.

But no one wants the average itself to fall to 30. After all, the capitalizations of the 30 companies don't change. The value of the U.S. economy doesn't suddenly fall by half. The companies simply split their stocks, to bring the prices down to where investors are more likely to buy them. Something has to adjust, right, to keep the average where it was?

What adjusts is the average's divisor. (For those who don't cotton to mathematics, that's the number on the bottom—the denominator.) The current prices of the stocks are $30. Multiplied by the 30 stocks gives $900. But this time, we don't divide by 30; we divide the $900 by only 15. The result: The average remains at 60. To reflect the stock splits, the divisor is moved downward.

As companies have grown and stock prices have risen, thousands of stock splits have occurred. The divisor of the Dow Jones Industrial Average has gone down, down, down. It's no longer 30, 15, or even 1. It is now just a small fraction of 1. As reported in a recent issue of *Barron's*, the divisor is 0.14452124.

Let's assume that the Dow Jones Average is exactly 10,000, and that the prices of the 30 stocks average $48.1737. Multiply by 30, and you get 1445.211. Divide by 0.14452124, and the average comes to 10,000.

The Dow Jones Industrial Average is price-based. The calculation works fine when you assume that only one share of each of the 30 stocks is included. The stocks whose prices are high have a greater impact on the average than the stocks whose prices are low.

Let's say the price of ABC is $100. It falls during the day by 2 percent, from $100 to $98. This causes the average to fall by 13.84 points ($2 divided by the 0.14452124 divisor).

XYZ's stock is priced, not at $100, but at $50. It also falls during the day by 2 percent, from $50 to $49. The Dow Jones average declines by only 6.92 points ($1 divided by the divisor). As you can see, the higher-priced stock has a greater impact on the average than the lower-priced stock.

In the long run, the differing price levels all come out in the wash. ABC might have a 2-for-1 stock split, bringing its price down from $100 to $50. (The denominator of the Dow Jones average would fall slightly.) But XYZ might enjoy a rapid increase in earnings, causing its price to rise from $50 to $100. The price positions of the two companies would reverse.

With 15,000 publicly traded stocks in the United States, the 30 that are included in the Dow Jones Industrial Average may seem of little consequence. But the Dow stocks are biggies. Those 30 companies constitute approximately 28 percent of the $12 trillion market value of all U.S. stocks.

The Standard & Poor's 500 Index: In 1943, Standard & Poor's, (a division of The McGraw-Hill Companies, Inc., publisher of this book), developed a different way of reflecting the market. Called an index, it reflects the changes in value of 500 of the largest U.S. corporations. Recall that a company's market value, the capitalization, is found by multiplying the total number of stocks outstanding by the current price. Standard & Poor's chose several hundred stocks it considered representative of the U.S. stock market (at first, there were fewer than 500 stocks). It calculated the capitalization of each of those stocks, added up those capitalizations, and assigned to this enormous number an index value of 10. Thereafter, as the capitalization of the stocks changed from day to day, the index changed by the same percentage. Standard & Poor's calculated the index back to 1926, when the index also happened to be 10. The S&P 500 Index is now 1123.09, higher than 10 by 112 times. This reflects the fact that the values of U. S. stocks have grown a tad.

Just as the Dow Jones is price weighted, the S&P 500 Index is capitalization weighted. To calculate the index, a single share of each of the 500 stocks won't do, as it does with the Dow. For each company included in the index, the price is multiplied by the total number of shares outstanding , resulting in the company's total market value. A percentage change in price of a company whose market value is $75 billion has three times more impact on the index than the same percentage change in price of a company whose total market value is only $25 billion.

Standard & Poor's thought it reasonable that its index be based on capitalization, because, after all, more money is invested in the stocks that have larger capitalizations. It seemed right that those companies should have a greater impact on the index than companies with smaller capitalizations.

The S&P 500 Index is top heavy. Even though the index includes 500 stocks, the market value of the largest ten constitute about 25 percent of the total. The five largest companies in the S&P 500 Index are General Electric, Microsoft, Exxon Mobil, Pfizer, and Wal-Mart.

Computers think fast these days. While the market is open, the Dow Jones and the S&P 500 are recalculated every 15 seconds.

Since the S&P 500 Index came into being, indexes have proliferated. Dow Jones and Standard & Poor's have each constructed numerous indexes based on various industrial groups. Morgan Stanley Capital International, Inc. (MSCI) has created indexes of foreign stock markets. The most inclusive index is the Wilshire 5000, designed by Wilshire Associates, an investment firm in Los Angeles. It covers more than 7000 stocks, representing about 98 percent of all publicly traded U.S. companies.

The Frank Russell Company, of Tacoma, Washington, offers three indexes: The Russell 1000 incorporates the 1000 largest U.S. companies. The Russell 2000 incorporates the 2000 next-largest companies. The Russell 3000 combines all 3000 stocks into a single index.

As the fortunes of companies change, the indexes change as well. If a company included in the S&P 500 absorbs another, for example, the index is left with 499 stocks. Standard & Poor's must select another to fill the hole. Also, if price changes cause a particular industry to bulk too large in the entire index, one or two companies might be removed from the index, replaced by companies from other industries. This is called rebalancing.

The Frank Russell Company gives its indexes a special, favorable twist. With almost all companies, some stock is unavailable for purchase. Stock owned by management or by certain investment institutions, for example, may never come to the market to be acquired by someone else. In determining the capitalization of a company, Russell removes from the calculation the unavailable stock. It multiplies the current price by the number of shares that are available for purchase by public investors. Companies whose shares are largely illiquid therefore have less impact on the index.

Now to the third floor, for mutual funds.

CHAPTER 3

Mutual Funds

A *mutual fund* is a pooling of funds belonging to thousands of investors, enabling them to share in the performance of a single portfolio of securities. Some mutual funds acquire just stocks, others bonds. A few acquire both. Some restrict the managers to certain kinds of securities; others don't.

Mutual funds are corporations, with shares owned by thousands of investors. The more money investors put in, the more of the fund they own. If the mutual fund holds stocks, for example, it's important to keep straight that the shares of stock owned *by* the mutual fund are different from the shares of stock *of* the mutual fund owned by the investors.

The tax code of the Internal Revenue Service exempts mutual funds from paying corporate income taxes. Instead, most of the tax consequences derived from the fund's investments are passed through to the investors who own the fund in proportion to their interests. An investor who owns a big chunk of the fund may have to report considerable taxable income in his or her individual tax return. (Mutual funds are not permitted to pass through losses.)

If you own shares of an individual company, like General Motors or AT&T, you have the option of taking delivery of the shares. You receive certificates, consisting of heavy paper with pretty engravings. The owners of some open-end mutual funds have the option of taking delivery. (Here, the paper's not so heavy, and mutual funds skip the pictures.) But most mutual fund owners do not take delivery of the shares. Instead, the number of shares held is recorded on periodic investor statements.

Although exchange-traded funds are easy to use, they're complicated. They bear similarities to each of the three types of mutual funds: open-end funds, closed-end funds, and unit investment trusts. The type they most resemble is open-end mutual funds.

OPEN-END MUTUAL FUNDS

(If the people who run mutual funds were literary purists, they'd say open-ended mutual funds. But I guess they aren't, because they don't.)

When you buy shares of an open-end mutual fund, you buy them *from the fund*. The fund creates new shares to accommodate investors who wish to buy, and it redeems shares to accommodate those who wish to sell. The demand for shares may be high or low, but the supply always exactly equals the demand. Each day, the fund creates or absorbs just the right number of shares. In effect, IPOs and redemptions occur daily. When investors want to invest in the mutual fund, the fund supplies additional shares to meet the demand. When they prefer to sell, the fund redeems shares, and those disappear.

As the public's demand for the fund fluctuates, the portfolio owned by the fund changes as well. On the days when the public's net demand for the fund is high, cash flows into the fund. The fund managers have the option of holding the cash, buying additional shares of the securities already owned, or buying shares of additional securities. On the days when the public wants, on balance, to sell shares of the fund, the fund must supply the cash that day, either by dipping into the cash already held or by selling some of the securities in the portfolio. When the stock market undergoes panic selling, as occurs infrequently, the mutual fund owners want to move out quickly. This requires the fund to engage in considerable selling, compounding the panic.

If you're a novice investor, you should understand right from the start that the days when most investors are in a panic to get out are almost always the days when you should be in a panic to get in. If you have not previously gotten out, you should certainly regard panic selling as a time to *stay* in. If you teach yourself to operate in opposition to public opinion, the press, and those who purport to be investment experts, believe me, you'll generally enjoy far better results. How will you know what those opinions are? Some of the time, you won't. But when investment professionals, investors, and the press are caught up in a wave of investment fright, believe me, you'll know it. If you happen to hold cash on those occasions, no matter how bleak the economy and the stock market may seem, you should hold your nose and jump in. More likely, since you should not have sold at the beginning of the price downturn, you should simply stay in.

Where was I? Oh yes, the number of shares of open-end mutual funds constantly fluctuates to match the demand.

An important term widely used in connection with mutual funds and exchange-traded funds is net asset value—NAV, for short. To calculate NAV, the fund determines the current market value of each of its holdings (the capitalization—the market price times the number of shares). The fund totals the values of all of its holdings and adds the cash on hand. It deducts any liabilities. (Some mutual funds acquire additional shares through borrowing, increasing risk.) Finally, the fund deducts its operating costs for the day (more about this later). The result is the net value of the fund's holdings, or the NAV. Most mutual funds compute their net asset values once a day, after the close of trading. A few compute their NAVs more often.

Going one step further, the fund divides the net asset value by the number of shares of the mutual fund held by the public at that moment. The result is the net asset value *per share*. (People refer to this number as the NAV, too, because it's usually obvious which number is meant, the total net value of the fund or the total net value per share. The NAV for the entire fund is in the millions or billions, while the NAV per share is usually less than $100.)

When people use the term "mutual fund," they generally mean open-end mutual fund. Mutual funds require minimum investments. For example, Vanguard's minimum is generally $3000. Schwab's is $5000. Some funds have minimums of $25,000 or more. The minimums for IRA accounts are usually lower.

With open-end mutual funds, the net asset value per share is also the price of the fund—the price that appears in the newspaper.

Since open-end mutual funds create and redeem shares to match the demand, the NAV per share of such funds is always equal to the fund's price. I say this emphatically, because with closed-end mutual funds, which comes next, the NAV per share and the price of the fund are seldom the same.

CLOSED-END MUTUAL FUNDS

Again, there is a portfolio of stocks or bonds, with shares of the fund owned by investors. But the number of shares of the fund does *not* fluctuate. The fund doesn't continually create and redeem shares, and the number of shares remains fixed.

To acquire shares of a closed-end fund, an investor cannot acquire them from the fund. She must buy them from someone who already owns them.

How do the shares get into the hands of investors in the first place? Through an Initial Public Offering, just like that of any stock. But once the IPO is completed, that's it. Thereafter, the shares of the fund pass from one investor to another. (Most closed-end mutual funds are traded on the New York Stock Exchange.) The price per share is whatever the buyers and sellers agree to. The price is not necessarily the same as the fund's net asset value per share. It is, in fact, seldom the same as the NAV. When a closed-end fund is hotly in demand, the price stands at a premium above the NAV. This is the exception. Most of the time, the prices of closed-end funds stand at discounts below the NAV.[1]

Most closed-end mutual funds own portfolios of bonds. On occasion, closed-end funds issue new shares through stock splits, stock dividends, or secondary offerings. But continual offerings and redemptions? No, this they do not do.

Dividends earned by the securities in the portfolio of closed-end funds are reinvested by the fund manager in the purchase of additional securities. Over time, the dividends cause the net asset value to rise, and usually the price as well. But most of the time, the dividends are not paid out to investors. They are used to purchase more shares of stock in the fund's portfolio. As a general rule, the managers also reinvest capital gains in the purchase of additional

[1] For those whose understanding of the time value of money is more advanced, the discount for closed-end funds is approximately equal to the present value of the fund's expected operating costs. Assume, for example, that a fund's NAV is $100, with operating costs expected to be 1.4 percent for the next 20 years. Discounted at 6 percent for 20 years, the price would be approximately $84, for a discount of 16 percent.

securities. But not always; the managers sometimes choose to pay out the capital gains to shareholders in cash.

Since investors in closed-end funds buy the shares from other investors, and not from the fund, the funds do not take in new money on a regular basis. The managers can change the securities held in the portfolio. But generally the fund's growth of assets stems from the appreciation in value of the securities, not from additional investor money.

Like open-end funds, closed-end funds are managed. A professional investment company chooses the securities held by the fund, changing them from time to time. This sets both open-end and closed-end funds apart from the third type of mutual fund, unit investment trusts.

UNIT INVESTMENT TRUSTS

Here again, a portfolio of securities is selected by the fund manager, with shares of the unit investment trust owned by investors. But the portfolio remains unchanged. The fund is not managed on an ongoing basis. The composition is determined at the beginning, and the fund is offered to the public through an IPO. Thereafter, there's little change; the securities just sit there, with no replacements.

Most unit investment trusts (UITs) hold bonds, not stocks. Interest, dividends (if any), and capital gain are paid out to investors. (Bonds create taxable gains when they're sold for a profit.) Mutual fund families that offer both unit investment trusts and open-end mutual funds offer the opportunity for payouts from the UITs to be invested in open-end mutual funds. But the payouts may not be reinvested in the unit investment trust from whence they came.

Investors may redeem their interests in unit investment trusts. To provide the cash, the fund manager sells a portion of the portfolio. Shareholders who choose not to sell may nevertheless be allocated capital gains.

ADVANTAGES OF MUTUAL FUNDS

Mutual funds have three advantages, with the first the most important:

Diversification: You recall that industry risk is less than specific risk, U.S. market risk is less than industry risk, and worldwide risk is less than U.S. risk. The more diversification, the safer your money.

When you spread your funds among many companies and several asset classes, those that are doing well partially offset those that are doing badly, and the volatility lessens. During bad times, it's easier to sleep nights. All three types of mutual funds—open-end funds, closed-end funds, and unit investment trusts—benefit from diversification. Your money is not invested in just one or two issues; it's invested in many.

Professional Management: Your funds are invested by those who spend full time at the job. Unfortunately, the managers like to get paid. We'll get to this down the line. I wish I could say that professional money managers exempt themselves from the prevailing tenor of opinion. I wish I could say that when others are losing all semblance of common sense during investment panics, the managers ride serenely above it all. They don't. They generally don't see the forest for the trees any better than other investors. Since they're *in* the forest every day, many of them see nothing but trees.

Not long after I first became a stockbroker, the market suffered panic. Watching the prices go down, down, down was mesmerizing. The decline finally came to a halt. The volume slowed way down, and the market seemed exhausted. A large order of what had been a popular stock came across the tape. This was the end of the decline; prices thereafter started to rise.

Several weeks later, I met a mutual fund manager at a party. We discussed the panic sell-off I had witnessed. He told me with chagrin that the sell order of that popular stock smack dab at the bottom of the market had been entered by him. The sale was not forced by redemptions from his investors. He just couldn't stand watching the price of the stock fall so far and panicked out of it. Had he remained serene, his fund would have enjoyed a significant rise in the price of the stock thereafter. Yes, professional money managers aren't always the panacea that mutual fund advertisements make them out to be. But diversification, the most important advantage of mutual funds, remains a blessing.

Adding and Withdrawing Funds Automatically: A third advantage applies to open-end mutual funds. These make it easy for investors to add small amounts on a regular basis, or, when the time comes, to withdraw them.

Before discussing this further, let's first get something straight. Most people in the investment world look with favor on dollar-cost averaging. Don't put everything into the stock market at one time, they advise. If the prices go down right after you invest, you'll be sorry. Instead, the advisors suggest that you invest a portion of your money a little at a time. When the prices go down, you'll buy more shares. When they go up, you'll buy fewer shares.

I consider this advice to be unhelpful. A majority of the time, stock prices go up. Yes, I know, they haven't done all that well lately. But the generality remains true: Unless the earth gets belted by an asteroid 10 miles in diameter, stock prices rise in the long run. Occasional "short-term" declines extend for even a decade or more. But even during those periods, you're more likely to preserve the buying power of your money in stocks than you are in competing investments. Those decade-long unfavorable markets are usually caused by errors in government policies. Big increases in tariffs in 1930 and big increases in income tax rates in 1932 come to mind. Those disasters, not to mention other mistakes of "social engineering," created and greatly extended the length of the Great Depression.

Errors of this magnitude are highly unlikely to be repeated in the foreseeable future. On the contrary, the legislators of most nations are squabbling about how much to *reduce* taxes, not raise them. In any event, during the course of any down market, the advance of technology and the work performed by the people of the world will eventually cause the advance of stock prices to resume.

Price downtrends are usually a lot shorter than a decade. No one consistently predicts when stock prices will begin going down for those "bear" markets. One can, however, reliably predict that stock prices always go up in the long run.

Let's cover that again, because it's important. We can't predict when stock prices will fall in the short term. But we can predict that they'll rise in the long run. Therefore, don't try to guess the market. Don't hold back cash for lower prices. The odds are against you. Instead, make your stock investments as soon as the money becomes available. Here's a good way to deal with the vagaries of the short term. Just assume that no matter what you do, you're going to be wrong. Assume that, in the short run, the market will go out of its way to get you. If you buy a security, its price will fall. If you sell, the price will rise. By taking it for granted that you have no control in the short term—which you don't—you are relieved from anxiety and guilt. The stock market is so much bigger than we are that in the short term, it controls. But widely diversified portfolios of stocks are so marvelously profitable in the long run that it is essential to get in as soon as you can. Never mind the uncertainties of the short term. Close your eyes, hold your nose, and dive in.

Investment professionals have every reason to recommend dollar-cost averaging. They don't know when stock prices will fall any more than we do. They like to give the impression that they know. But they don't, not consistently. They can't very well advise their customers to close their eyes, hold their noses, and jump in. If stock prices rise thereafter—the more likely alternative—investment advisors get no credit, because they're expected to know about those things. But if the stock prices fall thereafter, the advisors get the blame, and they quickly lose the customers they just worked so hard to land.

But what if you don't have much money now? You anticipate setting money aside as you earn it. Basically, the situation is the same: You're investing as soon as you get the money. But you have to earn it as you go along. This requires that you add small amounts to your investments every month. In effect, you're dollar-cost averaging. But it's not because you want to; it's because you have to.

Open-end mutual funds offer wonderfully convenient ways to add a small amount every month, every quarter, every year—whatever you like. You don't even have to sign checks. With your written approval, the mutual fund reaches its gentle electronic hand into your bank account, withdraws the amount you request (often a minimum of $50), and places it in whatever fund or funds you want. (Some mutual fund organizations—each one referred to as a "family"—offer more than 100 funds.)

Later on, when you need to draw on your capital, the fund on a regular basis will automatically deposit whatever amount you want into your bank account. Whether the money is coming in or out, the fund terminates the transfers immediately upon request. The fund is just trying to be helpful. The automatic transfer of funds is very helpful indeed.

Statistically, stock prices tend to rise on the last two trading days of each month and on the first four trading days of the month. I therefore suggest that you arrange for automatic investments to occur on the twenty-sixth of each month. This allows for weekends and for February being a short month. If you want automatic withdrawals, arrange for them to take place on the seventh of the month. The month's fourth trading day is unlikely to occur after that date.

Reinvestment of Dividends, Interest, and Capital Gains: Some of the stocks held by open-end mutual funds pay dividends. When you open the account, you are asked whether you want the dividends paid out in cash or whether you prefer that the money be used to purchase additional shares of the mutual fund in your account. If the latter, the price at which the purchase is made is the mutual fund's price (the NAV per share) on that day. Most investors prefer to reinvest. Very convenient this is, too. Assuming the shares are not held in a brokerage account, no time is lost while the check is in the mail. You needn't bother to deposit the money and then decide what to do with it, with more time lost while the funds are mailed for reinvestment.

If you need money from the mutual fund, go right ahead and take it. If you need a certain amount on a regular basis, arrange for that. But you're well advised not to remove the dividends just so you can "see" the money. You'll be tempted to spend the dividends, when you otherwise wouldn't. Besides, the amounts will be uneven.

Do not suppose that the reinvestment of dividends or interest in additional shares of the fund enables you to avoid paying taxes on those amounts. It doesn't. True, the money doesn't pass through your fingers; automatic reinvesting makes this unnecessary. But since you have the *option* of taking the dividends in cash, your friendly IRS agent says, sorry, they're taxable in the year they're made available to you. (Actually, IRS agents don't say they're sorry.)

When you open an account with an open-end mutual fund, you are given another choice: What to do about capital gains? After all, when the fund buys a stock (or a bond, for that matter) and later sells it for a profit, a gain results. If there are net gains over a period of time, your share can either be paid out to you or reinvested through the purchase of additional shares of the fund. Most investors choose reinvestment. Congress nixes the idea of losses being passed out to shareholders. Losses incurred by mutual funds are absorbed by the fund and not passed through to investors.

The reinvestment of dividends and of net capital gains generally applies only to open-end mutual funds. With closed-end funds, payouts to shareholders are seldom offered, because the money is reinvested by the fund manager. With unit investment trusts, dividends, interest, and capital gains are all paid out. Mutual fund families that have both unit investment trusts and open-end mutual funds offer a chance to reinvest distributions from the unit investment trust into open-end funds.

Exchange-traded funds do not offer automatic reinvestments. When you receive a payout of dividends, interest, or capital gains, you must take action to acquire more shares of the exchange-traded fund.

DISADVANTAGES OF MUTUAL FUNDS

Capital Gains and No Cash: Back to capital gains. When you buy the stock of an individual company, sure, you pay taxes on any dividends it pays. But until you actually sell the shares, you pay no capital gains tax. If you do sell for a gain, the proceeds provide the cash to pay the tax.

With an open-end fund, you may remove the gains in cash or reinvest the gains by buying additional shares of the fund. In either case, you pay tax for the year in which the gains are made available. But unless you specifically ask for cash from the mutual fund, you may have insufficient money to pay the tax.

This is a problem for mutual funds. With individual stocks, you pay capital gains tax only when you take action to sell. But with mutual funds, you pay capital gains tax, not because of something you did, but because of something the fund did. The fund may have sold stocks because it preferred to hold different ones. It may have sold because other shareholders redeemed in large quantities. In any event, the capital gains are not generated because of action taken by you. You are therefore well advised to choose funds that incur few sales of the stocks (or bonds) they hold. More about this later.

High Costs of Managed Funds: Many mutual funds—far too many—are managed with the objective of outperforming the market as a whole. Hardly any of them consistently succeeds. Let's say you flip a coin several thousand times. Besides ending up with sore hands and a painful back, you'll find that the tosses form a pattern as to the number of times in a row the coin comes up heads. Twice in a row will occur frequently. Three times in a row less frequently. Fifteen times in a row very infrequently. On each toss, the chance of the coin coming up heads is 50 percent. It's a matter of chance— a very slight chance—that the coin will come up heads 15 times in a row. Overall, the frequencies of consecutive heads (or tails) form a random pattern.

Academics have found that the number of years in a row that managed mutual funds outperform the market form roughly the same pattern as the random tosses of a coin. Two years in a row is frequent. Three years in a row less frequent. Fifteen years in a row, almost never. No matter how well a fund has performed in the past, the chances of it doing so in the next year are always 50 percent. Like the coin tosses, the performance of mutual funds form a random pattern.

Actually, I exaggerate the successes. Except for the pain and suffering of the hand and back, coin tosses involve no costs. But managed mutual funds incur costs—boy, do they ever! In most industries, as the volume increases, unit costs fall. Not so in the mutual fund industry. Despite the gargantuan growth in assets managed by mutual funds in the last 50 years, unit costs have generally risen! Investors must be so befuddled that they allow themselves to be taken to the cleaners by egregious costs, contravening the normal law of economics, which provides that the higher the volume, the lower the unit costs. Because of current costs, the average fund does not equal the market—nowhere near it.

When a mutual fund is acquired through a broker, both the brokerage firm and the broker look with favor about getting paid. Fund organizations provide (at least) three classes of the fund. They differ largely as to how the commission is charged to you, as follows:

- Class A shares pay commissions of about 5 or 6 percent at the time of the investment. The money is charged against the investor's account right at the beginning. Only the net amount is actually invested in the fund.
- With Class B shares, all of the investment goes to work in the fund, and the money to pay commissions is provided by the mutual fund organization. But the organization is repaid by extra charges against the investor's account. For about

eight years, the account is charged an extra 1 percent or so per year. Investors who withdraw are subject to additional withdrawal charges, usually amounting to 6 percent during the first year, 5 percent in the second year, and declining by 1 percent a year, reaching 0 in the sixth year. Brokers can proclaim that "all of your money goes to work for you." But the truth is, the deductions over time amount to more than if you had selected the A shares.

- Class C shares pay commissions that are somewhat lower, perhaps 3 percent. Again, the mutual fund organization pays the commission up front with its own money. The organization gets refunded by extra charges of 1 percent per year against the investor's account. These extra charges do not stop in eight years; they continue indefinitely.

The broker always gets paid up front. With A shares, the investor is also charged up front. With B and C shares, the charges are incurred later, but the investor usually ends up paying more than he would with A shares. The cost may be referred to by the fund and the broker as a "charge," not a commission. But don't be fooled. No matter what they call it; the commission comes out of your money.

Additional classes of funds have been created, other than A, B, and C shares. But no matter whether the commissions come out at the front, middle, or end, they reduce your net return. In all cases, the investor's account is charged at least 0.25 percent, just to keep the broker interested.

No-load mutual funds pay no commissions. To reimburse the fund for transaction costs in connection with investor redemptions, and possibly to discourage such redemptions, some no-load funds charge modest redemption fees, with the fee paid to the fund.

Unfortunately, the percentage of money invested in no-load funds has diminished in the last few years. Whereas 50 years ago, mutual funds numbered in the hundreds, now they number in excess of 13,000, including the various classes. Investors must find the possibilities daunting. They turn to brokers under the misguided notion that brokers know what's best. Brokers do have knowledge of various investment vehicles. But they do not know what will happen in the future any better than the rest of us. In fact, brokers are likely to be more wrong about the future than the rest of us because they pick up the prevailing tenor of customer opinions and spout it back as their own. The prevailing tenor of opinion is usually wrong. Most people are most optimistic when the market is high and most pessimistic when the market is low. Brokers absorb these beliefs and, to persuade people to act, reinforce them.

When the stocks of a certain industry perform particularly well, mutual funds take advantage by creating a fund that specializes in that industry. Investors buy them and the fund prices rise, inducing even more investors to buy. But then the industry is overbought, and the prices tend to decline severely.

One of the first sector funds was the Fidelity Select Technology Portfolio. For the year ending June 30, 1983, its price soared 162.1 percent, attracting $670 million in assets and earning its manager an appearance on *Money* magazine's cover. During the next 12 months, however, the fund fell sharply. A few years later, health care and biotechnology came to the fore. Sector funds for these two industries gained an average of 63.8 percent for 1991, and their assets nearly quadrupled. But during 1992 and 1993, those funds trailed the market averages significantly. In 1993, utility stocks took a bow. New utility funds came to the market, attracting a great deal of money. Sorry, they got belted by the rising interest rates in 1994. In 1996 and 1997, real estate funds turned red hot. Sure enough, they got their comeuppance in 1998 and 1999. And as you well know, the Internet stocks that flourished in 1999 subsequently became disasters.

Brokers become especially damaging with regard to such funds. It's a cinch to sell an investment that most people expect to sizzle. This is why mutual fund organizations come out with the funds in the first place. But these are the very ones to avoid. When investment professionals, investors, and the press consider any investment to be a sure winner, restrain yourself from climbing on board.

Funds that charge no commissions are called no-load funds. No broker is involved, and you must take the initiative to call the fund, obtain a prospectus, fill out the application, and mail it in. Oh yes, don't forget to sign a check and send that in as well. You must do all these things without a broker urging you on and telling you what a great job you're doing. You must have gumption. If the stock market is down and everyone else is pessimistic, you must have plenty of gumption. But the mere fact that you're reading this book shows that you have gumption and curiosity in ample quantities.

The lack of commissions represents an important savings, especially in the short term. But even no-load funds charge marketing costs. They're called 12(b)1 costs, a burdensome moniker named after the SEC code section that permits such charges. If you spot an advertisement for a no-load fund, think 12(b)1.

So much for brokers and marketing costs. How about the people who operate the mutual fund? They want to get paid, too. Research, trading, legal costs, dealing with government regulators, dealing with investors, printing prospectuses and other materials—all of this costs plenty. Every trading day, the fund is charged a portion of these costs. If there are 250 trading days in the year, 1/250th of the estimated annual cost is charged each day.

Another way in which managed mutual funds incur excessive costs is by trading excessively. Not only are losses incurred because of the commissions and spreads, the trades burn up the investor's cash because of excessive short-term capital gains that are taxed at high rates.

Spreads

Let's say you want to sell your car, and you don't happen to know anyone who wants to buy it. To avoid the hassle of advertising and hanging around for phone calls, you go to a car dealer, whom we'll call a market maker. The dealer pays you, say, $8000 for the car. He spends a little money on it and sells it for, say, $12,000. That's the dealer's spread. His "bid" price is $8000, and his "asked" price is $12,000. Net of costs, the spreads are how the dealer makes his living. He owns the car in the interim. The spreads of car dealers seem large, but most dealers don't sell cars every other minute. They have to work hard and smartly to make a good living.

Market makers in fur coats and diamonds make trades very infrequently. To get by, they mark up their products about 100 percent.

Most stocks, on the other hand, trade frequently. The markups by stock market makers are therefore small. A market maker may buy a stock for $20 a share and sell it for $20.05. On 100 shares, she makes five bucks. On 100,000 shares, the kind of order entered by a mutual fund, the spread might widen to $19.90 bid, $20.20 asked. The market maker, you see, buys the stock with her own money. The amount of money is large, and the market maker may have to wait before someone wants to buy it from her. Because of the added risk in holding so much stock, she widens the spread to compensate for the risk.

You may have heard television business commentators speak about what "traders" think concerning something that's going on in the market. The unstated implication is that the traders are profiting from their opinions.

This is unlikely. Many of the so-called traders are probably market makers. They make money, all right. But they make it from the spreads, not by being consistently right in predicting short-term price moves. They may have opinions about the short-term future; most of us do. When a television person asks for those opinions, they're happy to respond. But traders put on their pants one leg at a time, just like the rest of us. The chances are, they're not betting their money consistently on their opinions. If they did, they probably wouldn't remain in the market for long. After a while, they'd have nothing left to trade with. Spreads are how they make their living.

John Bogle, founder of Vanguard and now head of the Bogle Financial Markets Research Center, analyzed 384 managed, stock mutual funds for the 15 years from 1984 to 1999. Here are the average costs he found:

- Front-end commissions: 0.5 percent per year.
- Opportunity costs, because of the funds holding about 7 percent of their assets in cash rather than in stocks: 0.6 percent per year.
- Commissions and spreads from high turnover rates: 0.7 percent per year.
- Federal and state taxes on dividends and capital gains, mostly because of the rapid turnover: about 2.7 percent per year. (Traditional IRAs and 401(k) plans are temporarily tax free.)
- Management fees and operating expenses: 1.2 percent per year.
- Total average costs: 5.7 percent per year.

Before these costs, the returns of the 384 funds Bogle analyzed approximately equaled that of the market, namely, 16.9 percent per year. But after costs, the after-tax returns to shareholders were only 11.2 percent per year (16.9 percent less 5.7 percent).

16.9 percent versus 11.2 percent: That's a whale of a difference.

Let's assume a $10,000 investment in a hypothetical managed fund, which has costs of 5.7 percent per year. Compare this with a $10,000 investment in an index fund or exchange-traded fund, which we'll assume to have costs of only 1.7 percent, including ongoing taxes on dividends and capital gains. Both investments continue for 25 years and gain 12 percent a year before costs:

Fund A, in the managed fund, has a net annual return of 6.3 percent (12 percent less 5.7 percent). In 25 years, $10,000 grows to $46,061.

Fund B goes into an index fund or ETF with costs of only 1.7 percent per year. The net annual return is 10.3 percent (12 percent less 1.7 percent). In 25 years, $10,000 becomes $115,981.

$46,061 versus $115,981—a difference of 151 percent in 25 years. After 30 years, the lesser-cost alternative would be 203 percent larger. The investment returns are the same, mind you. The difference in the final balances is due entirely to costs. Which alternative would you choose?

Restricted Time and Type of Executions: We're still on the disadvantages of mutual funds here. Mutual funds cannot be acquired at just any old time. Most open-end mutual funds can be bought or redeemed only after the close of trading. You cannot specify that you want to buy only if the execution price is below a certain level. (These are called limit orders. For more on this, see Chapter 10.) Neither can you specify that you wish to sell only if the price is above a certain level. No, only market orders will do; you must accept the current price. If you want to acquire a certain mutual fund at the opening, you can't. The order is executed only after the close of trading, many hours later. The price may then be very different from what you anticipated. Some brokerage firms have an early cutoff time. Mutual fund orders submitted to TD Waterhouse after 2:00 p.m. eastern time, for example, are executed after the close of the *next* day's trading.

This limitation, of course, does not apply to closed-end funds. Those are traded like regular stocks, from investor to investor throughout the day. With closed-end funds, you may use any kind of order you like, whenever you like. With unit investment trusts, you buy only when it's first offered, at the IPO. That's it. If you miss that opportunity, you must wait for another offering. The redemptions of UITs are executed only after the close.

Lots of Paperwork: When you acquire an open-end mutual fund or unit investment trust, you receive a prospectus, which is difficult to follow because it's written to please the Securities and Exchange Commission. From unit investment trusts you receive annual reports. From open-end mutual funds you receive semiannual reports. From both, you receive statements about your particular account. These are no cinch to understand. Whatever affects the number of shares you own is reflected in the statement. This is appropriate, of course, but sometimes the changes are hard to follow.

Complicated Taxes: Year-end tax statements from open-end mutual funds are very difficult to follow. This generally isn't the fault of the mutual funds; it's the fault of the government for making income taxes such a swamp of complexity. Dividends and interest are reportable as ordinary income—that is, as income taxed at the same (high) tax rates as your salary. The sale of securities generates capital gains taxes, handled one way if they're short-term gains and another way if they're long-term gains. A third category of gains is set forth regarding securities that have been held for at least five years. Taxes paid to foreign governments are treated separately.

Most confusing of all, dividends, interest, and capital gains that have been reinvested require you to increase the tax basis of your holding. For example, let's say you buy shares of a fund for $10,000. During the tax year, dividends of $200 and capital gains of $700 are reinvested. You pay taxes currently on those items, but you have no desire, of course, to pay tax twice on the same income. Therefore, you must increase the cost basis of your holding from $10,000 to $10,900. Later, if you sell your shares for $15,000, you report capital gains of $4100, not $5000. Most mutual funds don't make these adjustments; you must make them yourself.

If you use the standard deduction on Form 1040, the laborious calculations just referred to become unnecessary. But your taxes might be reduced by using the long form and working the complexities yourself. If you utilize an accountant or a tax-preparation service, well, they like to get paid, too.

Capital Gains Payable Even Though You Don't Sell Your Mutual Fund Shares: As mentioned above, when the portfolio manager sells one security to buy another, a gain or loss is usually incurred. When investors redeem their shares in great numbers during periods of adversity, the manager is forced to sell securities to provide the cash. These actions have tax ramifications for you, even though you've taken no action with regard to your shares.

There's worse. Let's say you acquire $10,000 of an open-end mutual fund in January of 2003. For 18 months, stocks perform well, and your shares of the fund appreciate.

In June of 2004, the fund manager sells some of the fund's holdings at a profit and reinvests the proceeds into other stocks. The stock market then takes a dive. Six months later, your shares, having started at $10,000, are worth only $9000. You haven't sold, and your fund holding has suffered a net loss of $1000. Despite this, you must pay taxes on the *gains* that were incurred from the sales of stocks made in June 2004.

Even worse, assume you delay the purchase of the fund until July 2004, at the top of the market, right after the stocks were sold and new stocks were acquired. (Don't blame yourself for buying at the top of the market; no one anticipates bear markets consistently. Just buy when you get the money.) By the spring of 2005, your loss is larger than if you had acquired the shares earlier. But you must still report the gains on the profitable sales made in June 2004— gains that were incurred even before you bought your shares. A ticklish problem, right?

If you hold the fund for several decades, as you should, it all comes out in the wash. Just assume that the market will go out of its way to undercut your interest in the short term. Never mind days, weeks, or months; think of the long term being at least five years. Investment time horizons are a lot longer than most people think.

Do not confuse the time horizon of your investments with the time horizon of your retirement. The former is much longer. By definition, you have a 50-percent chance of living longer than your life expectancy. Plan on it. If you're married, consider your investment time horizon as being the year that the younger of the two of you reach age 100.

Avoid piling onto bandwagons. Fund organizations offer new mutual funds specializing in investments that are popular. And why not? They want to make money just like the rest of us. But you don't have to buy such funds. Investments that are popular have a way of turning unpopular when the prices return to earth from stratospheric heights. Case in point: Telecommunication and Internet stocks went wild in 1999 and early 2000, with many a mutual fund in tow. But subsequently, their prices crunched. So did the mutual funds that favored them.

Skullduggery: There's another sticky problem with managed mutual funds. Mutual funds being hotly competitive, they strive to attract investor funds by developing favorable records of performance in relation to their peers. To make the job easier, they diminish the size of the peer group. A fund may find, for example, that among growth funds of a size between $500 million and $750 million, its record was the best between March 1, 1984 and March 1, 1999. As long as the fund can find a category, a size range, and a set of dates during which its record was superior, the fund can boast all it wants.

The investing public tends to act like sheep—present readers excluded, of course. People are induced to buy funds that have a superior short-term record. But once they buy, inertia takes hold. When the fund's record subsequently deteriorates, the investors dislike selling, and they hang on for dear life. Therefore, mutual funds do whatever they can to establish a short-term record they can boast about. Here are a couple of ways they go about it:

1. Many funds, according to their prospectuses, are restricted as to what types of stocks they can acquire. If they buy other kinds, they have to do it on the sly. For example, a fund might be restricted to stocks that have relatively low price-earnings ratios. They describe themselves in the prospectus as "value" investors. Such a fund is not supposed to buy a high-tech company with a PE of 180, for example. On the dates when the fund's semiannual reports reveal what it owns to the public, it doesn't own such stocks. The fund is then as clean as a whistle.

But the periods between the reporting dates may be quite another story. In an effort to improve the fund's performance relative to its peers, the fund may sell the kinds of stocks it's supposed to own and climb on board the "hot" stocks that have risen more rapidly than the rest. Before the next reporting period comes around, the fund slinks back to the kinds of securities it purports to hold. Mutual funds do not disclose their holdings between reporting dates, so we don't know whether they're doing these things or not. Such "style drift" is sometimes unintentional, to be sure. A new manager, new company objectives, or price changes might cause the effective style of a fund to shift. But in other cases, the style drift is deliberate and surreptitious.

2. Some mutual funds engage in "window dressing." Just before a disclosure deadline, they dump the stocks that have performed poorly over the previous six months and buy recent winners. This doesn't improve the record of performance, but it does spruce up appearances.

3. Here's another trick some fund managers use. On the day funds must report their holdings to the public, they acquire additional shares of the stocks the fund already owns. This temporarily forces up the prices of those shares, thereby improving the values of the stocks as shown in the report. A 1999 study showed that the hottest stocks tend to peak during the last hour of the day of reporting periods—and decline during the first hour of the next trading day.

With all this trading, is it any wonder that the turnover rate of the average fund exceeds 80 percent per year?

As I say, it's managed mutual funds that incur excessive costs. But there are certain kinds of open-end mutual funds that don't

---

Bulls and Bears

A *bull market* is a period of time when stock prices are generally rising or thought to be rising. A *bear* market is a period of time when stock prices are generally falling or thought to be falling. Here's a good way to remember. A bull endeavors to kill you by thrusting his horns upward to stab you. A bear endeavors to kill you by pulling you down to the ground to bite you. But don't allow these analogies to frighten you. Over the long run, the stock market is a pussycat.

incur such heavy costs. They're attractive investments, too. They're called index funds, and they're on the fourth floor.

INDEX FUNDS

An increasing number of open-end mutual funds are called index funds. These select a market or industry index and acquire the actual stocks that are included in that index. Otherwise, index funds are unmanaged. The fund is not set up to beat the index, just to equal it. The company that produces the index, such as Standard & Poor's, chooses the stocks. The fund merely follows along. Recall that indexes are capitalization weighted. Stocks with greater market value have greater impact on the index than those with smaller market value. A fund that endeavors to track the index therefore buys more of the stocks that have larger capitalizations and less of the stocks with smaller capitalizations. In any event, no stock research is needed. The fund just buys in the proper proportions the stocks that are selected by someone else. This cuts costs considerably, because no stock research is required.

Vanguard launched the first index fund on August 31, 1976. Called the Vanguard 500 Index Fund, it tracks the most widely followed market index, the Standard & Poor's 500 Stock Index. Other money managers greeted the launching with derision.

If you "settle" for matching the market instead of outperforming it, said one mutual fund executive, "you're conceding defeat."

"Indexing is a sure path to mediocrity," said another.

Some mediocrity! The Vanguard 500 Index Fund has outperformed most other funds. With $120 billion under management, including institutional investments, it's now the largest fund in the world.

The general equity funds in existence in August 1976 numbered 356. Of these, 160 can no longer be found, a fallout of 45 percent. Some were absorbed by other funds, no doubt. Others just disappeared. But none would have fallen off the board, I warrant, if its performance had been successful enough to equal that of the Vanguard 500 Index Fund.

The broadest index of the U.S. stock market, the Wilshire 5000 now includes over 7000 stocks. Several fund families (that is, groups of funds managed by the same company) track the Wilshire. But

7000 are too many stocks for a fund to acquire. The Vanguard Total Stock Market Index Fund, which tracks the Wilshire, holds about 3000 of the stocks that are included in the index. To buy more would raise transaction costs too high. Despite the selectivity, the fund has nevertheless tracked the index remarkably closely. Since inception on April 27, 1992, the average annual total returns for the Wilshire 5000 have been 11.86 percent. For the Vanguard Total Stock Market Index Fund, the average annual total returns, after its annual fee of 0.20 percent, was 12.64 percent. By making the results even better than that of the index it followed, Vanguard certainly earned its fee. No doubt the winnowing of stocks from 7000 down to 3000 had beneficial effect.

The stocks that are included in indexes are seldom changed by the investment company that owns and keeps track of the index. Most of the time, the changes occur because a company that's included in the index is bought by or merges with another company. When buyouts or mergers occur, the company that promulgates the index must select another stock to fill the place of the one that was absorbed. But ordinarily, the stocks that are included in indexes are not changed. The turnover of the Standard & Poor's 500 Index, for example, amounts to only 2-to-4 percent a year. Because indexes have relatively little turnover, the funds that track them have little turnover themselves. This reduces capital gains taxes.

Indexes, such as the S&P 500, are hypothetical portfolios that are presumed to hold no cash. The mutual funds that track those indexes, on the other hand, are real-world accommodations that must bend to the desires of investors. To allow for the possibility of redemptions, index funds must hold somewhat more cash, on a percentage basis, than the indexes themselves, which are presumed to hold none.

The low level of cash on the part of index funds can cause a problem. When the market falls and investors turn pessimistic, they are inclined to liquidate. To provide the cash, the index fund must sell some of the stocks in its portfolio, and quickly. For those investors who do not sell—I hope you may count yourself among this number—capital gains or losses are nevertheless incurred. In other words, the investors who do not sell must report taxes precipitated by the actions of people other than themselves. This is not the case with a regular stock. If you don't sell, you incur no capital gains.

On a percentage basis, index funds tend to hold less cash than managed funds. The managed funds prefer to keep more of their powder dry, in case a stock they find enticing comes to their attention. In the long run, however, this doesn't pay off. Being fully invested in stocks engenders the best returns.

Advantages and Disadvantages of Index Funds: All of the advantages that apply to mutual funds in general apply to index funds, namely:

- Diversification: For a broad-based index fund, such as the S&P 500 or the Russell 3000, you can't beat the diversification.
- Professional Management: Here, the index funds do the managed funds one better. Oh sure, the managers of index funds take charge of the details of investing your funds according to the style set forth in the fund's prospectus. But they do not exercise their own judgment in the selection of securities. They just follow the index. As the index goes, so goes the fund. Relinquishing stock selection results in significant reductions of management and trading costs.
- Adding and Withdrawing Funds Automatically: Index funds are just as accommodating as managed funds with regard to the periodic transmission of funds from your bank account or to your bank account as you so direct. No problem there.
- Reinvestments of Dividends, Interest, and Capital Gains: On this score, index funds fill the bill admirably.

Index funds share some of the disadvantages of managed funds. But not all of them, by any means. Here are comparisons:

- Capital Gains, But No Cash to Pay the Taxes: Index funds can incur capital gains without your having sold your interest in the fund. But since the rate of turnover of stocks in index funds is far less than the turnover rate of most managed funds, the likelihood of your being taxed on capital gains but having no cash to pay the tax is considerably reduced.
- Worst Case: As more and more money flows into index funds—as has certainly occurred—funds have bought more stock than they've sold. Older index funds, such as the Vanguard 500 Index Fund, own stocks that were bought years ago at very low costs. The market value of the stocks

held by the Vanguard 500 Index Fund (not counting institutional funds) amounts to about $72 billion. In the unlikely event that every one of those stocks was sold at current prices (the market would have a hard time stomaching such monumental selling), approximately $13 billion of capital gains would be incurred. The IRS would enjoy raking in all those taxes. I realize that the chance of such massive sales being necessitated is slim, and one hopes that income taxes and the IRS will be done away completely with before it occurs. But the possibility continues to lurk in the shadows.

♦ Costs: Here, index funds are far preferable to managed funds. With no research, the cost of management is reduced. And fewer turnovers cause fewer transaction costs and less capital gains taxes.

♦ Restricted Time and Type of Execution: Like managed funds, index funds can be bought only at the close. No special kinds of orders are permitted; only market orders will do.

♦ Lots of Paperwork: Yes, index funds suffer from this malady, too.

♦ Complicated Taxes: With index funds, the poor investor must wrestle with the complexities of the tax code, just as he does with management funds.

♦ Capital Gains Even Though the Investor Made No Sale: My guess is that buyers of index funds are a little smarter and a little wiser than the buyers of managed funds. Does this make them less likely to submit sales during times of panic? Maybe, a little. I hope that you will not sell at times of panic. Those occasions are more often than not the most promising times to buy. But anyway, even with index funds, there is the risk of your incurring capital gains solely because of the actions of others.

♦ Skullduggery: Index funds don't change their style between the dates of shareholder reports. They do not, just before a disclosure deadline, sell the stocks that have performed poorly and buy recent winners. They do not, on the last day of the report period, purchase additional shares of the stocks already held to increase the valuations of those stocks on the last day of the reporting period. Such activities would run counter to their objective—to track an index.

CHAPTER 4

The Basics of Exchange-Traded Funds

We come at last to the penthouse—nice view.

An exchange-traded fund (ETF) is a cross between an individual stock and an index fund. Short-term traders treat ETFs as stocks that have characteristics of index funds. The U.S. Securities and Exchange Commission regulates exchange-traded funds as mutual funds that have characteristics of stocks. Take your pick; ETFs resemble both.

Exchange-traded funds are simple to use. Like individual stocks and closed-end mutual funds (but unlike open-end funds) they can be bought and sold continuously throughout the trading day. Yet each ETF represents an entire index. Some track broad U.S. indices, such as the Dow Jones Average (that's an average, not an index). Others track the S&P 500, the Nasdaq 100, the Russell 3000, or many others. Some ETFs track value stocks, others growth stocks. Some track market sectors or industries, such as energy or technology. Others track foreign markets, such as those of Sweden or Taiwan.

Despite the complexity standing behind ETFs, you may trade them as often as you please—a hundred times a day, if that's what turns you on. I hope you won't fall pray to any such nonsense. By trading ETFs seldom, you avoid becoming a loser. I want you to utilize these marvelous vehicles as long-term holdings and become a winner.

SPIDERS

The first exchange-traded fund came into being on January 29, 1993. It was called Standard & Poor's Depositary Receipts. If you take the first letter of each word and add an "s," you come up with "SPDRs," but people add a couple of vowels and refer to them as Spiders. ("Depositary" seems to me to be misspelled. But who am I to challenge a document that has been approved by the Securities and Exchange Commission, the federal government's most profitable agency? Profitable? Oh yes, when you sell shares of stock, a few little pennies pass into the hands of the SEC. A penny here and a penny there, pretty soon we're talking real money.)

It took three years for the Securities and Exchange Commission to understand and approve Spiders. Members of the Commission had to relate it to something they were already familiar with, so they could figure out how to regulate it. They classified Spiders as a unit investment trust. As you recall, UITs are mutual funds that have fixed, unmanaged portfolios. But unlike UITs, the portfolios of ETFs are not completely fixed. The components of indexes change occasionally, and when this occurs, the portfolio of an ETF that follows the index changes as well.

But the managers of ETFs exercise no discretion as to the choice of stocks. For the most part, the managers simply hold the stocks that are included in the index. The index is controlled by one organization, and the ETF is controlled by another. The index is a hypothetical portfolio; the exchange-traded fund is a real portfolio. As the index goes, so goes the ETF. Spiders, for example, track the Standard & Poor's 500 Index by buying in the proper proportions the stocks that are included in that Index.

The Spider fund is a trust. The prospectus identifies it as "SPDR Trust, Series 1 (A Unit Investment Trust)." Trusts were developed in England back in the Middle Ages. They connote the ownership and management of property by one party for the benefit of another. One reason trusts were developed is because women at that time were not permitted to own land. Precious few machines had been developed. Oh, there were wheels, carts, harnesses, and tools. But almost all workers were farmers, and land was the predominant productive resource. Fathers who wanted their daughters to inherit their land therefore placed it in trust. The trustee would be a man, but the beneficial owner would be the daughter. Cagey, huh?

The trustee of the Spider Trust is the State Street Bank and Trust Company, one of the old-line banks of Boston, Massachusetts. The beneficial owners of the trust are the owners of Spiders, which might include you. The trust, says the prospectus, is a "Pooled Investment Designed to Closely Track the Price and Yield Performance of the S&P 500 Index." Tracking the S&P 500 worked for Vanguard. Why not for Spiders?

As an ETF shareholder, you cast your vote on the proxies that are sent to you by the trustee's board of directors. But you do not vote the proxies of the companies whose shares are owned by the fund. These are voted under the direction of the ETF board. It's a good thing, too. If you owned an ETF that holds several thousand stocks, you'd have time for nothing else besides voting proxies.

Behind each Spider share stands considerable complexity. The stocks in the S&P 500 Index are apportioned, as you recall, according to their capitalization, or total market value. Yet practically in the blink of an eye, you can buy or sell a single Spider share, costing, at the time of this writing, $116. This represents an undivided interest in that entire portfolio—all 500 stocks, in the proper proportions. The value of that Spider also tracks the collective performance of all those stocks almost exactly, from minute to minute. How can this be?

Good of you to ask.

Undivided Interest

If you have a spouse, the chances are that you own your home jointly. If the house is in joint names, each of you has an undivided interest in the entire house. You don't own the north side and your spouse the south side. You don't own the first floor and your spouse the second. Each of you owns the whole thing. Lawyers love abstract concepts like this, and so do I. It's sort of like seeing a colored picture through two pieces of clear plastic .

Anyway, undivided interest means that a single Spider share, currently costing about $116, represents an infinitesimal amount of the smallest company in the S&P 500 Index and a still tiny amount of the largest company. It represents an interest in about 77 percent of the productive resources of this mighty nation. That one little Spider share trembles with excitement in the knowledge that it stands for so much.

THE CREATION AND REDEMPTION OF SPIDERS

When you acquire Spider shares, you do not create them; the shares have already been created. You buy them from another investor, as you would a closed-end fund. The Spider shares were not created all in one fell swoop in an initial public offering (IPO), as would occur for an individual stock, a closed-end fund, or a unit investment trust. Spider shares are created and redeemed by the trust. In this regard, Spiders resemble open-end funds, which create and redeem their shares according to shareholder demand. What makes exchange-traded funds unique is that the creation and redemption of the shares are called for by third parties. They engage in this activity because they find it profitable. Indeed, everyone benefits.

Not just anyone can call for the creation or redemption of Spider shares. You have to be rich, or, more likely, a rich financial institution. At this writing, 50,000 shares or multiples of 50,000 are the number of shares acceptable to the trustee for creation or redemption. At the current price of Spiders, 50,000 shares amount to $5.8 million. You also have to be willing for the profits to be ordinary income because the creation and redemption of exchange-traded fund shares usually involves quick turnover. The shares come in one door and out the other—hardly any are held for even a week, never mind five years.

The creation and redemption of exchange-traded funds would be impossible without a high-tech infrastructure, which includes electronic and fiber-optic equipment. Let's say you have some big bucks under your belt and you want to buy $30 million of the 500 stocks included in the S&P 500 Index. Not in equal amounts, such as $60,000 in each stock. Oh no, the S&P 500 Index is structured to include the 500 stocks in unequal amounts, in accordance with the current capitalization of each. You want to buy the shares in the proper proportion.

You don't have to jump through hoops. You or your trusty associate simply enters $30 million into your computer and pushes the Return button. Poof, every one of the 500 stocks are acquired within a few seconds, no matter whether the trades are executed on the New York Stock Exchange, another exchange, Nasdaq, or an electronic communication network (see Chapter 10). The investment world is a far cry from the days of ticker tapes, when every order to buy stock passed through the hands of about 10 people to complete an execution. Today, it's quicker and, since electronic equipment knows how to add and subtract flawlessly, less prone to error.

Okay, let's say that Spear, Leeds & Kellogg, a prominent player on Wall Street, buys $30 million of the stocks included in the S&P 500 Index. It immediately presents all of the S&P 500 stocks in the proper proportions to the State Street Bank & Trust Company. More infrastructure is involved here. No one carries 79 pounds of stock certificates by train from New York to Boston. It's all done electronically, quick as a wink. If trading in one of the S&P 500 stocks has temporarily been shut down for some reason and Spear, Leeds is unable to acquire the shares of that stock, it delivers cash to State Street Bank equivalent to the value. When trading in that stock resumes, State Street acquires the proper number of shares itself to fill the bill.

Okay, delivery is made from Spear Leeds to the State Street Bank. In another blink of the eye, the State Street Bank's trusty mainframe confirms that the delivery of 500 shares was correct, and the bank immediately delivers Spider shares electronically to Spear Leeds. Those are new Spider shares, the very Moment of Creation. It's a good thing that everyone takes it easy on the Sabbath.

How many shares of Spiders? Well, it depends on the price. If the price of Spiders on the most recent trade was $122 a share, State Street delivers to Spear Leeds 245,902 shares ($30 million divided by $122). All of this takes place within seconds. It's amazing enough to me that when I approach an airport terminal, the door kindly swings open to accommodate my entrance without a soul being in evidence to tell the door what to do. But the complexity involved in the speedy creation of millions of dollars of exchange-traded shares, well, I find it mind-boggling.

All right, Spear Leeds is now the proud owner of 245,902 shares of Spiders. It can do with them whatever it likes. It can keep them for 30 years. But the chances are Spear Leeds chooses not to retain the Spiders. Instead, it sells the shares immediately on the American Stock Exchange to normal, everyday investors like you and me. (Well, some of us aren't completely normal, but you get the idea.)

The newly created Spider shares thus enter what is referred to as the secondary market. When you cast your eye on the business pages of your newspaper and see the results of the previous day's trading, almost all of it takes place in the secondary market, wherein preexisting shares are passed from one investor to another. Some 50 years ago, for example, shares of Ford Motor stock first came into the hands of the public in a massive IPO. Ever since, those shares have passed from one party to another in the secondary market. The great majority of trades on the New York Stock Exchange, the American Stock Exchange, Nasdaq, and other exchanges throughout the world are secondary trades.

Alternative to the creation of Spiders, Morgan Stanley, another prosperous Wall Street player, might think it profitable to redeem shares of Spiders, in the amount of—oh, $20 million sounds like a nice round number. The process is reversed. Morgan Stanley enters orders on the American Stock Exchange to buy at market some 164,000 shares of Spiders from people like you and me. It delivers the shares to the State Street Bank. State Street immediately delivers to Morgan Stanley in the proper proportions shares of all 500 of the S&P 500 stocks, which Morgan Stanley immediately sells in secondary markets. Just like that, 164,000 shares of Spiders disappear.

As the public's interest in Spiders has grown and trading activity in the security has increased, the total amount of shares of stock held in the Spider trust has also increased. Over the years, more creation has occurred than redemption.

To engage in the creation and redemption of Spider shares, you must have heavy dough behind you, as mentioned. You must have computers and other infrastructure to enable you to engage in these multitudinous, complex transactions. And you must obtain the permission of State Street Bank to engage in the process. By so doing, you become what the Spider prospectus refers to as a "Participating Party."

Most people in the industry refer to participating parties as "Authorized Participants." This is probably because the participating-party term is too indefinite. It sounds like it might include the thousands of normal, everyday investors. But "participating parties" do not include riffraff. You have to be loaded. For all exchange-traded funds, there are so far only 20 to 30 Authorized Participants. That's it—no more than 30.

We now leave the Authorized Participants for a while. We'll discuss certain aspects of the secondary markets for exchange-traded funds and then return to explain why the Authorized Participants go to the trouble of creating and redeeming exchange-traded funds, such as Spiders.

SECONDARY MARKETS FOR ETFS

Exchange-traded funds, now numbering about 200, are multiplying like rabbits. The American Stock Exchange was the first to trade them, and it remains the secondary marketplace for the majority of ETFs. But, sensing rich plums, other exchanges are getting into the act. On July 31, 2001 the New York Stock Exchange began trading exchange-traded funds based on the S&P 100, the Dow Jones Industrials, and the Nasdaq 100. These ETFs have large volumes of trading, and since any exchange charges a tiny amount for each share traded, securities that trade heavily are the most profitable. Nasdaq, U.S. regional exchanges, and foreign exchanges are also offering trading opportunities for ETFs. The Nasdaq 100 is traded in nine different venues, and an option on that ETF is traded on the AMEX. Even the Chicago Board of Options Exchange is stepping up to the plate, trading Spiders.

There are three basic categories of exchange-traded funds:

The Broad U.S. Stock Market: Some ETFs track broad indexes of the U.S. stock market. These include the S&P 500, the Wilshire 5000, the Russell 3000, and the Nasdaq 100.

Portions of the U.S. Stock Market: Some exchange-traded funds track particular U.S. industries, such as the chemical or Internet industries. In some cases, there are problems in this regard. An industry may be dominated by a single, large company. Indexes, remember, are based on capitalizations. If the capitalization of a particular company is considerably larger than that of other members of the same industry, the company in question would have a disproportionate effect on the index. Amgen, for example, bulks large in the biotech index. Buyers of the biotech ETF should know that their investment is not widely diversified. Long-term appreciation depends more heavily on Amgen than on the other components of the index.

One ETF might track only those stocks in the S&P 500 Index that have relatively high price-to-book ratios. These are termed growth stocks. Another ETF might track only those stocks in the

S&P 500 Index that have relatively low price-to-book ratios. These are termed value stocks.

Foreign Markets: An important category of exchange-traded funds tracks indexes of foreign markets, such as those of France or Brazil. The indexes are creations of Morgan Stanley Capital International, Inc. (MSCI). With these ETFs, a single company, again, may dominate. The capitalization of Ericsson, for example, is considerably larger than that of any other Swedish company. The effect of that company on the ETF for the Swedish stock market is disproportionate.

THE ANTECEDENT OF ETFS: WAREHOUSE RECEIPTS

I had the privilege of talking with Mr. Nate Most, the father of exchange-traded funds. As a member of the staff of the American Stock Exchange, Nate designed the ETF concept in 1988. He took it to the Securities and Exchange Commission in 1989. With the enthusiastic support of the Chairman, Richard Breeden, the SEC gave its thumbs-up in 1992, leading to the introduction of Spiders in early 1993. Going strong at 87 years of age, Nate now designs new products for Barclays Global Investors.

I asked him, "What was the flash of light that brought the concept into your head?"

Nate said, "There was no flash of light. I'd worked in the commodity business for 20 years. The idea of exchange-traded funds came out my knowledge of warehouse receipts."

That was my flash of light. Here's an explanation.

Futures contracts were originally developed to accommodate the producers of agricultural products. When a grain elevator accepts 10,000 bushels of wheat into storage, for example, it gives the owner a warehouse receipt. The receipt is the title of ownership, similar to the title of ownership of a car. It's a negotiable instrument, meaning that it can be bought and sold. Whoever holds the receipt has the right to obtain from that warehouse 10,000 bushels of wheat. Warehouse receipts have a considerable history. In seventeenth-century England, goldsmiths issued warehouse receipts for gold left with them by merchants. While the gold remained stationary, the receipts then circulated as money.

The futures market is the buying and selling of products that have yet to be delivered. All futures contracts have maturity dates. Warehouse receipts don't apply to every product traded in futures markets. But where they do apply, the receipt is used instead of the physical commodity to make delivery of the product, in satisfaction of the contract when it matures. All the while, the product itself sits in storage.[1]

After maturity, the purchase and sale of the product continues in the cash market as represented by the warehouse receipt, until, finally, the processor who will use the product buys the receipt and presents it to the warehouse. The receipt is cancelled and the commodity withdrawn for processing. (Actual practices are more complicated than I describe. I'm trying to keep this simple enough so that even I understand it.)

When you buy shares of Spiders in the secondary market, you are in effect buying a warehouse receipt on the stocks included in the S&P 500 Index. You can't actually redeem the Spiders for stock unless you accumulate 50,000 shares and become an Authorized Participant. When you buy and sell an ETF, you're not trading the stocks that underlie it. Those sit quietly in the trust. You're trading an intermediate security, which represents, but is not the same as, the underlying stocks.

Smart fellow, that Nate Most.

CHARACTERISTICS OF ETFS

Reinvestments of Dividends and Capital Gains: One of the services that open-end mutual funds offer, as we've discussed, is the reinvestment of dividends, interest, and capital gains via the purchase of additional shares of the fund from which they came. This, unfortunately, exchange-traded funds cannot do. The mainframe computers of the trustees, the Authorized Participants, and the exchanges have all they can handle taking care of creations, redemptions, and deliveries. The reinvestment of dividends, interest, and capital gains

---

[1] Some agricultural products, including corn, have replaced warehouse receipts with shipping certificates. There are no warehouse receipts for livestock, oil, and natural gas; these are too perishable or too dangerous to store for long. Neither are there warehouse receipts for contracts on stock indexes and other financial products. Such intangibles have nothing physical to store.

would give the equipment indigestion. Assuming the computers could handle reinvestments, the tax statements calling for you to report said dividends, interest, and capital gains in your personal tax return and requiring that you add reinvested items back to the cost bases of your shares would drive you bananas. In any event, automatic reinvestments are not an option.[2]

Some ETF sponsors assert that they handle the reinvestment of dividends. Don't be confused by this. Here's what the sponsors mean: As is true of regular mutual funds, the dividends paid by the stocks owned by the ETF are added to the ETF's cash value and become part of the net asset value of the trust. These reinvestments take place within the trust. But at the shareholder level, reinvestment is not available. In every case, after being reduced by costs, dividends are paid out to the ETF shareholders.

As the holder of an exchange-traded fund that pays dividends (not all do), you must therefore deal with the receipt of cash every quarter. Not that the money arrives with a big red bow at your personal mailbox. Nothing in connection with ETFs arrives at your personal mailbox except your brokerage statements and annual or semiannual ETF reports. ETF trustees issue certificates of ownership to no one. If they did, costs would soar. The evidence of your ownership of the ETF appears in the statement you receive from the broker. You cannot acquire ETFs except through a broker, and brokers are required to render statements. As time goes on, more brokerage houses may deliver their statements electronically rather than by mail. This would cut costs further.

When an ETF dividend pops into your brokerage account (the cash is transferred to the brokerage firm electronically, of course), it may be "swept" by the firm into its money market account. But there it sits until you at least receive your monthly statement and observe that the money has been received or until your broker advises you of its receipt and suggests investment. If the amount is small, the dividend may stay there for longer, awaiting other cash inflows, until the balance builds to a level high enough to make it worthwhile to spend a minimum commission on the purchase of additional shares of equities. All of this causes delays. Those who

---

[2] On the ex-date of a stock dividend, the price of the stock—all other things being equal—falls by the amount of the stock. The same is true of ETFs.

consider themselves in the know refer to it as "dividend drag." It's one of the disadvantages of ETFs, although not a huge one, and it contrasts with the immediate reinvestment of dividends into additional shares of open-end mutual funds. How you might utilize the dividends to your best advantage is discussed in Chapter 11, which concerns asset allocation.

After the year-end, you receive a tax statement from your brokerage firm informing you of the amounts of dividends, interest, and capital gains to report in your personal returns. If you acquired additional shares of ETFs, you're stuck with adjusting the tax cost bases of your holdings upward.

Capital Gains: ETFs are less likely to generate capital gains than index funds, and they are far less likely to generate capital gains than managed, open-end mutual funds. As mentioned above, managed funds engage in too much buying and selling of the securities in their portfolios. The result is too much in the way of capital gains, especially the onerous short-term variety.

Indexes have very low turnover. The index funds that track them therefore report few capital gains, and the gains they do report are generally long-term. The same also applies to exchange-traded funds. But when the headlines are dour and index fund investors feel the grip of panic at their throats, some of them redeem their shares, precipitating unwanted sales of stock by the managers and causing tax ramifications for those shareholders who do not sell. ETFs do not have this problem. It doesn't matter how many ETF holders engage in panic selling. No selling of the underlying stocks by the trustee results. Exactly why is explained in the next chapter.

Capping: Some indexes are "capped." Recall that the Securities and Exchange Commission regulates exchange-traded funds as mutual funds. One of the many rules it imposes on mutual funds requires that no individual security may constitute more than 25 percent of the value of an entire fund. To accommodate this rule, some ETFs reduce the assumed capitalization of a particular company, to reduce its proportion down to a maximum of 25 percent of the fund. This brings the ETF "mutual fund" into compliance with the rule.

ETFs are reviewed quarterly for compliance purposes. In early 2000, the price of Nortel rose so much that its market value exceeded

40 percent of the value of the iShares MSCI Canada ETF. A significant number of shares had to be sold to bring the value of the Nortel holding down to only 25 percent of the fund. Later, as the price of Nortel fell, purchases were made. All of this increased the turnover rate of the fund significantly.

No such paring needed to be done for the MSCI Canada Index itself. Since indexes are hypothetical portfolios, the SEC exercises no jurisdiction over them. But when an ETF is adjusted to comply with SEC rules and the index on which it's based is not adjusted, the ETF falls out of alignment with the index and becomes of less value to investors.

CHAPTER 5

Keeping ETFs on the Straight and Narrow

We return, now, to the Authorized Participants. Why do they bother to create and redeem big quantities of Spiders and other exchange-traded funds? What's in it for them? More importantly, what are they doing for you?

Recall the notion of the net asset value (NAV) of mutual funds. The fund adds up the values of its holdings, adds the cash, subtracts liabilities, and arrives at the total value of the fund at that moment. That's the net asset value. Dividing this by the number of shares outstanding results in the net asset value per share. The NAVs of most mutual funds are calculated once a day at the close, if not more often.

The secondary market in Spiders is active throughout the day. The prices of the Spiders may vary from the "true" net asset value of the underlying securities in the trust. What is the true value? It has a lot of names. The most common one is "underlying trading value."[1]

Recall that the prices of closed-end mutual funds vary from the net asset values per share of the fund. In that case, the fluctuations are considerable—15 percent or more. The prices of exchange-traded funds vary from the underlying trading value of the trust, too. But in this case, the fluctuations are small.

---

[1] Other names mentioned in ETF prospectuses and marketing materials are "intraday indicative index value," "indicative optimized portfolio value," and "intraday value."

The underlying trading value of an ETF is calculated every 15 seconds during the day. It represents the value of the stocks held by the trust, plus the cash, all divided by the number of outstanding shares of the exchange-traded fund. The value of each stock in the trust is based on the last traded price and does not allow for an estimate of any change in the price due to the possibility that, for example, trading in the stock may have been halted. For Spiders, the underlying trading value may be found with electronic equipment, using the symbol SXV. The underlying trading value is calculated throughout the day, and the net asset value is calculated only at the day's end. Otherwise, the two terms mean essentially the same thing.

The prices of Spiders during the day (SPY) are seldom the same as the underlying trading value (SXV). But they're close, because the Authorized Participants and other institutional parties cause them to be close. The process engaged in by the Authorized Participants to bring the ETF prices within a narrow range of the underlying trading value has a fancy French name: *arbitrage*. Those who engage in arbitrage are called *arbitrageurs*. But since this word does not fall easily from the tongue of an English-speaking person, most people refer to arbitrageurs as "arbs."

Let's say that a roadside stand offers a bunch of tomatoes for $1.50 a pound. You happen to know that the local supermarket is selling the same kind of tomatoes for $2.00 a pound, and you figure that the supermarket is buying them for $1.90 a pound, enabling you to profit by 40 cents per pound.

The light of opportunity flicks on in your fertile brain. From the roadside stand, you buy 200 pounds of tomatoes for $300 ($1.50 times 200 pounds). Rushing to the supermarket, you sell them at $1.90 a pound, for a total of $380. After deducting five bucks for the gas and oil, you clear a quick $75 ($375 less $300). Nice going; you're an arb. (Actually, a supermarket is unlikely to buy tomatoes from you or me, for fear that we laced the little beauties with arsenic.)

Let's say that, after figuring the currency conversion, Coca-Cola stock is selling for $44 in London. At that moment, it's selling for $44.10 in New York. Bingo! You buy 20,000 shares in London and immediately sell them in New York. Before costs, you clear two grand (20,000 times $.10).

Arbitrage is the purchase of an item in one market and the sale of the item in another, with the goal of profiting from a difference in price between the two markets. Arbs do everyone the favor of bringing the two markets into alignment.

Let's say that the person who runs the operations of an Authorized Participant has her mainframe going full blast. The computer picks up that the Spider's underlying trading value (SXV) is $145.[2]

The computer detects that Spiders are trading at the moment on heavy volume at $144.70. Presto! The Authorized Participant immediately buys 100,000 shares of Spiders at $144.70 (for a cool $14,470,000), submits the Spiders to the State Street Bank, and receives shares of the 500 stocks that make up the S&P 500. The underlying trading value at that moment is $145 per share, making the shares worth $14,500,000 (100,000 shares times $145). In the final step, the Authorized Participant immediately sells the shares on the markets where the various stocks are traded.

The Authorized Participant bought for $14,470,000 and sold for $14,500,000. He clears $30,000.

For simplicity, I assumed above that the purchase of the Spiders and the sales of the stocks do not change the prices. Actually, they would change the prices. The purchase of the Spiders would tend to bring the price up from $144.70 to perhaps $144.75. And the sale of the 500 stocks would tend to lower the prices of the stocks, bringing the net asset value per share of the trust down from $145 to perhaps $144.95. This still leaves a gap of 20 cents ($144.75 and $144.95), which another arbitrageur might step in to close.

Arbitrage brings the two prices closer together. It diminishes the variances between the prices of the exchange-traded fund and the trust's underlying trading value per share. The arb makes a good buck, of course. But he also enhances the ETFs desirability. Investors in Spiders and other ETFs can feel confident that the shares they're buying are as close to the true value of the index as possible. The volume of trading increases, providing greater liquidity. The arb wins, sure, but so does everyone else.

---

[2] Spiders were initially priced at 1/10th the value of the S&P 500 Index. If the Index were 1200, the price of Spiders would be $120. All ETFs are initially priced at a specified fraction of the index it tracks (for example, Diamonds: 1/100th; Qubes: 1/40th). But over time, the relationship does not hold true. Dividend accumulations and daily tracking errors gradually draw the ETF price away from the index value. Not that any such deviation makes ETFs funds less attractive as investments; it doesn't.

Let's go at this one more time. Say the price of Spiders is currently $160. The net asset value per share as of a few seconds ago was $159.60. The arbitrageur endeavors to buy all of the S&P 500 stocks at prices that would enable the underlying trading value of the trust to remain at $159.60. He comes close; his purchases cause the prices of the 500 stocks to rise slightly, so that the underlying trading value increases from $159.60 to $159.70. The purchases cost the arb $15,970,000. He delivers the shares to the trust and immediately receives 100,000 Spiders ($15,970,000 divided by $159.70 equals 100,000 shares). The arb endeavors to sell those Spiders for $160. But the actual sale price is $159.90, and the arbitrageur receives $15,990,000 (100,000 times $159.90).

The arb nets $20,000 ($15,990,000 less $15,970,000).

The arb also reduced the price variance from 40 cents ($160.00 and $159.60) to 20 cents ($159.90 and $159.70), making Spiders all the more desirable. Investors feel assured that the difference between the price and the NAV per share is as close as possible.

All of this takes place in short order. Within seconds, thousands of accurate bookkeeping entries are recorded, and thousands of accurate transmissions take place, all with huge amounts of money. It's a marvel.

You yourself may observe an opportunity for arbitrage. Check SXV and SPY and see if there's a difference. Sometimes one will be higher; sometimes the other. The arb buys whichever is cheapest and sells in the other market.

Some arbitrages involve creations or redemptions with the underlying trust; others don't. An arb may buy the underlying 500 stocks in the market, for example. But instead of receiving new Spiders from the trust and selling them outright, he may simply sell Spiders short in the secondary market. (See below regarding short selling.) As long as no creation or redemption is involved, the person doesn't have to be an Authorized Participant.

Not all arbitrage trades are profitable. The variance the arb is counting on may narrow significantly before the trades are executed. Another party may be trying to execute an arb at the same time . But the arbs keep at it. One prominent arb arranges approximately 100 arbitrages every trading day in various ETFs.

I heard an active participant in the ETF industry say in a lecture that, in connection with arbitrage, "greed works." Indeed, he's correct. Nevertheless, I'm uncomfortable with the word "greed." It casts the task of arbitrage in an unfavorable light. Almost everyone wants more. Opportunism is part of human nature. If a potential employer offers you a job for a certain pay, you're unlikely to suggest that the pay is excessive. If you see a $20 bill in the street and no one who could have dropped it is nearby, you would be a fool if you didn't slip it into your pocket.

Arbitrageurs make good money, or they wouldn't bother. But they're in sharp competition with each other. If the earnings for all of them were wildly excessive, their success would be no secret. More institutions would pile into the business of arbitrage until the profit potential dropped back to the level of reasonableness. Opportunism is neither criminal nor immoral. When individuals have the freedom to pursue good fortune, the invisible hand described by the Scottish economist Adam Smith in his 1776 *Wealth of Nations* causes everyone to gain the maximum benefit.

Where was I? Oh yes, arbitrage narrows the gap between ETF prices and the net asset values of their respective trusts. It tightens the variances, making investment in ETFs all the more attractive. By the way, arbitrage is undertaken by more people than Authorized Participants. Unauthorized participants cannot engage with the trustee in the creation and redemption of shares, but they can trade the ETFs against the stocks that underlie them and against options, futures, or other ETFs.

Spiders, Diamonds (the Dow Jones), and QQQs (Nasdaq 100) are by far the most popular and widely used exchange-traded funds. Indeed, the QQQs are the most heavily traded security in the world. The volume of each is higher than that of the other ETFs, giving arbitrageurs more opportunities to trade in big numbers. Therefore, the variances of those funds tend to be narrower. During the course of the trading day, the variances on Spiders are very small—just fractions of one percent. Unlike mutual funds, the more trading there is, the more efficient ETFs become. As a general rule, the higher the volume of trading, the more you may be sure that the price reflects the true supply-demand conditions. In addition to the hedgers and arbitrageurs, who are not gamblers, you can rely on the day traders, who are indeed gamblers—and foolish ones at that—to help create a better product for you, simply because of the trading volume they generate.

With a variance of perhaps 15 or 20 cents, arbitrageurs are inclined to step in. As of this writing, the current price of Spiders is $113.13. A variance of 20 cents is only about 2/10ths of one percent. That is 0.177 percent, or 18 basis points, which is remarkably little.

Basis Points

Stock market commentators frequently use the term basis points. A single basis point is 1/100th of one percent. Maybe the commentators prefer the term because "th" makes them tongue-tied. Every professional group likes to develop vocabulary of its own. Using special terms makes members feel like they are comfortably a member of the clique. Anyway, 0.50 percent is 50 basis points. If the Federal Reserve raised the fed funds rate from 1.75 percent to 2.00 percent, it would have done so by 25 basis points. One percent is 100 basis points.

But the variance is, nevertheless, a cost. Let's say you buy and sell 1000 shares of Spiders. On both occasions, the underlying trading value of the trust is exactly $122.00 per share. (For simplicity, I will refer to underlying trading value as NAV.) But you happen to buy when Spiders are selling at a 20-cent premium. You acquire 100,000 shares at $122.20, for a cost of $122,200.

Later—it could be minutes later or months later—you sell when the NAV is exactly the same, $122.00 per share. But this time, Spiders are selling at a 20-cent discount. You sell 100,000 shares at $121.80 and receive $121,800.

Not counting commissions, you lost $400. This is only about 3/10ths of one percent of your investment (30 basis points, right?), but it's a cost over which you have no control. You therefore want those arbitrageurs to stay on the ball and step in as often as they can.

You, however, should not step in as often as you can. You should trade as seldom as you can. The more often you trade, the more you incur potential variance costs. Let's take it to an extreme. Let's say you execute 100 trades a day. That's 50 round trips. Let's say the average variance combined with the average spread is 20 cents, or 3/10ths of 1 percent. Your ETFs must gain 15 percent a day (0.30% x 50 round trips) just to break even. If you trade 200 days a year, your ETFs must gain 3000 percent a year (15 percent profit per day times 200 days) to break even. You don't think you can gain 15 percent a day, every day, do you? If so, dream on, kiddo, dream on.

Variances aren't the only costs. Anyone who day-trades in such a manner is a fool. Being a reader of this book, you, on the other hand, are as wise and intelligent as they come.

Trade as infrequently as possible. Acquire ETFs that represent thousands of stocks from throughout the world and don't sell them. Let the millions of people who work for those companies do the work for you, just as your work benefits the shareholders of the company that employs you. You are riding on the shoulders of those millions of other people, and they're riding on yours. Buy, but except for modest rebalancing, as explained in Chapter 11, do not sell. Let time and patience make you a financial winner.

Trading Volume: The average daily volume of the most active ETF, the Nasdaq 100 (the symbol is QQQ; they're referred to as "Qubes") is about 70 million shares. This is about one-ninth of the 600 million shares outstanding, implying that the average share is turned over about once every nine trading days.

But 80 percent of the volume of actively traded ETFs is generated by a small percentage of the shareholders, including arbitrageurs. Reports to the government reveal that about one-quarter of the Spider and QQQ shares are held by institutions. Indeed, the average trade for the QQQs is 2500 shares. This many shares involve a hefty chunk of money, on the order of $100,000. Does that sound like Joe Sixpack to you? To me, it implies that a handful of larger investors, including arbitrageurs, dominate the trading. There are day traders, sure, but clearly the average investor of modest means is hanging on to their ETF shares longer than most people think. The frenetic activity that underlies these holdings is part of the strength of exchange-traded funds. The incessant arbitrage continually ensures that the prices of the ETFs remain as close as possible to the values of the indexes they represent.

Most ETF investors, however, are not hanging on for 30 years. I want you to break the mold. I want you to assemble a spectrum of exchange-traded funds, as described later in this book. Except for rebalancing, I want you to hold them for decades, through thick and thin. With the long-term investments, the benefits are thick, and the problems are thin.

SPECIAL PROBLEMS REGARDING VARIANCES

During a brief period every day, variances become a bigger problem. Describing it requires a brief foray into futures markets.

Let's say you're Nebraska producer of wheat. You have supplies, machinery, employees, weather, and other complicated things to worry about. Speculating on the price of wheat isn't your bag. At the time you plant 10,000 bushels of wheat in the spring, you sell them in the futures market for delivery in the fall. Until you actually deliver, you receive no money, but the price for which you sell in the spring determines how much you'll receive. A price drop during the summer doesn't disturb you, because you have transferred the price risk to others, and they take the loss. A price rise benefits the speculators, but the price for which you sell in the spring should earn you sufficient profit.

After computers came into their own, futures contracts in financial securities were developed. If you buy a single S&P 500 futures contract that matures six months hence (and don't sell the contract prior to maturity), you are required to buy about $300,000 worth of the S&P 500 stocks. Alternatively, if you sell an S&P 500 contract maturing in six months and don't buy the contract prior to maturity, you must then sell about $300,000 worth of the S&P 500 stocks. Most futures trades are unwound prior to maturity. The contracts can be bought or sold quickly, with low commissions, and the trader of a single contract on the S&P 500 is required to furnish only about $20,000 to support the $300,000 trade.

Financial futures are widely used as hedges. Let's say that a mutual fund manager holds $100 million of stocks. During the next two weeks, he expects the stock market to be vulnerable. (How he could expect any such prediction to be reliable is beyond me, but money managers frequently act on such predictions.) The manager doesn't want to sell his entire portfolio and buy it back again in a couple of weeks. (For that, we'll give him a gold star.) Instead, he sells up to $100 million of S&P 500 futures contracts. This nullifies his positions. If the market falls, he loses on the stocks but gains on the futures. If the market rises, he gains on the stocks but loses on the futures. If he's fully hedged, no matter which way the market goes, he makes or loses nothing.

The trading of stocks comes to an end, as you know, at 4:00 p.m., New York time. But futures trading continues for another 15 minutes. During that quarter-hour, the fund manager could hedge his position in the futures market, but not, historically, in the stock market.

The sponsors of Spiders didn't like that situation one bit. They didn't like fund managers hedging in the futures market when they could do the same with Spiders, even during those last 15 minutes. Therefore, the sponsors arranged for trading in Spiders to continue until 4:15. Sponsors of other ETFs have followed suit, even though, for many sector or foreign market ETFs, there are no equivalent futures contracts.

But as to variances, the 15-minute extension of trading creates a problem. The underlying trading value of the Spider trust, you recall, is based on the current prices of the S&P 500 stocks. When stock trading comes to a halt, the NAV of the trust remains fixed. But Spider prices do not remain fixed; they go on trading for another 15 minutes, when no arbitrage can be undertaken. The earth keeps turning during this quarter-hour. In the financial world, things change from second to second. As the time passes, Spider prices may stray further and further from the 4:00 p.m. net asset value of the trust. If surprising earnings of one of the major S&P 500 stocks, such as Microsoft, should be announced during that time, Spider prices might diverge considerably from the 4:00 p.m. net asset value of the trust. It's not that Spiders suddenly become mispriced during those 15 minutes; they remain properly priced. It's just that important new information changes investor expectations.

Despite all this, the end of stock trading is when variances are formally recorded every day. But the close of stock trading is a problem for ETFs because this is when the variances are generally wider than at any other time. The published records paint a more unfavorable picture of the variances than prevails until 4:00 p.m. Disregard the published records. During most of the trading day, the variances of the broad-based ETFs with big volumes are remarkably narrow.

So far, we've been talking about the major ETFs, like Spiders, whose underlying stocks can generally be bought and sold quickly and easily. If you have the equipment, trades in those stocks can usually be executed in seconds. But the underlying stocks of some exchange-traded funds cannot be bought or sold quickly. The volume of trading in those stocks is relatively light, and so is the volume of the corresponding ETFs. Try though they might, arbitrageurs cannot get their trades executed quickly. The variances in those exchange-traded funds therefore range more widely than they do for the more active ETFs.

The same applies to the ETFs of foreign markets. Many foreign stocks are not as liquid (that is, cannot as readily be bought or sold) as U.S. stocks. The trading volume tends to be lower. Also, an arbitrageur may take a position on one side of the market for ETFs in America and, because of a time difference, be forced to delay taking an opposing position until the market opens a few hours later in the foreign nation. This, too, disrupts the task of arbitrageurs and widens the variances.

Short Selling

A short sale is undertaken in anticipation of the price of the stock going down. The stock is borrowed from the brokerage firm (no interest is charged). The firm obtains the shares from someone who holds it on margin. The margin agreement signed by that person—and by every margin buyer—authorizes the firm to lend stock held on margin without the owner's knowledge or permission.

Okay, you have now borrowed stock, which you sell in the open marketplace. The buyer of the stock doesn't know you're selling short, but this doesn't matter. You're selling short because you think the price will fall. The buyer thinks the price will rise. In time, perhaps you'll both be right.

Anyway, you happen to be correct; the price falls. You then buy the stock in the open marketplace. This is called "covering" the short. You need not buy from the person you originally sold to, because every share of a particular company has exactly the same value as every other share.

You bought low and sold high, only you did the selling first. When you own stock, you are said to hold it "long." When you sell stock short, you are said to be "short."

Many institutions, including the trustees of exchange-traded funds, make available for short-selling purposes the stocks they hold long. For them, it's a source of income.

CHAPTER 6

The Costs of Exchange-Traded Funds

Variances: As discussed, variances are one of the costs of exchange-traded funds, always minimized by arbitrageurs.

Operating Costs: The operating costs of most ETFs are very low, partly because they avoid such complexities as mailing out certificates of ownership and reinvesting dividends and capital gains. The costs are deducted from the dividends. The quarterly dividends that pop into your brokerage account are net of the ETF costs. Some exchange-traded funds track high-tech industries whose companies pay little or no dividends. To the extent that the dividends do not cover the operating costs, the costs are deducted from the net asset value of the trust.

Royalties: An exchange-traded fund that tracks a particular index must pay an ongoing royalty to the company that owns the index. Dow Jones, Standard & Poor's, Wilshire, Russell, Morgan Stanley Capital International, and other companies that generate indexes all receive income for their use by ETFs .

Spreads: Recall that we discussed a car dealer being a market maker with a spread of $8,000–$12,000 on a used car.

Since the trading volume of stocks is high, the spreads are low. The trading volume of the popular ETFs is very high, and the spreads are very low. But you pay a spread only if the other party with whom you're trading is a market maker. That's how he makes his living. Most market orders for Spiders, for example, are handled by the specialist or by market makers. But the Spider post on the American Stock Exchange is crowded, not only with market makers, but with non-market-making brokers, who endeavor to execute trades for their clients with other brokers. They may bypass the market maker. (On an exchange, the principal market maker for any particular stock is called a specialist.) In many such cases, the price is set between the bid and the asked prices.

For active ETFs, as I say, spreads are very narrow. On Spiders, they're likely to be a nickel. Say the quote is $120.00 bid, $120.05 asked. Buying 100 shares would cost you $12,005. If you sold the shares immediately, before the price changed, you'd receive $12,000 (not including commissions). On the investment of $12,005, the spread would cost you $5.00. That's 4/100th of one percent, or 4 basis points. Not very much, although even insignificant costs become onerous when the trading is frequent.

Great Britain imposes on foreigners a "stamp tax" on the purchase and sales of securities in England. This is reflected in the spreads on iShares MSCI United Kingdom. Let's say that you buy 10,000 of iShares MSCI UK. The market maker doesn't happen to have any shares in his inventory. To accommodate your purchase, he goes short. But being short $150,000 of British stocks is not his idea of fun, because he doesn't know whether the prices are going up, down, or sideways. As soon as possible, he therefore buys, in the proper proportions, $150,000 of the British stocks represented in the MSCI UK Index. This removes his price risk and hedges his ETF position. If the prices fall, his profit on the ETF is offset by the loss in the stocks. If the prices rise, his profit in the stocks offset his loss in the ETFs. This is all very well, except that the stock purchases in the UK trigger payment of the pesky stamp tax. The market maker passes the cost of the tax to others by widening the spread. Not that I blame him; ultimately, all taxes are paid by consumers.

When Americans are heading home for dinner, the Japanese and Australians are just rising for breakfast. Let's say that, at 10:00 in the morning, New York time, a U.S. investor enters a market order to sell $50,000 worth of iShares MSCI Singapore, the exchange-traded fund of Singapore stocks. The market makers for this ETF are required to accommodate the sale. Market makers don't like risk any more than everyone else. For about 12 hours until the Singapore stock market opens, the market maker who buys the $50,000 worth of iShares MSCI Singapore cannot hedge the risk by selling short the underlying Singapore stocks.

Alternatively, if the investors at 10:00 o'clock in the morning buy, instead of sell, $50,000 of the Singapore ETF, the market maker would have to sell his holdings (or sell the shares short if he had none in inventory.). To hedge the risk, he would prefer to buy the individual stocks on the Singapore stock market. But for about 12 hours, he can't do this either.

Unable to hedge for a full trading day, the market makers run risks that are not run when the positions can be hedged immediately. To compensate, the market makers increase their spreads. They widen the gap between the bid and asked prices, making more on each trade, to provide a cushion to offset unhedged risks.

Market makers include specialists. With any single security, such as Spiders, there is generally only one specialist, although there may be many market makers. For ETFs with low volume, a single person may serve as specialist for something like eight ETFs. The specialist controls the trading, especially when the orders are large. He can decide how much of a trade he will offset with his own money (or his employer's money) and how much he'll pass off to others. He keeps the "book" of outstanding limit orders, and he's the only person who has access to the book. After a buildup of limit orders overnight, the specialist has a special opportunity for profit when the market opens in the morning. But in return, to the extent he can, the specialist is required to keep an orderly market. If the price is trending down, for example, he must keep it falling in stages. Unless the selling is overwhelming, which occurs during periods of panic, he must spend his own money to prevent the price from gapping down unduly.

There are approximately 20 market makers for Spiders. Inactive ETFs have many fewer market makers.

The amounts that specialists and market makers deal with can be substantial. For example, the maximum order for an ETF that a brokerage firm can submit to a specialist on the American Stock Exchange is 99,999 shares. With Spiders, that's about $12,000,000.

You may recall that back in 1987, the U.S. stock market suffered a devastating, one-day decline. During parts of the day, the stock market and the futures market were not open at the same time, making hedging between the two markets impossible. Hedging alleviates risk. Without it, price fluctuation is increased. ETFs trade in the same markets as the underlying securities. Since the ETFs are used as hedges, market stability is increased.

Operating Costs: The operating costs of exchange-traded funds are remarkably low. There are no 12(b)1 charges to pay for market costs. The operating costs range from 9 basis points (0.09%) to 99 basis points (0.99%) per year. The high-cost varieties are the ETFs of foreign markets. The deduction of operating costs from the trust on a daily basis is one aspect of ETFs that favors the trader. (This is true of mutual funds as well.) If there are 250 trading days a year and you hold an ETF for only a day, you pay only 1/250th of the operating cost. But don't count on this one little goody making you a ton of money. Trading still isn't worth it.

Commissions: If you're investing only $100 a month and paying $45 commission each time, you're hitting your head against a brick wall. Almost half of your money disappears to the broker. Even with commissions of only $8, investments of $100 are foolish. For small monthly investments, use index funds.

But with modest-sized investments, the situation improves greatly. With commissions of $8 a trade, for example, $10,000 in iShares S&P 500 Index, which charges 0.09% per year, would have to be held for about two years to beat the Vanguard 500 Index Fund, which charges 0.18%. This isn't bad. As a long-term investor, you should plan on holding for at least 2 years. Try 30 years. There, that's better.

Capital Gains Taxes: In the capital gains department, ETFs have mutual funds beat—all mutual funds, even the index variety. When you buy an ETF, you avoid taking on the burden of someone else's capital gains. Say an open-end mutual fund buys stocks whose prices rise a lot. You then buy shares of the fund. After you get in, the fund sells some of the profitable stocks and buys different ones. The market falls, with the result that you own shares of the mutual fund at a loss but must nevertheless pay taxes on the capital gains from the sales that took place after you bought your shares. Don't think this hasn't happened. Thousands of people who bought mutual funds at the market top in the spring of 2000 have suffered this very problem.

One reason why people are inclined to buy at the top is because the economy is then strong and employee pay is plentiful. Finding themselves with extra money, people step into the market.

Nor do they do wrong. It's best always to buy stocks when you get the money. Any other prescription causes more problems than benefits. Neither the market nor the economy, you see, is polarized. Both are continuums; they're not way up or way down. They usually move gradually one way or the other (although, to be sure, the market falls fall faster than it rises).

Let's say that both the market and the economy are on the rise, and you've accumulated some money. Some time in the future, both the market and the economy will top out (not at the same time; stock prices make their moves first). The market might reach a temporary peak next week, or it might do so three years from now. You don't know, and neither does anyone else. Just assume that if you buy now, the market will start falling immediately. If you wait, the market will continue to rise indefinitely. Assume that the market will make you wrong about the short term. This partially reduces your anxiety and induces you to stop trying to exercise judgment about the short term. It helps you to buy with an oh-to-heck-with-it attitude. You're always correct to buy. Just hold your nose and do it.

Back to capital gains. In the short term, some investors must report gains that were generated by the mutual fund, even though they hold the shares of the fund at a loss. This is more likely to occur with a managed fund than with an index fund.

But even the short-term unhappiness of your having to pay capital gains taxes when you hold the fund at a loss is highly unlikely to occur with ETFs. Exchange-traded funds seldom buy and sell their underlying stocks. Oh, the trustee creates and redeems shares of the ETF, and it gives and takes delivery of underlying stock. But it seldom actually buys or sells its stocks in the marketplace. It does this only when the components of the index are changed. It may also be required to do so to comply with SEC requirements. But both of these incidences are infrequent. Ordinarily, the trust just follows along behind the company that operates the index. Yes, the assets in the trust do change, but the key is that the trustee seldom executes purchases and sales. Receipts and deliveries of the underlying stocks by the trust take place *in kind*. The stocks pass in and out without being bought or sold. The arbitrageurs do the buying and selling; it is they who must bear the tax consequences. But when Authorized Participants receive stock from the trust, the cost basis of the stock becomes the value as of the date of delivery. Any low tax basis in the trust is wiped out by the delivery. The stock has a new tax basis in the hands of the Authorized Participant. Capital gains are not a factor for Authorized Participants. If the arbitrage is successful, the Authorized Participant pays ordinary income tax on the overall profit.

But let's get back to the main person around here, which is you. Capital gains are generated by sales, not by in-kind exchanges. One of the remarkable aspects of this relatively new investment is that, since the normal fluctuations of the assets of the trust involve in-kind exchanges with third parties, and not purchases and sales by the trust, the tax consequences of those fluctuations do not affect you. With rare exception (and almost never with the actively traded ETFs), you pay capital taxes only when you choose to sell your shares, not when strangers choose to sell theirs.

There's more. When Spider shares are redeemed, the Authorized Participant, as you well know by now, submits Spider shares to the trust and receives shares of the stocks that are included in the S&P 500 Index. But the trustee doesn't distribute just any old shares of each of the 500 stocks. The trust owns some of those shares at low prices and others at high prices. The trustee selects for distribution the shares of each stock that have the lowest cost. The trust is continually getting rid of its low-cost assets. The Spider trust is the oldest of the exchange-traded funds. If ETFs had to carry stocks at their original costs, Spiders would hold very low-cost items indeed. But the fact is, the Spider trust does not hold assets with net gains. Recently, the net assets of the Spider Trust were $25.5 billion. The cost of those investments for federal income tax purposes was $35.5 billion. The trust holds losses, not gains. If you should happen to be the owner of Spider shares when all of the trust assets must be sold, you would have no tax liability whatsoever. Any calamity that forced the trust to sell everything would be of far greater concern than any tax problems.

In contrast, open-end mutual funds do not receive and deliver assets in kind. They must actually buy and sell them. In the (unlikely) event that all of a fund's assets are sold, the tax consequences could be grave. With ETFs, you're not buying into tax problems caused by others. With rare exceptions, you incur the tax consequences of actions taken only by you.

Whenever it can, the trustee gets rid of low-cost stock. High-cost stock is what it wants. On the rare occasions when Standard & Poor's decides to remove a particular stock from its index and replace it with another, the trustee must sell from its portfolio the stock that has been removed. Over time, the trustee has gotten rid of its low-cost shares, so that when the time for a sale rolls around, unless circumstances are unusual, little or no gain results. For the entire nine years from the beginning of 1993 to the end of 2001, for example, the total capital gains distributed to Spider shareholders were—get this—12 cents. We're talking about shares worth on the order of 100 bucks a pop during that period. In comparison, $0.12 amounts to remarkable little.

On the less active, less liquid ETFs, capital gains are more likely. If the market value of a single company within an industry increases so as to cause the stock's value to exceed 25 percent of the index's value, the ETF must reduce its holdings of that stock, to bring it into compliance with SEC requirements. This would occur after the price of the stock has risen considerably. Since creation and redemption takes place at a slower pace with industry ETFs than with the major ETFs, the trustee doesn't have the opportunity to get rid of its low-price stock. The sale of the stock by the trustee, to "rebalance" the portfolio, is therefore likely to generate significant capital gains.

A Visit to the American Stock Exchange

What was once the mezzanine visitors' platform overlooking the trading floor of the American Stock Exchange is now the trading area for exchange-traded funds. I had the pleasure of observing the proceedings.

All of the traders face computers and are equipped with earphones and microphones at the ready. With little space available, almost everyone is stationary. A family-sized television carries CNBC with the sound off, although the spoken words are spelled out in real time. Large black panels display the current quotes above.

Three metal counters, arranged end-to-end with walkways between, are the focus of trading for the three major ETFs: Qubes, Spiders, and Diamonds. Behind the counters, in front of black partitions, stand the specialists and their aids, each such group being employees of a major trading company.

The specialist faces a "crowd," numbering something like 25 people for the Qubes, and 20 each for Spiders and Diamonds. Crowd members remain standing, with laptops resting on wooden stands.

On one side of the mezzanine area is the entrance. Ringing the other three sides are two rows of brokers, market makers, hedging facilitators, and specialists for other ETFs, all seated.

Short-term positions are the rule here, mostly with borrowed money. The goal is to scalp a penny or two per trade. Most positions are hedged immediately. A purchase, for example, would be offset by one or more sales of futures, options, other ETFs, or the underlying stocks. When the position is exited, the hedge is undone.

It's a young man's game. Almost everybody I saw looked to be in their 30s. Many of them are in amicable competition with one another. If you plan to trade, they'll be competition with you. Their experience is considerable. Their reactions are quick. If you think you can beat them at their game, I suggest you think again.

For the Qubes, Spiders, and Diamonds, small orders coming in to the AMEX floor are usually accommodated by the specialists. Big orders, whether buys or sells, elicit immediate shouts from members of the crowd, indicating their eagerness to fill the other side of the order. The specialists decide how much of the trades they want, and the rest are parceled out among members of the crowd. On a large order I overheard, one member of the crowd immediately took charge of allocating the order, calling out numbers representing thousands of shares: "I'll take 15; Billy, you've got 20; Jimmy, 10, . . ." On other orders, different members do the parceling. When working together helps, the traders work together. When it comes time to compete, they compete. Capitalism is what you call it.

Qubes, as mentioned, are the most actively traded securities in the world—not bad for an item created only a few years ago. The total trading of Qubes is approximately 70 million shares a day. This includes trades on various U.S. exchanges. It also includes trades on electronic communication networks like Island and REDI (see Chapter 12), not to mention trades handled on both sides by a single brokerage firm. At $40 a share, 70 million shares amount to $2.8 billion a day. For Spiders, total consolidated trading amounts to $1.7 billion a day. About a quarter of all this is handled on the American Stock Exchange. We're not just whistling Dixie here. By scraping off a penny or two per share, those 30-year-olds have plenty to shout about.

CHAPTER 7

Balancing Short-Term and Long-Term Goals

INVESTMENT GOALS

When you embark on an investment program, figure out how much you're starting with. If you have no more than $250 to launch an IRA, this is no big challenge. But plenty of people who already have investments are unaware of what they hold. If this includes you, make a list. Write down each item, the amount held, the price, and the current value. Categorize the investments into groups: cash or cash equivalents, types of mutual funds, types of bonds, types of stocks, etc.

Write down what you need to spend the money on, and when. Single out those items that will come up within the next 5-to-10 years. Education for children would be a good example. Nail down the details; get as close to the amounts as you can. Do you think the quality of a kid's college education comes from the college or from within the kid? How much can the child earn while in college? Do you have a big trip planned? Do you want to purchase a second home?

Here are some guidelines in connection with short-term financial needs:

A) The shorter the time before the expenditure is needed, the less you can spend on risky investments. For the next decade or two, I consider five years to be the chancy period. If you need the money within five years, stick it into a money market fund, certificate of deposit, Treasury security, or other cash equivalent. If you're certain of an expense to be made in two years, for example, buy an investment that matures in two years.

B) The less money you have, the less you can spend on investments, such as stocks, that can fall in value in the short term. Alternatively, if you have plenty of money, you can accept the risk, because you'll still have enough left, even if you lose. Most of the time, the stock market rises. It's a good thing to be in the market as much as you can. But the less you have, the less you can afford to be in for the short term, for fear the market then happens to go against you.

C) If the stock market has recently taken a significant tumble, the economic news remains bad, market experts are pessimistic, and companies are laying off workers, this is probably a favorable time to invest (although others at such a time would be frightened to do so). Under those circumstances, you might invest money in stocks that you know you'll need to spend in, say, three years.

If the deadline for big expenditures will arrive in more than 5-to-10 years, I believe you're okay for the stock market, especially if a bear market has occurred recently. But no matter how favorable the prospects may seem, don't horse around with individual stocks. Exchange-traded funds are preferable, because each one represents a multitude of stocks. Diversification pays. When you acquire equities, I strongly recommend an asset allocation program, as presented in Chapter 11.

When you buy equities, make sure your expectations are realistic. If you say to yourself, "I want to make a lot of money with no risk," you're in a quandary. If you take no risk, you make little gain. Guaranteed investments, especially those that are guaranteed by the government, make remarkably little.

Here's a more promising expectation: "I'd like to make a reasonable return. I don't anticipate having to use my long-term money for at least 10 years, and I want my investments, collectively, to be worth considerably more then than when I started."

That sounds fine. But here's what you want to guard against: Let's say that, six months after you buy stocks, the market crunches by 20 percent, and your stocks are down. Your reaction may be quite different from the reasonable approach you took originally. You might be inclined to say, "Whaaat! I've lost a fifth of my money?

I don't go for this, man! I'm finding some investment guy who knows what he's doing!"

The investment you bought originally may have been entirely appropriate. But there's no guarantee that those investments wouldn't drop by 20 percent over a couple of years, only to perform magnificently over 5 to 10 years. . The strain of the decline, however, induces you to find an investment person "who knows what he's doing." That advisor senses that your top priority is to *change* what you're doing. Off you go, spending commissions, spreads, and taxes, buying other investments that are safer in the short term or pay higher levels of current income but have less promise of long-term growth.

Many people feel that when their investments are doing well, they're doing a great job, but when their investments are doing badly, the broker really screwed up. Take responsibility for your investments and buy them online. The suggestions in Chapter 11 would enable you to avoid using a broker.

Bear markets can activate emotions that can damage your long-term performance. The most difficult aspect of successful investing is emotions. Learning the niceties of exchange-traded funds is all very well, but when things go against you—and they inevitably will—unpleasant emotions will arise that are vital for you to become aware of from the beginning. Recognize these reactions. Allow yourself to feel them. But do not allow them to cause your investment results to deteriorate.

All of us may want our investments to live in 20-year periods or longer. But we ourselves don't live in such long periods. We live in the moment. We live only a fraction of a second at a time.

During the painful periods of declining stock prices, the pain of the moment can easily take over. Your 5-year, 10-year, and 20-year investment time horizons fly out the window. The chances are you'll find a broker or advisor who goes along with your need to relieve your pain. You sell your stocks and your ETFs at the very time they're perched for a long-term advance.

There are plenty of normal people who fall prey to this kind of reaction. As to your personal life, your sex life, your working life, and whatever else you're doing, by all means live in the moment. Get a Zen teacher. Squeeze every drop of fulfillment you can out of the now. But as far as your investment life is concerned, take it in 10-year lumps. Say you invest primarily in a broad variety of stocks for 10 years. But you fall victim to a long-term bear market , and the buying power of your portfolio, after adjusting for inflation, is down from where you started. Despite this, the chances are excellent that your buying power would have been even worse had you acquired anything other than stocks. Stocks are volatile in the short term. But in the long run, they're the best things around. As the investment time period lengthens, the risk diminishes.

Given all this, you're faced with having to turn risk on its head. We all live, as I've said, in the now. Emotionally, it's the near-term future that concerns us most. Ten or 20 years seem so covered with mist that it's difficult to come to terms with time so far removed. The near term is what we want to control. The more-distant future seems beyond the pale.

But as far as investments are concerned, the reality is quite the opposite. In the near term, the market controls. We can't fathom its month-to-month movements any better than, as swimmers, we can calm the ocean waves. It's discomforting to subject ourselves to conditions in which we have no control in the now. But to be successful investors and enjoy long-term gains, we have no alternative but to subject ourselves to short-term forces we cannot control.

The long term is quite another story. Over the long pull, the stock markets of the world go up. As billions of people create wealth, how can stocks help but do so? Buy exchange-traded funds representing companies that employ the workers of the world, so that you may ride on their shoulders. When they buy shares of the company that employs you, they ride on yours.

Don't be an investment groupie. If you fail to set yourself apart from the investment crowd, you will be more inclined to act on hot tips. You will be more inclined to buy when your friends are supremely confident and to sell when your friends are in despair. Buying high and selling low adds nothing to a fulfilling retirement.

It may be too lonely a road to think of yourself as a loner. But at least set yourself apart regarding your investments. Do not share with your friends the pride you feel about your gains. Do not seek commiseration about losses you may have suffered. When it comes to your investments, stay quiet.

Here's what can happen to a groupie: You buy stocks, and over a couple of years, the market rises. Your friends say, "It can't go on like this."

You sell.

But the market continues to rise. Your friends say, "Golly, the economy is strong, and earnings are terrific. Maybe this bull market is for real." Figuring that you were a fool to sell, you buy.

Immediately, the market begins to fall.

Rome wasn't built in a day, right? You have to take the bad with the good. Having been wrong before, you'd feel really stupid selling at a loss now. You'll just ride it out.

The market falls in earnest. "Oh God," you say to yourself, "I'm no good at this game." But you hang on.

The market is now down 30 percent. You've lost your previous gains, and you're behind. Your friends are warning you to get out, get out, get out; there's no telling how far this thing can fall.

They prove to be right; it falls further. One afternoon, the market falls hugely on enormous volume. Just that morning, you could hardly look at yourself in the mirror without thinking how stupid you are. The additional selling you just can't accept. You sell.

Fifteen minutes later, the panic is over, and prices start rising. By the end of the day, the market has recovered half the day's losses. The whole thing makes you sick.

Several months later, the market is higher. But the economic news is dreadful. Corporate earnings have fallen through the floor and layoffs are big news. You and your friends agree that the market can't stay up in the face of all this. You're glad your money is safely in money markets funds.

But the market doesn't fall. It begins to rise rapidly. After a few months, the news improves.

Never mind, you say to yourself, the record is amply clear that investing just isn't your bag. You'll have a less-fulfilling retirement, maybe, but that's okay. At least you'll have money when you get there.

But the market goes even higher than it did at the beginning. The news is wonderful. Your friends tell you, why accept ordinary income taxes on the interest from that money market fund, when you could earn capital gains in the stock market, capped at 20 percent, and even 18 percent if you hold for five years? Things look good. Whaddaya say, man? How about buying stocks?

You pull your money out of the money market fund and buy stocks.

Just a few weeks later, the market . . .

Meanwhile, one of your friends, who doesn't talk about her investments, invested about the same amount into the market when you first did. She didn't find it pleasant when the market turned sour and the economic news was poor. But she stopped reading the business pages, stopped checking her stock prices, turned off the business shows, and kept assuring herself that she was no fool for having bought stocks. She knew that the work performed by the people of the world would eventually carry the day and that the bad news wouldn't last forever. Except for rebalancing every 13 months, as described in Chapter 11, she did whatever was needed to avoid selling. She held through the bear market. Having started with about the same amount as you, she now has a great deal more.

You're also wise to confront, up front, an elemental childhood fear: the fear of abandonment. Every child senses the possibility that his parents might somehow withdraw, subjecting him to wants and dangers that cannot be met alone. Such fears come up at the prospect of having no control over short-term market fluctuations and at the prospect of confronting market uncertainties without the support of friends. If you feel fears of this nature, do not try to suppress them. It is altogether healthy to feel them. By so doing, you may prevent them from controlling your actions.

Do not decide what you want to do in life and count on the market making it all possible. Put the horse before the cart. The market is the horse. Instead, select investments that, as a group, should provide the best possible long-term returns with the best long-term level of risk. Put your long-term funds into those investments and keep them there. Then accept what the market gives you. You can do no better.

The most difficult part of investing is emotions. And the most difficult action to take is . . . no action. Treating investing as a form of recreation leads to rapid buying and selling. This is the most expensive recreation you can find, because you'll lose a ton of money. Leave your investments alone and find another way to have fun.

You may have heard people say that at that particular time, they were uncertain what to do, because "the market's funny." Remember this: The market is always funny. Short-term uncertainty never dissipates.

Bring your fears to the surface and confront them. Here are some of them:

+ Confront the fear that you might need the money just at the time when stocks are down. You probably won't need the money then.
+ Confront the fear that just because things are bad, they're certain to get worse. This is the thought of a seven-year-old who believes in magic.
+ Confront the feeling that, since you bought investments that went down, you must be a fool. You were not a fool. You bought when you got the money, and you bought well. Archie (that's me) told you to expect stocks to go down in the short term. The market's decline is not your fault.

Do not suppress these fears. Their presence proves that you're a normal human being. Let them come up. Allow the wiser part of you to do a half-Nelson and pin them to the floor.

Here's an important reaction that is normal for most living things. We feel pain and loss about twice as intensely as we feel pleasure. Investors feel the pain from a given percentage loss far more intensely than they feel pleasure from the equivalent percentage gain. This probably stems from our forebears, who had to deal with grizzly bears to their left, tigers to their right, and glaciers up front. Without reliable alarm mechanisms and copious adrenaline, they never would have made it. News programs and newspapers thrive on bad news. When there's an automobile accident, drivers passing by slow to a crawl, straining their necks to catch the sight of blood. All of us have more emotions tied up in bad news than we do in the good.

Develop a tolerance for short-term losses, especially of individual securities. By having the patience not to sell, you may enjoy the security of long-term gains. Your reactions to adversity are normal. Be aware of them, but prevent them from doing harm to your financial future. Do not sell a broadly diversified portfolio just because the news is bad. Give yourself time to benefit from the labor and creativity of the people of the world.

The Long Term: When asked your long-term investment goals, you might say, "I don't know what the future holds. After retirement, my spouse and I want our lives to be as fulfilling as possible. We want to be able to support ourselves when our health deteriorates, and, who knows, maybe leave a few bucks to the kids."

This sounds fine to me. But I urge you not to make the mistake of many others. Your investment time horizon as far as stocks are concerned should not end when you retirement *begins*. Plan on your investment time horizon continuing until your retirement *ends*. Dying is getting harder these days. Medical science is performing miracles without half trying. You should expect to remain active in retirement for many years—and inactive for years after that. My guess is that, by the end of the century, dying will become an option, not a certainty. You yourself, reading this at around the beginning of the century, may not have that fortuitous option. But children born in the year 2000 and thereafter may indeed squeeze under the wire.

Many people in retirement find that they need significant funds during two periods:

- Shortly after retirement, when they plan to do elaborate things such as an extensive trip to the Andes Mountains— things they've always wanted to do, but couldn't while they were working.
- Old age, when disability requires the expenditure of substantial funds.

If and when you kick off, we will all be regretful, of course. But your investments will go on living right here on earth, to benefit your surviving spouse, other members of your family, and your charitable interests.

Do not plan on your investments in stocks coming to an end when you retire. In fact, don't plan on your investments in stocks coming to an end ever. Holding no stocks in retirement is silly. Plan on living for a long time. Your investment time horizon should properly be the year that you or your spouse (whichever's younger) attains the age of 100. Now that's more like it.

Here's a good way to think about risk: It's okay for a particular investment to lose in value, even over a period of several years. The performance of the entire portfolio is what counts. At the time you need the money, it's not okay for all of your investments, collectively, to be worth less than you started with. The performances of individual investments don't matter so much. What matters is the performance of the value of the entire portfolio. Don't sweat the small stuff.

LONG-TERM PROSPECTS AT THE BEGINNING OF 2002

Accepting risk for long-term rewards takes faith. You have to feel assured that hundreds of millions of people throughout the world are going to continue creating value, as they have in the past. I have tremendous faith about this. Here are the basic ingredients for rising stock prices:

+ A rapid pace of technological advance;
+ Money created at a suitable pace;
+ A low risk of terrorism; and
+ Government not doing too much harm.

Technological Advance: The floodgates are opening! The reduction of tax rates in the early 1980s enabled huge amounts of money to be invested in new business ventures, resulting in a wave of new developments in the 1990s. Additional venture-capital investments made in the 1990s will fuel mind-boggling advances in the early part of the twenty-first century. By 2030 or so, even cheap computers costing about $1000 in today's money will probably have the capability of a human brain—20 million billion calculations per second. By about 2060, a single inexpensive computer will equal the brain power of everyone in the entire world. You don't suppose the stock market will fall, long term, in the face of such technical advances, do you?

Money Creation: The Federal Reserve Bank makes possible the creation of America's bank deposits, which constitute over 90 percent of our money supply. The Fed has been far from perfect. It bears part of the responsibility for the economic slowdown of 2000 and 2001, for example. Nevertheless, the Fed is learning. When it goes astray, it returns to the proper course within a year or two. I believe that the Federal Reserve Bank will not again engage in the dreadful policies that persisted for so long in the 1960s and early-1970s.

Terrorism: In September 2001, terrorism became a severe shock for Americans. At the time of this writing, the U.S. government is knocking the possibility of further terror down to size. I'm an optimistic sort, and I believe that the effort will succeed. Within six months after the World Trade Center disaster, by March 2002, I think the risk of terrorism will be at least 60-percent reduced. The risk will be reduced 85 percent by 2003, and 95-percent reduced within five years thereafter.

Government: Ah yes, government. This one's always a stickler. Here are the essential roles any government should play:

- Protection of private property rights;
- Enforcement of contracts;
- Preventing people from hurting others directly by force or fraud; and
- National defense.

Including state, local, and county governments, there are about 4000 tax-raising governmental authorities in the United States. The principal ones, of course, are the federal government and the 50 states. Over the years, American governments have performed the four essential functions mentioned above remarkably well. The result has been the most extraordinary economy in world history.

But as you well know, the governments of the world, including ours, have taken on many other functions besides the four basics. I believe that government policies other than the basic four do more harm than good. The *actual*, long-term results of such big-government policies are opposite to the *intended* results. Since American governments have performed the four essential functions well, the economy has done well despite government's other activities, not because of them.

To me, the evidence is overwhelming that the people of the world are beginning to realize that nonessential roles of government cause more harm than good. Russia is starting down the road toward honoring private property. President Putin has put forth a bill making it legal to sell land. It's about time! China is becoming Communist in name only. India is beginning to limit the powers of a huge bureaucracy. Elections during the year or two prior to this writing have favored the reduction of government in Mexico, Italy, British Columbia, Japan, Peru, Spain, and the United States. Despite heavy campaign spending, the parties favoring bigger government lost. Only in most of Africa has the sunlight of capitalism not yet dawned. Indeed, in Mauritania and the Sudan, slavery is still legal. But even on that benighted continent, television and the Internet should bring changes within the decade.

The framework for economic growth and individual liberty is created by government, and that framework has improved immeasurably. Just a few decades ago, China, the Soviet Union, Eastern Europe, most of Central and South America, most of Africa, and most Asian nations were ruled by dictators. Now, except for Africa, few dictatorships are left. Many nations are cutting tax rates, not raising them. The number-two man, even in the quasidictatorship of China, has reduced the number of ministries from 40 to 29, and he wants to cut China's bureaucracy by half. Man, let's put that guy to work in America!

Consider the changes from only about 60 years ago. Hitler murdered something like 21 million people. Mao Tse-tung killed about 35 million people and starved an additional 27 million from government-induced famines. Lenin and Stalin murdered 20 million and set up a slave labor system that claimed another 40 million lives. Soviet government murders alone tripled the number of deaths from the African slave trade. The total number of governmental killings in the twentieth century exceeded 200 million. And without help from their enemies, the dictators of the Soviet Union and China brought their massive economies to a standstill.

Much of this governmental psychosis has disappeared. Castro killed about 30,000 political opponents. But compared to his forebears, Castro's just a piker. When China tortures a few followers of a religious sect, it's big news. The world hasn't yet turned into Disneyland, but the comparison with just a few decades ago is stunning.

The thrust for a bigger American government came into its own with the well-meaning but disastrous "social engineering" of Herbert Hoover, perpetuated by Franklin Roosevelt. Tariffs were raised in the early part of the century, but especially in 1930. Tax rates were increased in 1932. Hoover's effort to keep labor costs high caused the real income of the employed to rise while unemployment increased enormously. These and many other such policies caused the Great Depression, bringing distress to the entire world.

The last big-government effort to solve social and economic problems in America that had the wholehearted support of the American people consisted of the well-meaning but destructive policies of Lyndon Johnson.

Since then, it's true that the ranks of government have expanded apace. Government subsidies are hard to stop. The benefits mean a lot to relatively few, while the costs are spread among many. But people are catching on that big government causes more harm than good. Yes, the fear of terrorism has induced Americans to appeal to government for help. In some respects, this is appropriate. But I doubt that the expansion will be sustained. America now has about 100 million investors. They're starting to sense that government doesn't butter their bread. The richer people are, the more they need government to carry out the basic essentials and the less they need it to perform all the other dumb things it does. Eventually, voters will induce government policies to become less intrusive. U.S. voters haven't yet realized that big government hurts the poor more than the rich. When they do, the changes will be momentous.

Meanwhile, the huge nations of Indonesia and the Philippines recently ditched rotten presidents, constitutionally. Street demonstrations in Argentina forced a miserable president to flee two years before the end of his term. At this writing, Iran's overzealous theocracy is shaky. For the first time, Asian governments are coming to see the value of a free press. Approximately two-thirds of the U.S. currency lies outside of the United States because people consider it the most likely currency to hold its value. All of this is positive, not only for the poor, but for the world's stock markets.

Those who oppose globalization are dead wrong. The more that the people of the world trade with one another, the stronger everyone gets. Moreover, people that trade a lot don't fight a lot. They don't fight at all, in fact; they talk. It would be enormously healthy for everyone if all U.S. tariffs and all of its barriers to international trade were repealed.

Terrorism is frightening and awful. But it isn't going to last forever. I doubt it will even last for long. It is severe and extended economic downturns that are disastrous for humanity. These are creations of government. The chances of such conditions returning are small and diminishing. So are the chances of great wars. Wars are coming to resemble international police work. Many of the world's nations are becoming democracies. Democracies don't fight. They talk.

When government spending grows faster than the economy, the stock market tends to fall. From 1994 to 1999, for example, government spending grew more slowly than the economy. Sure enough, the stock market soared. It concerns me that, beginning in the year 2000, even before the terrorist attack, the prospect of a government surplus caused the U.S. Congress to go wild with expenditures. The rapid growth of government in 2000 and 2001 no doubt contributed to the bear market of those years. The security concerns to protect against terrorism, necessary though they may be, are adding even more to government spending.

The key factor is the awareness and opinion of voters. Once the terrorist scare subsides, voter suspicions about big government will come to the fore. Technological and political advancements are improving the conditions for mankind, stocks, and the earth. The world's long-term prospects are luminous.

CHAPTER 8

Setting up a Brokerage Account to Buy ETFs

If you've accumulated just a little money and intend to invest a few hundred a month or less, don't bother with a brokerage account. The commissions on buying exchange-traded funds would cut your net returns severely. Buy a broad-based, no-load index funds. Don't buy it through a brokerage firm either, because even though the fund is supposedly no-load, the firm is likely to charge some kind of commission anyway. Contact the no-load fund directly, either by phone or over the Internet.

If you already own a no-load fund whose annual operating charges are low, and you've held it long enough to have accumulated a significant capital gain, my inclination would be to keep it. Do not sell the fund, pay capital gains taxes, and invest the reduced amount in exchange-traded funds. Even if the costs of the ETFs, including the commissions, are low, you are unlikely to catch up with the amount that would have accumulated had you left the money where it was and delayed the payment of tax. But if your mutual fund is held within an IRA, that's quite another story. You could be better off transferring the money to a brokerage firm and buying ETFs, also within an IRA. I'll have more to say about this in Chapter 11.

Otherwise, to buy exchange-traded funds, there's no way around it, you need a brokerage account. They come in three basic varieties:

- *Traditional Firms* charge fairly heavy commissions, say, $40 and up. Orders are placed with an individual broker. If they're asked, such brokers are only too happy to share their opinions about what you ought to do. Some share their opinions even if they're not asked. Such firms also employ stock analysts, who write reports recommending individual stocks. In the long run, these opinions and these analyses are likely to do more harm than good. Plus, they cost money, which you pay for with high commissions.

- *Discount Firms* charge lesser commissions. You deal with a broker, who answers questions about the nature of various investments. But the brokers of discount firms are trained not to give advice or to offer guesses about the future, even if asked. Some discount firms supply stock research. Others don't.

- *On-Line Firms* charge very low commissions. Orders are placed over the Internet or by pushing buttons on your telephone. With some firms, you may place orders verbally, but in this event the commissions are higher. Ameritrade, for example, charges $8 when an order is submitted over the Internet, $12 when it's submitted by pushing buttons on a phone, and $18 when the order is given to a broker. For confirmations sent electronically, there's no cost. For confirmations sent by mail, the firm charges $2. These charges are very reasonable. There is no brokerage firm I like better. (See www.ameritrade.com or call 800-454-9272.)

After reading this book, you should be primed to use on-line firms. By all means, do so. But like all brokers, even the on-line firms thrive on rapid turnover. This you must resist.

Brokers: Brokers can be helpful about the specifics of investment vehicles. But if you happen to talk with brokers associated with traditional firms, do not, ever, ask their opinions about anything having to do with the future—not about individual stocks, the economy, the market, or anything else. You'll obtain more reliable answers by flipping coins. At least you'll be half right. Most brokers are fine people, but the dynamics of the brokerage industry cannot help but cause them to be wrong often. Brokers earn commissions only if they persuade clients to act. It's easier for brokers to persuade anyone to act if they reinforce what the person already believes.

When prices are high and investors are generally bullish, this is usually the very time that brokers suggest buying. They especially favor investments that are hot—the ones that most people feel sure to be certain winners. But when prices are low and investors are generally bearish, many brokers are inclined to recommend that their customers accumulate tax losses. Commissions come in faster when brokers reinforce what customers already believe. Here's the key: Customers—present company excepted, of course—tend to believe the wrong thing. They're bullish when prices are up and bearish when prices are down. Therefore, brokers often find themselves reinforcing the wrong thing. Many brokers believe what they're saying. It's not in their financial interest to question it. Besides, precious few brokers would wax enthusiastic about your buying exchange-traded funds and holding for 30 years. Those who encourage their customers to do such a thing would starve.

Sector Rotation: In preparing for this book, I called a brokerage firm for information. In an effort to find the right person, I happened to speak with a regular broker. When I told him I was writing a book about exchange-traded funds, he responded enthusiastically, "Really?"

"Yes," I replied.

"Are you going to include everything, including sector rotation?"

"Yes."

"That's terrific!"

Before the advent of exchange-traded funds, "rotation" was restricted to the trading of individual stocks. All you have to do is sell the stocks that are going to go down, you see, and buy the ones that are going to go up. Decade after decade, gargantuan efforts have been wasted in the effort to carry off this feat successfully.

Now, lo and behold, exchange-traded funds enable the rotation of entire sectors. "Consumer cyclicals look a little high," says the broker. "Better sell 'em. But energy stocks look like they're ready to break through resistance and bust outta here."

Ah, the power of it. In the chess game of investments, no longer are people limited to shuffling pawns. They now have at their disposal knights, bishops, queens and kings, muscling money from one huge economic sector to another.

Don't be taken in. Do your muscling at the gym. No matter whether your investments represent insignificant parts of the economy or massive parts, their price action in the near future is unpredictable. Sector rotation benefits no one except the broker.

The Media: Most business news you hear about on television or read about in newspapers is not helpful. Here's a headline from a major newspaper, for example. (I don't reveal the name, because this kind of headline is so common that I don't want to ascribe any special blame to the particular paper.) The headline characterizes the stock market for the previous day, when stock prices fell. The headline reads, "Fed Rate Cuts Help Bond Markets But Don't Work Magic on Stocks."

The present tense ("Don't Work Magic") allows for the possibility that the Fed rate cuts will *continue* to not work its magic on stocks. Maybe they will continue to do so, and maybe they won't. Nobody knows about the near-term future, certainly not people who write headlines. It's not their job to predict the market accurately. It's their job to attract readers.

More accurately, the headline might read, "Fed Rate Cuts Have Helped Bond Markets But Haven't Worked Magic on Stocks." Changing to the past tense implies that what's done is done. A subheading might state, "As to the Future, We Don't Have the Faintest Idea Whether the Fed Rate Cuts Will Work Magic or Not."

I'm being picayune. I picked out this headline from the morning paper of the day I happened to be writing about this matter. But you might listen carefully to a rundown of the business news on a television program prior to the market opening. In describing recent trends, the present tense is often substituted for the past tense. A commentator might say, for example, "There was a net outflow of money from mutual funds last month. That's a negative." It's the kind of information viewers want to know, right?

True, except that the inference is wrong. Last month's mutual fund withdrawals may have caused stock prices to fall *last* month. But by saying that the selling pressure *is* a negative, the reporter implies that last month's selling is making investors do more selling *this* month.

If the stock market worked that way, everything would come to a screeching halt. *This* month's selling would increase pessimism and induce selling *next* month, causing even more pessimism and selling the month after that. The market would spiral downward until the prices reach zero. Sorry, there is nothing so inevitable about stock prices. (The only inevitability about stock prices is, in the long run, they go up.)

Assume that the reporter said correctly, "Last month, there was a net outflow of money from mutual funds. That was a negative." Our natural reaction is, well, thanks, but we're not all that interested in last month; we want to know about this month. And could you please give us an idea about next month as well? Smart as they may be, reporters don't know the answers to those questions. No one does.

Television commentators are attractive and articulate. They're well informed, certainly, about what *has* happened. But what has happened is water over the dam. Commentators don't know the future any better than we do. But they can't continually admit to any such incapacity. After all, television producers are in the business of attracting viewers; they want to enhance advertising revenues. If listeners make money because of the program, fine. But to producers, this is a secondary objective. Therefore, reporters engage, with the best of intentions, in a linguistic sleight of hand. Instead of describing what has occurred, they use the present tense, implying at least the possibility that the historic trend is continuing into the present and might even persist into the future. This reinforces on us listeners the impression we are already inclined to believe, namely, that what has occurred will continue to occur. If the economy has declined, it will probably go on doing so. Stock prices have been rising and will continue to rise. Without intending to, the press reinforces our natural inclination to become card-carrying members of the herd.

Opening a Brokerage Account: Whether you open a brokerage account by answering a broker's questions or by filling out a form on-line, be prepared for nosy questions. All brokerage firms are required by the Securities and Exchange Commissions to "know" their customers. The broker is not supposed to allow a customer to acquire an investment whose risk is inappropriate, given the individual's wherewithal, knowledge, and experience. You may be asked questions pertaining to these matters. You will certainly be asked about your employment.

You will also be asked if you are a director, a 10-percent shareholder, or a policy-making officer of a publicly held company. If the answer is yes to any of those possibilities, you're considered an "insider" of the company, and the purchases or sales you make in its shares of that stock must be reported to the SEC, which subsequently reports them to the public.

One of the first questions you're asked when setting up a brokerage account is how the account is to be registered: your name or joint name with right of survivorship. (There are other possibilities, but they're beyond the scope of this book.) Married people are often inclined to choose joint name and are not informed of the potential problems.

Joint name with right of survivorship means that if you die, the other party (we'll presume it's your spouse) automatically becomes owner of the property. This disposition takes precedence over your will. Even if your will provides that everything you own goes to your favorite horse, your will has no effect with regard to the brokerage account. The account goes to your spouse simply because of the account's registration. I have nothing against your spouse, you understand, and I would never stand in the way of enriching such a dear person. But there are two problems, both of which arise if one of you should die. Sorry, those things do happen.

As I've mentioned, if you buy an investment low and sell it high, you pay a capital gains tax on the difference. But if you buy the investment low, you die, and someone *else* sells it high, it's a different story. The cost basis (the low price you paid) is changed by reason of your death to the value as of the date of your death, which presumably is higher than when the item was acquired. If your beneficiary sells soon after your death, the price is probably about the same as the date-of-death value, in which case the capital gains tax is little or nothing. The investment is said to attain a "stepped-up basis." The cost, for tax purposes, is stepped up to the date-of-death value.

Here's the problem: Stepped-up basis doesn't apply to joint accounts. If you acquire an exchange-traded fund in joint name and hold it for 30 years, its value, presumably, is higher at the time of your death than when you bought it. Your spouse becomes the sole owner of the account. She sells, and . . . whoops! She pays a whopping capital gains tax. No stepped-up basis applies to property held in a joint account upon the death of the first to die. To get the stepped-up basis, both of you must depart the scene.

The solution for you and your spouse is to hold the property separately in your own names. Even better, place your property into a revocable living trust, the nature of which is way beyond the scope of this book. The legal costs to set up such a trust would probably run something like $2000 or more. If you're just beginning, such an expense should, of course, be postponed.

The other problem with joint accounts applies to federal estate taxes. Again, the problem arises for wealthier individuals, but since you're sharp enough to be reading this book, I have every expectation that you'll join their ranks.

All through life, the federal government, as you know, taxes what you earn. But when you give your property away, either during life or at death, it also taxes what you own. This is called the transfer tax, and there are lots of things that reduce it. I'll explain two:

- ◆ The marital deduction. Whatever amounts you transfer to your spouse, during life or at death, are deductible from the transfer tax.
- ◆ A large credit. The credit is $1 million in 2003 and will increase in steps to $3.5 million in 2009. If an estate is large enough in 2009 to call for a tax of $3.5 million, for example, the credit reduces the actual tax payable to zero.

Here's the key. If all of your property passes to your spouse because of joint-name registrations, your estate incurs no tax. But the credit available to your estate remains unused, because the marital deduction reduces the estate to zero, resulting in no tax against which to apply the tax credit.

When your spouse subsequently dies, his or her estate is piled high, not only with property the spouse owned previously, but also with property inherited because of the joint ownership. If the spouse doesn't remarry; the marital deduction is not available. Despite the use of the credit by the spouse's estate, the tax could nevertheless be large, on the order of 45 percent.

The solution? Each of you holds property in your own names—better yet, in revocable living trusts. Such trusts enable you to have control over your property. You may serve as trustee of your own property, and the trust can be revoked at any time. An estate-planning attorney can explain how both you and your spouse may be comfortably provided for as the survivor. Yet each estate has the opportunity to utilize its credit. Neither credit is lost.

If you think all this is ridiculously complicated, you're right. Write your representative in Congress a sharp letter calling for the immediate and permanent repeal of all death and gift taxes. The government takes in relatively little money from these taxes, but the disruption caused is enormous, and so is the cost of arranging one's affairs to reduce the taxes. You might add in your letter that wealthy people are the ones who provide employment for the others, giving the others, in turn, a chance to get wealthy. Tell your representative that the world needs as many wealthy people as possible.

Cash: Do not hold for long even a modest amount of cash at a brokerage firm. On small amounts the brokerage firm keeps the interest. On large amounts, you forfeit the opportunity to be invested mostly in stocks. Stocks are where you'll find the best long-term payoff. The best time to buy stocks is when you get the money.

Pertinent Dates: The date on which you acquire a security is called the trade date. The SEC requires that the cash in payment must be in the hands of the brokerage firm just three brief trading days later. Snail mail being unreliable, it's usually best for the money to be on deposit at the firm in advance of the purchase.

If a dividend is payable on a stock that you bought recently, are you entitled to receive the dividend or not?

It depends on the dividend's ex-date. You remember your Latin, don't you? "Ex" means "from" or "without," as evidenced by the word "exception."

If you buy a stock on the ex-date, you're one day too late to receive the dividend. On that day, the stock trades "without" the dividend. You receive the dividend only if you buy the stock *prior* to the ex-date. All other things being equal, the price falls on the ex-date by the amount of the dividend. Let's say the price of a stock at the close on the day prior to the ex-date is $100. The dividend to be paid is $.50. (For the year, the stock pays four times this amount, or $2.00, giving the stock a dividend yield of 2 percent, that is, $2.00 divided by $100.)

On the morning of the ex-date, assuming there are no other changes that would influence the stock price, the stock opens at $99.50, down a half. No one knows whether there are other influences or not, of course; these things are never exact. But during the course of a calendar quarter, the stock price gradually gains by the amount of the anticipated dividend, and on the ex-date, it falls by the amount paid. On the day a stock "goes ex," newspaper stock pages display some sort of symbol to indicate that that is in fact the ex-date.

Clearing: The SEC imposes special requirements on broker-dealers that handle the securities and cash of customer accounts. (These functions are referred to as "clearing.") The amounts of money handled by clearing firms are large, and the SEC requirements are expensive. A brokerage firm that is too small to bear the costs arranges for another, larger firm to do the clearing. The commissions are shared by both firms. It's as if the clearing firm is the wholesaler and the smaller firm the retailer. If you set up an account with a certain brokerage firm, you may at first be surprised to receive your statements from another firm. The latter is the clearing organization. The statement reveals that your account came to the clearing organization from the firm with which you opened the account.

Insurance: No one insures your brokerage account against the possibility of your investments going down in value because of unfavorable price action. When you buy stocks, bonds, or any other kind of securities, you must accept investment risk. But your account is indeed insured against the brokerage firm (or the clearing organization) goofing up its business. If there is fraud or business failure, a government organization called the Securities Insurance Protection Corporation (SIPC) is the first to step in. Things usually move slowly when government is involved, and you shouldn't count on receiving your money in a hurry. But the SIPC insures against fraud or business failure up to $500,000 per account, with a maximum of $100,000 for cash losses. (Brokerage firms are not banks. You are presumed to have most of the cash invested in securities.) But even if your account is larger than these amounts, most brokerage firms pay for additional insurance that protects clients against fraud or business failure up to far higher amounts, say, $10,000,000 per account or more. That should take care of your needs, to start with, anyway.

Everything on One Statement: A brokerage statement shows the securities you hold and the value of them as of the statement date. As you shall see in a later chapter, it's important to be able to compare the values of the various exchange-traded funds you own. Being able to do so from a single statement is a nice convenience.

CHAPTER 9

Investment Approaches to Avoid

As you probably know by now, I do not favor stock trading. Nevertheless, I feel the need to explain some of its ingredients. After all, exchange-traded funds were created partly to give investors the opportunity, for the first time, to buy and sell entire indexes just as easily as they can trade individual stocks. In case you feel the urge to lose your money and suffer financial disappointment over the long term, you can lose all the faster by, for example, trading with two-to-one leverage in a margin account.

Margin: Brokerage firms are only too delighted to lend you money to purchase more securities than you could acquire on your own. The interest that brokerage houses earn on margin balances is one of the industry's largest sources of income. But brokerage firms do not themselves have the money to lend. They obtain it from banks.

For its most reliable borrowers, banks charge the "prime" rate. If Sears Roebuck, for example, borrows money from a bank to tide it over until the Sears customers pay for their Christmas purchases, the bank will probably charge the current prime rate, which at this writing is 4.75 percent. Less reliable customers pay up from there. But for brokerage firms, banks offer a special deal. They charge the "call" rate, which is now only 3.50 percent. The call rate is usually lower than the prime rate, because the margin rules provide an extra layer of security. Unlike credit cards, brokerage firms cannot make unsecured loans. Any loan from a brokerage firm is secured by the borrower's investment assets held by the firm. Some securities are considered too volatile and risky to serve as collateral and are therefore excluded from margin borrowing. Margin accounts are continually scrutinized by specially trained margin clerks. The accounts are kept separate from cash accounts, from which the customer may not borrow.

For most margin accounts, the brokerage firm charges interest a bit higher than the call rate. The brokerage, of course, retains the difference between the two rates..

Assume you deposit $50,000 in a margin account. You borrow an additional $50,000 from the firm and acquire $100,000 of marginable securities. The loan is referred to as "margin." The difference between the market value of the securities ($100,000) and the margin ($50,000) is referred to as "equity," which in this case is also $50,000.

While the market is open, market values fluctuate continually. Once in a great while, when you're not looking, security prices go down. The brokerage firm's foremost concern is to take action before the value of the securities drops below the loan balance. The loan would then become unsecured, and the firm might not recover its money. The federal government, which regulates these matters, requires that the equity not fall below 25 percent of the market value.

If the market value of your account should fall to $66,667, (a decline of one-third from $100,000), you're still okay. The margin remains at $50,000. (Actually, the margin grows every day because of interest, but we'll disregard this for now.) Your equity is now $16,667 ($66,667 less $50,000), which is exactly 25 percent of the $66,667 market value. (A hefty chunk of your original $50,000 disappeared in a hurry, didn't it? The market value declined by 33.3 percent, but your equity fell by 66.7 percent.)

Now, if the market value falls the next day from $66,667 to $60,000, your equity is $10,000 ($60,000 less $50,000). It's now only 20 percent of the $50,000 margin, below the required "maintenance" level. You receive a "margin call," requiring that you add $5000 to your margin account, pronto. If the brokerage firm cannot reach you, it immediately sells $10,000 of your securities. When stock prices are dropping rapidly, as it may during a bout of panic selling, margin calls may be issued during the day and sales made immediately. If you cannot be reached, the firm sells whichever of your securities it chooses, whether you like it or not.

Given that the margin is continually growing because of interest, the actual situation would be worse than I've just described. If security values do not move as you intend, the results of margin borrowing can be devastating.

You'll be pleased to know that brokerage firms have all this down to a science and seldom lose money because of the failure of margin customers to repay loans. You'll be even more pleased to learn that banks practically never lose money from margin lending. In the unlikely event that the brokerage firm fails to obtain recovery of its loan because the security values fall too fast, the firm must nevertheless come up with its own money to repay the bank.

If you want to take a vacation water-skiing on the Mediterranean (and are willing to reduce your wealth at retirement), here's how you can do it. Place securities you already own into a margin account. The firm is willing to lend you half of the value for any purpose. Bingo! There's your cash. Have a ball. The interest is significantly less than that of most credit cards. You don't get the securities back, of course, until you repay the loan, but you can always hope that the security prices rise by 70 percent or so. This should provide enough to pay off the loan, plus the interest, plus the capital gains on the sales, enabling the return of the original value of your securities.

Short Selling: Exchange-traded funds, as I've mentioned, can be sold short. In a short sale, as you recall, you endeavor to buy low and sell high, only you do the selling first. Via your friendly broker, the stock to be sold is borrowed from another of the brokerage firm's clients who holds the stock on margin. That client is unaware that her stock is being lent. (She authorized such lending, however, when she signed her margin agreement.) If no customer of your brokerage firm happens to hold on margin the stock you want to borrow, the firm borrows the stock from another brokerage firm. If the stock held on margin has already been sold short and the stock cannot be borrowed from any source, you cannot short it yourself. If you embark on a short sale, but the shares later become in short supply because the margin holders themselves want to sell the stock, you may be required to cover your short whether you like it or not. In this case, the stock is "called" away from you.

Since the brokerage firm is lending you stock to sell, the arrangement takes place within a margin account. Whether the brokerage firm is lending cash or stock, it cannot make unsecured loans; collateral is required. You may deposit $10,000 cash and sell short $10,000 of stock. In this case you pay no interest. You are not required to borrow cash to make a short sale. But if you choose to, you can deposit $10,000 cash and borrow $20,000 of stock to sell short. In this event, you would pay interest on the $10,000 cash you borrowed.

While you're short a stock that pays a dividend, you must pay the dividend yourself. More likely, it would be deducted from your margin account. The brokerage house arranges for the dividend to be deposited in the margin account of the client who lent the stock.

For the last 60 years or so, short sales of stocks have been subject to the uptick rule. The government requires that a short sale may be executed only on an *uptick*, that is, at a price which is above the last price that was different. Sorry about that. Here's what I mean:

Assume that in a sequence , a stock trades at $20, $20, and $20.05. The last price is an uptick. It is higher than the last price that was different.

If the trades are $20, $20.05, and $20.05, the last price is again an uptick, because it's higher than the last price that was different.

If the sequence is $20.05, $20, and $20, the last price is a *downtick*. It's lower than the last price that was different. Regarding individual stocks, downticks are no-nos for short selling. The government doesn't want short sales to drive the market down, as occurred during the Great Depression. It wants shorting to take place only when there is offsetting buying pressure.

Every trade is either an uptick or a downtick. Even if a stock trades at the same price 22 times in a row, somewhere back there it traded at a price that was different. Computers are adept at keeping track of such things. How market makers did so before computers is beyond me.

The SEC is considering doing away with the uptick rule. On certain large stocks, like General Electric and Microsoft, no restrictions on short selling will be imposed. Since the trading volumes of such stocks are so large, the SEC figures that their prices cannot be influenced by short sellers, no matter what they do. Futures contracts on these individual stocks will be permitted soon. Futures contracts can be sold short without restriction. Therefore, to avoid "regulatory arbitrage," the SEC will remove all restrictions on the short selling of those stocks. On other stocks, the SEC intends to require that short selling may occur only when the latest best bid price (not the last price) is higher than a previous bid price that was different.

(Imposing restrictions on short selling probably makes bear markets worse, not better. The restrictions no doubt discourage people from engaging in the practice. The dearth of short sellers during bull markets enables stock prices to rise higher than they would if short sellers had free rein. The unnatural rise during the upturn causes the prices to fall unnaturally low during the subsequent downturn. As in so many cases, the actual long-term results of big government policies are opposite to the intended results.)

After taking your valuable time to explain all that information about short selling, I now advise you to forget it. Exchange-traded funds, you see, are exempt from the uptick rule. Why? Because the sale of an ETF is not a sale of the stocks that underlie the ETF.

With or without an uptick, let's say you sell Spiders short in sufficient quantity to drive the price down significantly. This causes the variance between the ETF price and the trust's NAV to widen to the point that an arbitrageur considers it advantageous to take a position. The arbitrageur buys Spiders and sells the underlying stocks short, thereby bringing closer together the Spider price and the underlying trading value. Short sales by arbitrageurs are always exempt from the uptick rule, which means that practically everyone associated with ETFs is free of the pesky requirement.

Short selling is risky business. Even if you put up the full amount as collateral and borrow no cash, shorting is still risky. In the first place, the mathematics are against you. For example, if you buy a stock at $50 and sell it at $100, you've made a profit of 100 percent. But if you sell a stock short at $100 and cover at $50, sorry, you've made only 50 percent. To make a 100-percent profit on a short sale (without borrowing cash), the stock must fall to zero. To avoid losing their jobs, the company's employees are doing everything they can to prevent this. When you sell short, you're bucking the tide.

Secondly, when you buy a stock without using margin, the worse that can happen is that the price goes to zero and you lose all of your investment. But when you sell a stock short, the worst that can happen . . . well, there is no worst. There's no limit on how high the price can rise and no limit on how much you can lose. Your potential loss is infinite. They tell me that's pretty high.

At any one time, approximately one-quarter of Spiders shares and about half of Qubes are held short. Some of those positions are held by arbitrageurs, market makers, and hedgers. But in my opinion, the percentages of short sales are nevertheless too high. In the long run, too many of those positions will be proven wrong.

Institutions that hold large numbers of shares get paid for making them available to short sellers. This is generally the case for exchange-traded funds. Making shares available for shorting is a source of income, thereby reducing the operating costs charged against the dividends.

Fundamental Analysis: When you estimate the future price of a stock based on what you expect its earnings to be, you're engaging in fundamental analysis. When you estimate the supply and demand factors of an entire industry, you're engaging in fundamental analysis. When you endeavor to judge the economic health of the various nations of the world, this too is fundamental analysis.

Stock analysts spend considerable effort on the fundamentals. Future demand for a company's products, costs, quality, competition, marketing, debt, management capabilities, the price-earnings ratio—the list of considerations is nearly endless.

In the short run, fundamental analysis of stocks doesn't work. If it did, the firms that hire the most stock analysts would outdo the others. They don't. The analysts may or may not have a good idea about next quarter's earnings. But they have no idea what multiple the stock market will place on those earnings. This makes their work useless. Some of them may outperform the market for a while. None of them beat it consistently. One observer opined that security analysts are little more than highly paid disseminators of corporate spin.

Sometimes, analyst results are amusing. On August 10, 2000, for example, Evolve Software brought its stock to the market in an initial public offering at $9, advised by Credit Suisse First Boston (CSFB). About a month later, after the price ran up sharply to $28, CSFB analyst David Sturtz initiated coverage of the stock, giving it a buy rating and a price target of $38. Two months later, after the stock's precipitous decline to $8, Mr. Sturtz emphasized that the Internet slowdown was "NOT hurting" the company's sales. He repeated his price target of $38. Ten months later, with the price only $0.24, Mr. Sturtz again gave the stock a buy rating. Just three weeks later, with the price at $0.22, Credit Suisse First Boston dropped its research coverage of the company. In the long run, Mr. Sturtz's predictions may prove correct. But in the short run, the professional analysis of the company's investment prospects was no more helpful than Captain Kangaroo.

Fundamental analysis does work if you look far enough out into the future, say, 10 years. That's a long time to wait, of course, to see if your predictions were correct.

For estimating long-term stock market trends, I have mentioned that the conditions for favorable stock prices are:

- Rapidly advancing technologies
- Favorable monetary conditions
- Suppression of terrorism
- Recognition by voters that big government causes more harm than good

Many stock analysts are employed by large financial institutions. But it's almost impossible for these big guns to beat the market, because they *are* the market.

Here's why fundamental analysis is unlikely to beat the market in the short term. Most trends in stock prices occur, not because of fundamental changes that are happening now. They occur because of fundamental changes that will happen in the future—three-to-six months in the future. No one is yet aware of those developments. Not the management. Not professional stock analysts. Not you or me. Certainly not the government.

So how do people who are buying and selling a stock now know what's going to happen down the line?

They don't know, exactly; they just guess. Some of the guesses are wrong, of course. But as a general rule, the collective guesses of all the participants in a stock are remarkably accurate. Let's say that the price of a stock starts to trend upward. About four months later, gosh, unexpected favorable news is reported. The price then moves down. Several months later, what a surprise, bad news comes out of the blue.

Let's say you uncover something bullish about a company. You're the only one in the world who knows it. You mortgage your house and buy a big chunk of stock to make a killing. But after you get in, the stock doesn't go up; it goes down. Why? Because several months ago, the stock went up in anticipation of the good news that only you now know for sure. To your dismay, the price is now falling because of unfavorable news that no one will know about specifically for several months in the future.

Do stock prices react to current news? Yes, of course they do, especially to changes in government policy. But as to economic and business news (and not changes in government policy), the temporary reactions of stock prices generally don't persist unless the reactions are in line with future news not yet known.

The stock market must make itself a continual surprise. It must act counterintuitively, meaning that it keeps everyone flummoxed. If it didn't, if it acted as people expected, making money in the stock market would be as easy as eating candy. People would borrow up to their eyebrows, throw everything into the market, and come out multimillionaires, simple as can be. This is impossible. The stock market has to keep one foot in the real world. Real wealth is being created all the time, of course, but not so rapidly as to make everyone a multimillionaire in quick time. No, the stock market has to make the majority wrong most of the time.

The majority thinks short term most of the time. I want you to think long term all the time. In the long term, the stock market acts as we expect. With some fluctuation as government policies lean toward good or ill, the stock market grows roughly in line with the creation of real wealth. (Good government policies enable the rapid creation of real wealth. Bad government policies slow the creation of wealth. Wretched government policies destroy it.)

On the whole, stock analysts aren't too bad at predicting corporate earnings. But they're no better than flipping a coin (and probably worse) at predicting future stock prices. Analysts may have a line on demand, quality, costs, management, competition, interest costs, and the other real-world events that lead to a reasonably accurate earnings estimate. But analysts have no idea how the market will value those earnings. Professional estimates of future price-earnings are no more than wild, unsubstantiated guesses.

When everyone agrees that the prospects for company earnings are favorable, they may well be correct. But at the time of those favorable expectations, the price-earnings ratio is also higher.

Is the PE ratio too high, too low, or just right?

No one knows. Just because you agree that the prospects for the company are favorable, you can't buy the stock and expect the price to make you a nice profit in the short term. Even given the excellent prospects, the PE ratio may be out of line on the upside. Oh, there are times when "growth" stocks seem as if they'd never fall. The years 1998–1999 were just such a time. But persistent trends like that don't last forever, either on the upside or the downside. Generally, you not only have to be correct about the prospects for the company; you must also evaluate whether the price has discounted those prospects too much or too little. Few people (if any) can do this successfully on a consistent basis. And even fewer of those people work for large financial institutions. The institutions are the ones whose opinions you learn about from day to day. Their opinions are generally worthless.

Evaluating the short-term prospects for a stock, or for the market, for that matter, is like trying to beat the odds on a football game. You may be entirely correct that A will beat B. But if A has to beat B by more than 13 points for you to win, you're in a quandary. Twelve points and you lose. Thirteen points, and everyone loses except the bookie. Only if A wins by 14 points or more will you pocket any cash. The prospects are well discounted. Only if you can see the future better than most of the others, including the bookies, will you be a consistent short-term winner. The chances are you can't.

Evaluating price-earnings ratios has been rendered all the more difficult, lately, by the failure of many companies to count all their costs as deductions from their earnings. Companies are prone to mislabel expenses that one should consider as normal operating expenses. They call them "special" or "nonrecurring" expenses and exclude them from counting against operating earnings. Since the bad stuff is not taken properly into account, the operating earnings therefore overstate the true earnings. The press, not bothering to look more carefully, promulgates the false earnings to an unsuspecting public.

Is the market therefore overvalued?

Don't ask me; I don't know. But I do know this: In the short term, the odds against making profits are against you. In the long term, however, stock prices are always undervalued.

From time to time, however, I do have an opinion or two about the short-term prospects of the market based on the level of pessimism abroad in the land. When panic selling occurs, I turn bullish. When panic occurs, but the market rises modestly and stays there for several months amid widespread expectations of bad things to come, I remain bullish. Can't help it; it's part of my crusty nature. Sometimes I'm wrong. Sometimes a bigger panic occurs at lower prices. But as a general rule, being bullish when panic occurs serves one well.

Do not infer from this that I would advise selling at market tops, holding cash, and stepping in later when panic occurs. Any such attempt is foolhardy. Prices fall faster than they rise. People are naturally inclined to experience bad feelings more intensely than good feelings. Market bottoms are usually accompanied by unanimity of opinion that things are just awful. Panic selling occurs, often signaling the end of the bear market.

The ends of bull markets, however, are signaled by . . . nothing. There is seldom unanimity of bullish opinion, even at market tops. Investors are uncertain about whether prices will drop or not. Successful investors almost never engage in panic buying. If you sell because you feel that a bull market just can't continue any longer, it will indeed continue. It will probably rise for another year or two. You'll be left kicking yourself at having been so stupid. Finally, in despair, you'll buy, whereupon the market will begin going down in earnest.

In its purest form, market timing means to be in cash during bear markets and fully invested in stocks during bull markets. You think you can do this, eh? Dream on, friend. Trying to guess the ends of bull markets is a fool's game. You're betting against the long-term trend, which is upward. In 1996, for example, Barton Biggs, a respected market analyst at Morgan Stanley, recommended the sale of stocks, citing evidence that prices were overheated, overvalued, and vulnerable. The S&P 500 was less than 800 at the time. Mr. Biggs has remained bearish since. Even after the September 11, 2001 World Trade bombing attack, the S&P 500 generally remained at more than 1000. At this writing, it's more than 1100.

Mr. Biggs is a fine, well-meaning fellow, and Morgan Stanley is a prestigious house. Had you taken his advice, you'd have paid capital gains on the sales. You'd have missed a gain of over 30 percent (from 800 to 1100). You'd have gained from having your money in the money market fund for five years, but forfeited the dividends on the stocks. Taking everything into account, including the capital gains paid, you'd be significantly behind. You probably could not live long enough that any market timing you attempt in the future would be accurate enough to make up such a loss of opportunity. More likely, any market timing you attempt in the future would sink you further into the hole.

You've heard the term "stock picker's market" bandied about on TV, haven't you? It means, of course, picking stocks that outperform their industries and stocks that outperform the market as a whole. Investment experts throw the phrase around as though accomplishing it were easy as taking a shower. Why, you just choose the stocks that are going to rise, that's all. Will Rogers, popular raconteur during the 1930s and 1940s, said, "Picking stocks is easy. You buy a stock. It goes up, and you sell it. If it doesn't go up, don't buy it."

Well, picking stocks that will outperform the sector isn't one bit easy. If it were, the investment experts would accomplish it. They don't, not consistently. Oh, the fellow who talks about the stock picker's market on television probably did accomplish it during the last 12 months. That's why he's being interviewed. He's the latest guru. But during the next 12 months, his stock selections are likely to underperform. The fellow will then be considered a dunce, and no one will want to see his face on TV.

Let's say that one institution is buying 50,000 shares of a stock, and another institution is selling 50,000 shares of the same stock. On most trading days, this kind of thing occurs hundreds of times. Both institutions are privy to the latest information concerning the company's value. Intelligent, well-educated individuals on both sides have evaluated the information and reached opposite conclusions. One wants to trade cash for the stock. The other wants to trade the stock for cash. At that moment, the price they agree upon is undoubtedly the stock's intrinsic value. Who's to say they're wrong? Subsequent events will prove them wrong and the price will change. But when the transaction takes place, they are probably correct.

It's in the interest of the brokerage firms to use phrases like "stock picking." If you're an accredited stock picker and jump from one stock to another, your broker loves you like a brother. You won't be a stock picker forever, of course. Eventually, you'll be as poor as a cotton picker, and the broker will bestow his affections on someone else. It's in the interest of money managers to use phrases like stock picking because they want to give potential clients the impression that they can succeed in jumping around among stocks. It's also in the interest of the television producer to use such phrases, because, to attract viewers, he wants to focus on what's hot. None of these individuals question the concept. They don't look at the record because it's not in their interest to do so. They're all trying, dear reader, to rope you in.

Never mind what's hot. You're better off watching sit-com reruns.

The whole notion of expertise in the stock market is altogether different from expertise in tangibles. If you want to design a new airplane, you turn to those who are expert in aerodynamics, electronics, metals, jet engines, and other complicated disciplines. Without such experts, you are well advised not to hitch a ride when the craft first attempts to stay aloft.

Expertise in the stock market, however, is quite another story. Oh sure, people know about the characteristics of various investments. You yourself are becoming something of an expert on exchange-traded funds. But when it comes to predicting stock prices in the short term, all of us are plain, dumb amateurs, more likely to be wrong than right.

Technical Analysis: Technical analysis is a study of historic price and volume figures to detect patterns that have a better-than-even chance of persisting into the future. Technical analysts believe that historic price and volume trends, to some extent, have predictive value. For example, if the price of a stock bounces up from 37 two or three times, the 37 is referred to as a support level. If the price again approaches that level, "techies" expect the support to hold and the price to rise.

By the same token, if a stock hits 56 and thereafter falls several times, this is termed a resistance level. If it hits this level again, you're supposed to sell or sell short.

If the price bounces up off a support level two or three times and, during the same period, bounces down two or three times from a resistance level, the price is considered to be in a channel. The line of support and the line of resistance are parallel. The channel may be horizontal, upward pointing, or downward pointing. If you buy at support and sell at resistance, you're supposed to get more bang for your buck.

Well, it's supposed to work, but it doesn't.

The head and shoulder pattern catches my fancy. The price rises sharply (the left arm), stays level (the left shoulder), rises to a rounded top and falls (the head), and stays level (the right shoulder). Get ready. The pattern signals that the price will fall down the right arm by about the amount that it rose up the left arm.

This doesn't work either. None of these patterns work well enough to result in consistent, long-term profits. After paying transaction costs and short-term capital gains, traders using technical analysis generally end up losers.

Here's why: Most of the people who take interest in a stock don't care about historic price and volume levels. That's water over the dam. Their sole concern is what's going to happen in the future. Historic price and volume figures have no predictive value.

Technical analysts respond that at least *some* investors are aware of stock charts and think they have predictive value. It's as if the techies are saying, "Well, I'm not so stupid as to believe that historic price and volume figures have predictive value. But other people believe they do. Therefore, I'm going to try to take advantage of their ignorance."

Sorry, it doesn't work.

When you challenge technicians as to the veracity of their calling, they'll probably say, "Oh, technical analysis is just a tool to be used in conjunction with fundamental analysis."

Baloney! If an investment technique has no predictive value on its own, it adds no value to any approach it's combined with.

The same goes for "relative strength," which doesn't work either. A stock whose price trend has been stronger than that of its peers doesn't necessarily continue to be stronger than that of its peers. When the relative strength becomes obvious, this might be the very time the stock turns into a 95-pound weakling.

Technical analysts are having a ball with exchange-traded funds. For the first time, they have volume figures, open, high, low, and closing prices for what amounts to mutual funds. These data are not available with indexes, which are hypothetical portfolios. Nor are they available with mutual funds, because those trade only once a day on unknown volume. Exchange-traded funds open up new windows for technical analysis. They trade during the entire day, with the spreads, prices, and volume figures widely promulgated.

But rest assured that analysts will have no more luck with ETFs than they've had with individual stocks. You haven't heard of multimillionaires who made their money from technical analysis, have you? I haven't.

Despite their uselessness, investment technicians continue to get paid by large financial institutions because charts look like they *ought* to work. After all, what's the poor professional stock picker supposed to do? In a highly competitive environment, money managers are responsible for choosing stocks in multimillion-dollar portfolios. They know as much as anyone about the future prospects of companies. But are the stock prices overvaluing or undervaluing those prospects? The managers don't know, any more than anyone else, and there's no way in the world they can find out.

Ah, but there are always those pretty pictures—that seemingly rock-solid evidence of historic price patterns. There they are, clear as day. Look at that line of support; it has to hold. Look at that head-and-shoulder pattern. We're just at the right shoulder; the price has gotta go down. That wretched money manager is swimming in uncertainty; he's desperate for dry land. Those beautiful patterns, crystal clear, seem to provide it.

They don't.

Do stock pickers keep trustworthy, long-term records of decisions they've made on the basis of technical analysis? Of course not. If they did, they'd find that technical analysis added no value whatsoever. They'd rather not discover this, thank you, because then they'd be left swimming in uncertainty with no dry land at all. Instead, they fudge the experience in their own minds. They say to themselves, "Maybe technical analysis doesn't work. But other people think it does, so I might as well go on using it."

If it doesn't work, it doesn't work, no matter who's using it. Forget about technical analysis. But the poor money managers don't want to forget it. If they did, they'd be left with fundamental analysis, which doesn't work all that well either. The poor managers are going cross-eyed reading company reports. They're getting dry in the throat from peppering questions to the company policy makers. They know about as much as anyone concerning the real prospects for the company. Yet, so often when they buy or sell, the prices moves opposite to their expectations.

When good luck provides them with a string of successes, the results are glorious. Their funds get good write-ups in financial magazines. They're interviewed on television, touted as some of the nation's top stock pickers, and given big pay raises. But when Lady Luck bestows her favors on someone else, they slink back into obscurity, wondering what they did wrong. It's no wonder that so many psychics and card readers make a good living on Wall Street.

In choosing to learn about exchange-traded funds, you've made a good move. If you will simply allow them to serve you with long-term results, you'll have those other guys whipped. John Bogle, founder of The Vanguard Group, said, "Exchange-traded funds are beautifully-designed shotguns. They can be used for self-defense or for suicide."

The self-defense applies to people who have accumulated substantial wealth. They can use ETFs to hedge certain risks. But it's the suicide we're talking about here, and it's suicide I want you to shun.

Market Letters: Beware also of market letters. The authors may or may not buy the stocks they recommend. But their primary business is not investing; it's publishing. The authors of course prefer that you make money in the market. But this isn't their primary objective. Their primary goal is for you to subscribe and keep subscribing to their publication. They don't have to be right. They do have to be interesting.

Newsletters have the same conflict of interest that brokers do. To attract readers, they tend, intentionally or not, to express the views that readers agree with. As a general rule, the readers are optimistic when prices are high and pessimistic when prices are low. These tend to be the very opinions that newsletters express. You'd probably be better off going opposite to newsletter recommendations. When they say to buy, sell. When they say to sell, buy.

Here's a headline I saw recently in an advertisement for a newsletter: "Where to Invest in a Changed World." Assuming that the investment suggestions made in the newsletter are good ones (which they may not be) and assuming that you have just completed the accumulation of cash for investment, the recommendations might be helpful. But many of us are already fully invested, or certainly should be. If your portfolio is properly diversified, there's no reason to change anything. The WTC attack was horrifying. But the United States has weathered such storms before, and it will again. Do not allow torment to knock you off your investment course. Buy and, except for modest and periodic rebalancing (see Chapter 11), hold. Acquire broad-based ETFs and participate in the market's long-term uptrend. Trading is a zero-sum game. Long-term investing is not. Beware of all those who offer equipment, brokerage, investment seminars, or other services to investors. They have no objection, of course, to your making money in the market, but their primary objective is for you to buy their services. During the California gold rush, a mere handful of people made money from the sale of gold. But lots of people who sold the miners equipment, lodging, food, liquor, and sex made money hand over fist.

Exchange-traded funds enable you to purchase packages of stocks just as easily as you can individual stocks. Right there you're ahead because they give you diversification. Diversification pays.

After all this preaching, get ready for a big laugh. In the next chapter, I provide suggestions on how to be a day trader. Some people succeed at that precarious occupation, but most don't. I recommend you not try. But just in case you can't resist, here are some helpful hints.

CHAPTER 10

The Ins and Outs of Day Trading ETFs

Exchange-traded funds were created to enable people, for the first time, to trade entire indexes. Ah yes, trading. No word sounds sweeter to a broker's ear.

I do not recommend short-term trading (often referred to as "day trading"). Most people who try it end up losing money. Only a few succeed, and remarkably few find it profitable over long periods. I myself have never tried day trading; I don't have the talent for it. I know a little something about it, but unless you have special and unusual talents, the ideas presented here will not help you in the long run to make money. If you have a craving to lose your money, these ideas may help you to do so in 24 months, say, instead of 12.[1]

Researchers estimate that something like 5000 "pure" day traders work at it every day from an office, doing dozens or even more than 100 trades a day and ending up flat at the closing bell. Less professional but hyperactive traders working from home probably number more than 200,000. At any rate, these were the estimates prevailing before the bear market of 2000–2001. The June 12, 2000 issue of *Forbes* reports that the North American Securities

---

[1] Books about short-term trading I have found helpful are as follows:
The Everything Online Investing Book by Harry Domash, 2000, Adams Media Corporation.
Trading Rules: Strategies for Success by William F. Eng, 1990, Dearborn Financial Publishing, Inc.
The Electronic Day Trader by Marc Friedfertig and George West, 1998, McGraw-Hill.
The Guts & Glory of Day Trading by Mark Ingebretsen, 2001, Prima Publishing.
Tricks of the Floor Trader by Neal T. Weintraub, 1996, McGraw-Hill.

Administrators Association analyzed the accounts of 124 day traders for the years 1998 and 1999, a period characterized by rapidly rising stock prices. Some 77 percent lost money. Of those who profited, the average over a period of eight months was only $22,000. Only 2 people out of the 124 netted $100,000 or better. The highest was $160,000. Given a two-year period of rapidly rising prices, these results are wretched.

All too often, in-and-out investors don't know, or don't want to know, that it isn't working. They resemble a person watching a football game who is so obsessed with the details of the game that he forgets to notice the score, which reveals that he's losing.

Most traders rely on technical analysis. I have stated in this book that historic price and volume trends do not have predictive value. Most successful traders believe that indeed they do. The failure of most traders to succeed only reinforces my belief that technical analysis doesn't work. But to avoid confusion in this chapter, I speak of technical analysis as traders do, with the implication that it works. I caution you not to test this assumption too assiduously.

For beginning traders, $50,000 is a suitable amount to start with. Expect to pay several thousand for a few intensive days of practice. Do not be a trader while holding down another job. So few are able to carry this off that it's not worthwhile trying. Trading is a zero-sum game. The professionals are full time. If you're a part-timer, the professionals will eventually own your sums. You'll own the zeros.

My suggestion that you toss your job to the wind is rendered, I realize, all too lightly. By forfeiting income from employment and also risking the loss of your capital from day trading, you render a double whammy to a fulfilling retirement.

Nevertheless, let's say you've decided to chuck it all and become a trader. Even after reading this chapter, other books on trading, and attending one or more trading seminars, do not expect to know the ropes. On-the-job learning is required. You have to know what style of trading fits your personality, and you must make that style work for you. None of this happens until you try. You might first engage in paper trading, keeping records of buys and sells without spending money. But since you're not actually entering orders, deduct at least 20 percent from the rates of return you purport to earn from paper trading.

Until you've proven your success and feel the need to share your knowledge, treat trading as a lonely profession. Do not disclose your positions or share your opinions with others. If you boast about your successes, you'll feel that you're better than you are. If you seek commiseration for your failures, you'll feel that you're worse than you are. When you broadcast your investment positions, you feel married to them. Stay married to your spouse, not to your stock positions. Much as you may prize your positions now, any of them may become throwaways in time, probably by lunch.

Day trading in Nasdaq stocks is more complex than day trading in listed stocks (although, indeed, both are impossible for most people). Since ETFs are traded on exchanges, I omit particulars about Nasdaq trading, making this chapter considerably shorter than would otherwise be the case.

Certain widely used phrases often used by professional money managers you might take with a grain of salt. In *The Wall Street Journal*, investment columnist Jonathan Clements revealed their true meanings, as follows:

- *The stock market was down on technical factors:* We have no idea why the prices fell.
- *The trend is your friend:* Stocks have been going up.
- *Trees don't grow to the sky:* Stocks stopped going up.
- *The market looks a little extended:* We're dumping everything.
- *The stock is fairly valued:* If it climbs a few more bucks, we're unloading this puppy.
- *Our portfolio has some great values:* The stocks have been massacred.
- *The stock's oversold:* We never imagined that the price could fall this far.
- *Don't miss this compelling opportunity:* I need the commissions.
- *We rate the stock a strong buy:* We need the company's investment-banking business.
- *We consider the stock attractive long term:* Next year is going to be rough.
- *We rate the stock a hold:* For God's sake, dump it.

Jesse Livermore (1877–1940) is considered by many to be the greatest stock trader that ever lived. Born on a farm in Shrewsbury,

Massachusetts, he went to Boston in 1891 with $5 in his pocket. By 1930, he was worth approximately $100 million, the equivalent of about $1 billion today, all from trading. Highly intelligent, Jesse had a remarkable capacity to calculate and remember numbers.

I wouldn't emulate Jesse too slavishly, however. He wasn't always successful, not by a long shot. At the beginning, he went broke three times in less than two years. Even after becoming a millionaire, he went broke again, and, for four long years from 1911 to 1914, he remained in debt. Alas, the man was addicted to beautiful showgirls. This caused his second wife, the love of his life (herself addicted to alcohol), to divorce him in 1932. Susceptible to depression all his life, her departure caused him to be consumed by despair. By 1934, only three short years after being worth $100 million, he declared bankruptcy. His third wife had been married four times. All four husbands had committed suicide. In 1940, Jesse did the same. As the saying goes, money isn't everything.

Jesse Livermore learned that the big money is not in the individual fluctuations, but in the main movement. The big money is made, not from reading the tape, but from sizing up the trend of the entire market. His principal trading tactic was to continue buying only if the price continued up or to continue selling only if the price continued down. Whether he bought or sold short made no difference to him.

From *Reminiscences of a Stock Operator,* here are some of Jesse's opinions about trading: [2]

  ◆ It never was my thinking that made the big money for me. It always was my sitting.
  ◆ It is natural for human beings to hope and to fear. But the successful trader must reverse these two deep-seated instincts. Instead of hoping he must fear. Instead of fearing he must hope. Most especially, he must fear that a loss may develop into a much bigger loss.
  ◆ There isn't a man in Wall Street who has not lost money trying to make the market pay for an automobile or a bracelet or a motor boat or a painting. I could build a huge hospital with the birthday presents the tight-fisted stock market has refused to pay for. In fact, of all the hoodoos in Wall Street, I

[2] *Reminiscences of a Stock Operator* by Edwin Lefevre, Copyright 1993, 1994 by Expert Trading, Ltd. Reprinted by permission of John Wiley & Sons, Inc.

think the resolve to induce the stock market to act as a fairy godmother is the busiest and most persistent.

- There are many thousands of people who buy and sell stocks speculatively. But the number who speculates profitably is small.
- The course of the market is always from six to nine months ahead of actual conditions.

In other chapters of this book, I maintain that the market is generally three-to-six months ahead of actual conditions. I did not develop my opinion from Jesse, but I was delighted to learn of his confirmation. I hold to the three-to-six months view, however, since the dissemination of information in our day is so much more rapid than it was in the early decades of the last century.

Jesse quoted another prominent speculator of his day, Thomas F. Woodlock, "The principles of successful stock speculation are based on the supposition that people will continue in the future to make the mistakes that they have made in the past."

In *The Guts and Glory of Day Trading,* Mark Ingebretsen highlights 12 individuals who have succeeded at day trading. Each has carved out a style that suits his or her personality. Many of them lost money at first. Some are in and out of the market quickly, going for 10 or 15 cents a share per trade. Others are swing traders, going for larger amounts intraday, or even for as long as two weeks. Some study fundamentals; others don't. None of the traders are natural gamblers. Only one ever bet on a horse race. All of the traders take great pains to minimize risks; this is absolutely key. All have faced huge losses in the past. Most of them have taken advice from mentors. None are drinkers. Many of these day traders look upon their trading rooms as a means of social interaction. They feel the need to share their knowledge, to teach others how to trade. All work hard. All have an aversion to risk, a deep desire to learn, and a subsequent desire to teach. It's likely that each of them would have achieved success in whatever field they chose.

WEB SITES

There are no end of Web sites regarding investments, some free and others not. They include the following:

www.supertraders.com

www.tradestation.com

www.metastock.com

www.telescan.com

www.cnbc.com

www.multexinvestor.com (company reports)

www.economy.com

www.beesoft.net (for Macs)

To view corporate reports submitted to the Securities and Exchange Commission, use www.Edgar-Online.com.

- www.bigcharts. com: Historical quotes shows charts based either on the current price or the price on a date in the past.
- Another fine Web site for real-time charts and quotes is www.wallstreetcity.com.
- *Investors Business Daily* highlights the relative strength of individual stocks, that is, the stocks that are performing better than others.

Pay heed to CNBC. Stocks mentioned before the opening are immediately in play.

STRATEGIES

A much-used rule of trading is to buy strength and sell weakness. If an ETF is hard to buy at the price you want, the buying interest is probably strong. If an ETF is hard to sell short at the price you want, the selling interest is probably strong. Baron Rothschild, who made a great deal of money as a trader on the Paris Exchange in the nineteenth century, said that he preferred to buy high and sell low. He meant that he bought stocks when they went to new highs and sold them while they were still rising but before others felt the urge to sell.

Buy on a scale up, obtaining lesser amounts each time. This is called pyramiding. Buying up keeps your average price on the low side. Buying less each time avoids your being overleveraged. By the same token, sell short on a scale down, again, in lesser amounts each time.

Orders to buy and sell mutual funds accumulate during the trading day. Except during bear markets, purchase orders ordinarily exceed the sells. By 3:30 p.m., New York time, mutual funds have a good idea how much stock they'll need to acquire. Therefore, prices tend to rise during the last half-hour of the day.

Market bottoms can often be identified by panic selling. If you're a longer-term investor and you're on the ball, you might even buy at bottom prices. But market tops are seldom signaled by panic buying and are much harder to identify. Don't jump the gun. Delay your short selling until after the prices begin to falter.

SPECIALISTS

Listed stocks are traded on exchanges, which include the New York, the American, and various regional exchanges, such as those in Boston, Chicago, and Philadelphia. Regional exchanges account for about 15 percent of the volume.

Trading listed stocks, rather than Nasdaq stocks, provides certain advantages. Since specialists dominate the trading and are aware of the true supply/demand conditions, they're more confident about the markets they make and more likely to provide liquidity than the less-informed Nasdaq market makers. There are tighter spreads, fewer restrictions, and usually greater liquidity. One person takes responsibility for executing orders fairly. (Specialists don't go overboard on the fairness business; they're not out to lose money.) Floor brokers on exchanges are not permitted to trade in those stocks for which they handle customer orders.

Specialists control the trading on all exchanges. For each stock or ETF, there's usually only one specialist. All orders in the stock flow through that person. Specialists are the only people who are privy to the limit orders on the books for their stocks, giving them a distinct advantage, especially at the opening.

Specialists are natural sellers when a stock is rising and natural buyers when it's falling. More than two-thirds of the time, customer orders are paired. If someone wants to buy at the same price at which someone else wants to sell, the two orders are matched. About 70 percent of the orders on the New York Stock Exchange are paired. In the other 30 percent of the orders, the specialist takes a position on the other side of customer orders.

Specialists are subject to requirements. If someone wants to sell and no one happens to want to buy at the moment, the specialist must fill the order with his own money whether he wants to or not. (Most specialists are guys.) Under most conditions, they must maintain orderly markets. If a stock ordinarily moves in steps of 10 or 15 cents, but moves by a whole dollar over a period of time, the specialist must usually arrange that it trades in increments of 10 or 15 cents during the move.

It is more likely for specialists to fill orders they would prefer not to fill than for Nasdaq market makers to fill orders they would prefer not to fill.

Specialists can quote whatever prices they want, as long as they honor them. A quote may represent the true supply and demand for the stock, or it may represent what the specialist wants the public to perceive about the supply and demand.

The best time of the day for specialists to make money is the opening. They're the only people who are privy to all the limit orders and therefore have better knowledge than anyone about the true supply and demand. They can open their stocks at any price they choose, as long as they fill all the market orders and fill any limit orders priced more favorably than the opening price. The acceptable range that the specialists can move stocks during the opening moments without arranging trades at each increment is larger than during the trading day.

For example, let's say that at the opening there are 50,000 shares to buy at market and 10,000 to sell at market.

As to limit orders, assume there are 50,000 shares available for sale at 40 or higher and another 20,000 shares for sale at 39.70 or higher.

Let's say the specialist is inclined to sell the stock. He might open it at 39.68. Neither one of the limit orders to sell is executed. (Both wanted to sell higher.) Out of the 50,000 shares to buy at market, the specialist matches 10,000 shares with the 10,000 market sells, all at 39.68.

40,000 shares remain to buy at market. The specialist fills these by selling 40,000 from inventory or, more likely, by selling 40,000 shares short, at 39.68. But unless the specialist genuinely wants to sell the stock, he is unlikely to open at 39.68 at all.

If the specialist is more inclined to buy, he might open the stock at 39.95. The 10,000-share market sell order is happy, and so is the 20,000-share order that was willing to sell for only 39.70. These two sell orders are filled from the 50,000 buy order, leaving 20,000 shares on the buy order. To fill these, the specialist shorts 20,000 shares at 39.95.

The specialist then broadcasts a quote of 39.80 bid, 40 asked. His purpose is to induce the buyer of 50,000 shares at 40 to give way and drop the limit to 39.80. If this succeeds, the specialist covers his short sale at 39.80, for a profit of $3,000 (20,000 shares times $.15). Nice work if you can get it.

Out of the 50,000 sell order that drops its limit from 40 to 39.80, the specialist buys 20,000 to cover his short sale. Thirty-thousand shares remain to sell, now at a limit of 39.80. The specialist is bullish on the stock, and his bid price is 39.80. He therefore buys the 30,000 shares at that price. If the specialist is not bullish and no additional buy orders have come in, the specialist must buy the 30,000 shares anyway. (The cost of 30,000 shares at 39.80 is almost $1.2 million. It's all in a day's work.)

To be a trader, you have to be quick, with a good memory for numbers. You have to be able to think on your feet, regardless of whether you're standing or sitting down. If reading the above description makes you feel awash in a sea of numbers (which I myself feel, even though I labored over the writing of it), you would probably find it especially difficult to become a successful day trader.

At the opening, there is often a rush of trading. Market orders from Europe and Asia await execution. If the buying pressure is strong, specialists open the stock as high as they can, taking short positions to accommodate the buyers. The specialists then endeavor to move prices down, enabling them to cover their shorts. The opening is when the specialists make their bread and butter. Some traders avoid trading at the opening, to let the specialists have at it.

But not all traders avoid the opening. Some try to think like specialists and to trade with them. During most of the day, you would endeavor to buy strength and sell weakness. But at the opening you would endeavor, like the specialist, to buy weakness and sell strength.

Twenty minutes or so after the opening, the prices may fade. If the price opens up, subsequent prices tend to fade down. If the price opens down, subsequent prices tend to fade up. During the fade, you might choose to take a position. If the prices are fading down, you would buy. If they're fading up, you would sell short.

Before the opening, you don't know whether the price will open up or down. You might enter several limit orders to buy at various prices above and below the previous night's close. No matter where the item opens, up or down, you have a chance of participating with the specialist. Use limit orders (see below) that are good only at the opening. If you use day orders, do not forget to cancel them, even before the day's end.

Most investors enter limit orders at round numbers, such as 30 or 30.50. The specialist takes advantage of this to scalp a few pennies profit, and you can too. For example, let's say that QQQ closed the previous day at 29.50. At the opening, there are sellers at 30. The specialist might open at 29.98 and place his quote at 29.93–29.98. He's trying to entice some of the sellers to come off their limits at 30 and hit his bid at 29.93. If he's successful, the specialist buys at 29.93. He then moves the price up, if he can, and sells at 30, gaining a seven-cent profit. If you have an order in at the opening to sell short at 29.97 or 29.98, you might cover, go long at 29.93, and sell at 30.

If a stock closes strong, the specialist might have taken short positions to accommodate the purchases. In this case, he would endeavor the next morning to open the stock down, to cover. If you had gone short on the previous close, you could enter your limit orders on the low side.

To express a bid (to buy), put the price first and use the word "for." You might say, for example, 29.93 bid for 1000 QQQ.

To express an offer (to sell), put the price last and use the word "at." You would express it 1000 QQQ at 29.98. Orders fly fast and furious. Big money is involved. To keep errors from abounding, everyone talks the same language.

Prices may not fade after the opening; the buying pressure may be too strong. Let's say the QQQ opens at 29.98, but the quote at 29.93-29.98 doesn't hold. Some trades occur at 29.97, but there's lots of buying at 30. You'd be well advised to cover your short for a two-penny loss and buy, in hopes of a strong morning.

As one prominent trader put it, "If you concentrate 100 percent of the time, you will be 100 percent effective. If you concentrate 95 percent of the time, you will be 90 percent effective. If you concentrate 90 percent of the time, go home."

Even though many stocks may have gap openings, the market as a whole may not. This is because the individual stocks are opening one at a time. The averages may therefore change rapidly but smoothly, without a gap.

To gain access to listed stocks electronically, traders use SuperDot. (DOT stands for Designated Order Turnaround. SuperDot is an improved version.) SuperDot is an electronic order system that links member firms directly to specialists. Orders of less than 2100 shares on SuperDot have priority over larger institutional orders. SuperDot is not easily available to individuals. But Internet systems, such as that of Ameritrade, offer similar executions and in some cases, better ones.

Some 80-to-90 percent of all orders are delivered electronically to American Stock Exchange specialists. Sixty percent of the *volume,* including of course the big institutional orders, comes to the specialist via brokers. Those orders cost a little more, but a floor broker often achieves a better price.

SuperDot is no piker, however. It can handle orders up to 99,999 shares per order. No floor broker is involved; the order is protected by the integrity of the specialist and the exchange. Specialists generally fill orders within seconds or place them in their books, to be represented in their quotes. During hectic markets, specialists can delay execution for up to two minutes.

ORDERS

Market Orders: You buy or sell at the current market. You endeavor to buy at the lowest asked price available and sell at the highest bid price available. Market orders have priority over all others.

Market Not Held: You authorize the broker to use discretion, delaying the order, if necessary, in an effort to get the best price. If the delay doesn't happen to work in your favor, the broker may not be held responsible.

Market On Open: A market order to be executed only at the opening.

Market On Close: A market order to be executed only at or near the close. Be wary here. Prices often range widely at the close, and professionals have ample opportunity to take advantage of traders at such times.

Limit: On a buy order, you specify the highest price you're willing to pay. On a sell order, you specify the lowest price you're willing to receive. If the last price of an ETF is 30, for example, you might enter a limit order to buy at 29.60 or lower. You might enter a limit order to sell at 30.40 or higher.

Most limit orders are called *Day Orders* and are good only until the close of the day's trading. A limit order that remains on the books until it's cancelled is referred to as *Good Til Cancelled* or *GTC Order.*

If a dividend is paid on a stock or an ETF on which you have a GTC order on the books, the limit price is automatically reduced by the amount of the dividend. If your limit price is 50, for example, and the dividend is $.25, the limit price is reduced to 49.75. If you don't want the price reduced by the dividend, mark the limit order *Do Not Reduce (DNR)*.

Market If Touched: On a buy order, if the price declines to the price you specify, your order becomes a market order and may be executed at a price higher than the one you specified. On a sell order, if the price rises to the one you specify, your order becomes a market order and may be executed at a price lower than the one you specified.

Stop Order: To protect a stock you own from incurring an excessive loss, you might enter a stop order to sell below the current price. As to the New York Stock Exchange, when the specified price is hit, the stop order then becomes a market order. The order would likely be executed at the current bid, which may well be lower than the stop price. As to the American Stock Exchange, only *Stop Limit* orders are accepted. If the last price is 50, you might enter an order to sell at 48 stop, 47.80 limit. If the 48 price is hit, your order becomes a limit order to sell at no lower than 47.80. If, after touching 48, the bid price immediately becomes 47.75 or lower, the order is not executed.

If you're short, you might enter a stop order to buy above the market. Again, the rules for the NYSE and AMEX differ.

Most people think of using a stop order to get out of a losing trade or protect a profitable position. But stops can also be used to enter a position. If an ETF has knocked up against resistance several times at around 40.50 and you want to buy it when it breaks out on the upside, you could put in a "buy stop" to buy at 40.85. When the ETF hits 40.85, the order becomes a market order.

Alternatively, you could enter a buy stop limit order at 40.85, limit 40.90. When the price hits 40.85, the order converts to a limit order to buy at no higher than 40.90. (On the AMEX, where most ETFs are traded, limits, as mentioned, are required in connection with stops.)

In the reverse, let's say you're bearish about an ETF, but it keeps bouncing off support at 20.25. You might place a "sell stop" to short at 20.10. After hitting that price, the order converts to a market order. If you add a limit at 20.05, the order will be executed at no lower than 20.05.

Cancel Former Order (CFO): This does the work of two orders. It cancels a prior order and replaces it with a new. Professional traders use CFO orders more frequently than *Cancel Orders* (CXL)

Fill or Kill Order: If the order is not filled immediately, it is killed. Do not use these orders. They don't provide better fills, and they aggravate the market makers.

Unexpected good news can be a nightmare for short sellers. Buyers rush in, and the short sellers rush to cover. But the buying by the short sellers drives the prices all the higher, causing larger losses for those who remain short. This is called a "short squeeze." Speculators in the nineteenth century sometimes tried to acquire all of the available supply of a stock or a commodity. The goal of such a "corner" was to create a severe short squeeze. In this connection, Daniel Drew, a prominent speculator back then, penned the following quote: "He that sells what isn't hisn must buy it back or go to prisn."

If buying is so persistent that you sense a short squeeze coming, by all means, go long.

Electronic Communication Networks (ECNs) are electronic systems that match trades automatically. An order is displayed only on the ECN on which it was entered. Market makers trade on ECNs. But ECNs do not have market makers and do not refer trades to market makers. Only limit orders are accepted—no market orders. If one party wants to buy at a certain price and another party wants to sell the same item at the same price, the trade is executed automatically. Approximately half of Nasdaq's volume is executed through Instinet, with some 80 to 90 percent of these entered by market makers. ECNs are used for both listed and Nasdaq stocks, although primarily for the latter. They include Instinet (INCA), Island (ISLD), MarketXT, Spear, Leeds and Kellogg (REDI), Teranova (TNTO), and Bloomberg (BTRD). Instinet is the biggest.

OPTIONS

An *option* is a contract that gives the buyer the right, but not the obligation, to buy or sell a specific asset by a specific time. Buyers of a call, if and when they choose to, have the right to buy the asset, that is, to call it away from the other person. If the call is thereby exercised, the seller (or "writer") of the call is required to sell at the agreed-upon price.

Buyers of a put, if and when they choose to before the put expires, have the right to sell the asset, that is, to put it to the other party. If the put is thereby exercised, the seller (or "writer") of the call is required to buy at the agreed-upon price.

Let's say I own a stock that's priced at $20. I'm the writer of a call. You're the buyer. I give you the option, but not the requirement, to buy the stock from me at $20 at any time during the next six months. The $20 is the *strike price*. For this right, you pay me $2. This is the *premium*.

Since the strike price is the same as the current price, the contract is said to be *at the money*. The premium has nothing but *time value*. (If the stock price exceeded the strike price, the premium would be partly time value and partly *intrinsic value*.) If the price of the stock remains at $20 or below, the option is not exercised and expires worthless. You lose your two dollars, but no matter what the price does, you lose no more.

Say the stock rises by 10 percent to $22 within six months and you exercise the option. You pay me $20. You sell the stock for $22. But since you paid $2 for the option, you break even.

If the stock rises 20 percent to $24, you make $4 profit on the stock. Having paid $2 for the premium, you double your money. If the stock rises to $30 by expiration, you make five times your money. ($10 divided by $2).

Okay, the stock I own is again priced at $20. But this time, you contract to buy it from me at $22. With the price at only $20, the option is *out of the money* by $2. The premium is $1, all of it time value.

If the price rises from $20 to $23, you buy it from me at the $22 strike price and sell it at $23. Having paid $1 for the option, you break even. The price has to rise to $24 to double your money ($24 – $22) / $1). All options are risky, but out-of-the-money calls are especially so. But they can be profitable. For example, if the price rises to $30, you make eight times your money (($30 – $22) / $1).

Now let's set the strike price on the other side of the current price.

My stock is priced at $20. You buy a call with a strike price of $18. The stock is in the money by $2. You pay a premium of $3, consisting of $2 intrinsic value and $1 time value.

The price rises from $20 to $21. You buy the stock from me for $18 and sell it for $21. Having paid $3 for the option, you break even. The price must rise from $20 to $24 for you to double your money ($24 – $18) / $3). If the price rises to $30, you make four times your money ($30 – $18) / $3). Sounds good, right? But a rise of 67 percent in only six months is unlikely.

By expiration, any time value on an option declines to zero. Early in the life of an option, the time value declines considerably slower than it does closer to expiration. Therefore, early in the contract life, the premium of an in-the-money option rises and falls by almost the same number of dollars as does the security on which it's based.

Let's say that, early in the life of the contract, the price of the stock is $24, with a strike price of $18. The option is in the money by $6. It's priced at $8 ($6 intrinsic value and $2 time value). If the stock price rises from $24 to $27 quickly, the option rises from $8 to approximately $11.

Note the leverage. If you bought the stock itself at $24, a rise of $3 would gain you 12.5 percent. But if you buy the option at $8, a rise of $3 gains you 37.5 percent. In-the-money options have plenty of risk, but they're less risky than out-of-the-money options.

As a contract approaches expiration, the time value diminishes rapidly. If the contract has no intrinsic value at expiration, it expires unexercised and worthless.

Today, most options on securities are bought or sold through exchanges, not between individuals. If you buy a call, you pay the premium and hope that the stock rises. If you sell the option prior to expiration, you receive whatever the premium may be at the time. Even if the stock price remains unchanged, the premium diminishes. The closer to expiration, the faster the time value falls.

With puts, everything is reversed. You acquire a put if you expect the price of the stock to decline (or if you want to hedge against the possibility of the price declining). Buying puts is a highly leveraged way of going short. All the terms I mentioned in connection with buying calls are applicable to the purchase of puts, except that the values are reversed. For example, with an in-the-money put, the current price is below the strike price. For other details, review the aforementioned description of calls while holding the book upside down.

So much for buying options. Let's look at writing (or selling) them. When you write a call, you receive the premium as income up front. You then hope that the price of the stock falls, preferably below the strike price, so that the option expires worthless. If this occurs, the stock is not called away, and you retain the entire premium you received at the start. Writing a call is similar to going short. It's what you might do if you expect the price of the stock to decline.

If the option expires at a time that the price exceeds the strike price, the stock is called, and you receive the strike price, not the higher current price.

If the price of the stock goes up after you write the call, the premium rises. If you buy the contract to exit your position (called a "closing purchase transaction"), you pay more than you received up front and incur a loss.

If you own a stock against which you write a call (or you're short a stock against which you write a put), you are writing a *covered* option. Owning a stock is a bullish move. Writing a call is a bearish move. You're hedging your position by reducing your risk and increasing your current income.

If you do not own the stock on which you write a call (or you are not short the stock on which you write a put), you're writing a *naked* option.

So far, Spiders are the only exchange-traded funds on which options exist. But the options on the S&P 100 Index (OEX) are very popular. If you own Spiders, you might buy a put or write a call on the OEX to hedge your position. If you're short Spiders, you might write a put or sell a call on the OEX to hedge your position.

It is difficult enough to predict what the price of an individual stock will do within a year. Most option contracts last only three months, with time values holding up reasonably well for only part of that time. With a time horizon this short, you'll probably have better luck flipping a coin than to exercise judgment about which way the stock will move. But even flipping a coin will lose in fairly short order because, in relation to the amount of money spent, the commissions are higher for options than they are for stocks. If you expect to come upon a pot of gold by buying options, you're probably looking at the wrong rainbow.

QUICKIES

- ◆ Start slowly.
- ◆ The biggest moves tend to occur at the opening and at the close.
- ◆ Formulate your own rules and stick to them.

- Use limit orders, to keep from giving up the spread.
- Trade securities that are volatile. Choose stocks whose average daily range is at least five times the spread.
- A market that grinds slowly higher is a good buy. A market that grinds slowly lower is a good sell.
- Don't be deceived by big rate-of-return numbers. Let's say a trader is down 50 percent one year and up 80 percent the next. Another trader is down 10 percent one year and up 25 percent the next. Which one ends up with more? (Pssst: −10% versus +13%)
- When you lose 20 percent of your equity, do not take ridiculous shots to recapture the money you lost. Instead, get out, pull yourself together emotionally, and revise your trading tactics.
- If an ETF doesn't act right, leave it alone. If you can't tell what's wrong, you don't know where it's going.
- A price is never too high to begin buying and never too low to begin selling.
- Do not prefer a bull market to a bear market or a bear market to a bull market. Just keep focused on being right.
- To be angry at the market for going against you is counterproductive. Oh sure, you can *feel* anything you like. Feelings bubble up whether you want them or not. But the market couldn't care less what you feel. Do not act out in anger against the market by varying from your normal style.
- When the stocks that had been market leaders in a bull market falter, be prepared for a bear market, even if the rest of the market continues to rise.
- Beware of buying a stock that refuses to follow the group leader.
- Remove the monthly profits you make from your trading account and invest those funds more conservatively.
- Trade only one security at a time. Your option positions should represent only a small portion of your entire portfolio.
- Learning how to trade means learning how not to lose money.
- Limit the number of indicators you watch.
- Stay close to the market.

- When the market turns choppy, shorten your trading horizon.
- Never trade with money you need to live on.
- Don't go for windfalls. Try for consistent small trades. The market continually serves up new opportunities.
- Have a reason for every trade you enter, where you're reasonably certain you have an edge.
- Before entering a trade, always plan your exit strategy, covering both a profit and a loss.
- Don't try to time the market perfectly.
- At the day's end, go flat.
- If you rely on tips from other people, you lose your autonomy. You might as well work for the other person. Good tips are given to only a few. Bad tips are ubiquitous.
- Reward yourself by buying things you want, like vacations. Do not reward yourself by taking bigger risks.
- You've probably heard the maxim, "You'll never go broke by taking a profit." This is true, but the advice is nevertheless unhelpful. Instead, cover your losses quickly and let your profits run.
- Go short as well as long. But since bear markets last only about one-third of the time, expect to be long more often than short.
- Avoid following the crowd. The crowd is often wrong.
- The best trades are profitable right from the start.
- Use the "two-order" rule: When you enter any order, enter a stop order too, to protect against a significant loss. As the price moves in your direction, keep raising the stop (or lowering the stop on a short).
- When a position becomes profitable, the losing trader takes a profit. The winning trader tries to determine whether the position will continue to show more profit. She lets it runs its course.
- On a short-term basis, anticipating which direction the market will move is hard enough. How far it will move, and for how long, is even harder.

- To alleviate stress, some traders drink, smoke, or do drugs. Bad idea. Better find another profession.
- Today's leading stocks may be tomorrow's losers.
- Trade issues that have consistently high volume. They have narrower spreads and greater liquidity. Liquidity means that when you want to buy or sell, there's likely to be a seller or a buyer near the price you want.
- Trade on-line, electronically, and do not use a live broker. If you cannot rely exclusively on your own judgment, you shouldn't be a trader.
- The smarter you are, the more likely your mind will wander while you're trading. A bored trader is often a poor trader. If you're really smart, you might find a way to have a job and arrange your trades on off hours. I don't know how you could succeed at it, but maybe I'm just not smart enough. Some people—precious few—do succeed at part-time trading.
- Don't for a moment think you can will the market to go your way. You're just a swimmer in the ocean surf. When big waves start hitting shore, get yourself onto dry land.
- If the iSharesGS Semiconductor (IGW), for example, is up by 2 percent during the day, while Spiders are up only 1 percent, you might decide that IGW has good relative strength. You might buy IGW and short Spiders.
- To a trader, news is of some importance. But how the news compares with what investors are expecting and what their positions are just prior to the news is vital. You're not only forming your own opinions, you're trying to determine other people's opinions as well. Judge markets by observing how others react to news.
- Some people think that you haven't suffered a loss until you sell. This is nonsense. If the price has gone against you, you have already suffered the loss. The appropriate question is, "What investment will gain the fastest from here, the one I'm in, or another one?"
- Did I mention this? Before entering a trade, always plan your exit strategy, covering both a profit and a loss. Without this, you're a dead duck.

Here are firms I consider appropriate for day trading:

Ameritrade, Inc.
E*Trade Financial
ChoiceTrade[3]

REALITY

Okay, this is the real Archie talking now. Certain aspects of this chapter I consider fiction. I went along with the make-believe to talk the language that traders talk.

When a stock breaks through "resistance" on the upside, it does *not* have a good chance of becoming a profitable trade. On the contrary, the approach will probably fail every bit as often as it succeeds. The transaction costs are not worthwhile.

Sometimes, market leaders correctly anticipate bear markets. Sometimes they don't. If predicting bear markets were that easy, traders would succeed at it consistently.

A seemingly "choppy" market has no predictive value whatsoever.

The notion of a stock "acting right" has no meaning. When the price of a stock rises consistently enough for you to identify that it's acting right, and you buy it, the stock then has about a 50 percent chance of starting to act wrong. But you have a 100 percent chance of paying commissions. In combination, these are lousy odds.

Specialists love stop orders. Say you buy a stock at $40. A stop order you place to sell at $39.69 is like a ripe plum sitting in his book. To the extent the specialist can, he'll pull the market down, pick up your stock at $39.69, and let the market float back up to a sale at $40.

Forget the small stuff. Buy the darn stock at $40 and hold for the rest of your life.

---

[3] ChoiceTrade was founded by a very competent old friend. Brokerage for day trading is specialized. I consider ChoiceTrade among the best. But I have a modest financial interest in the firm's success, so I may be biased.

CHAPTER 11

The Best Way to Go About It—Asset Allocation

The best approach to long-term investing ever devised is asset allocation. It has a fine pedigree, arising out of Modern Portfolio Theory, for which the developer, William F. Sharpe, received a Nobel Prize.

Asset allocation provides a highly favorable combination of relatively high returns and relatively low risk. For a given level of risk, you can obtain the best possible long-term gains.[1]

Capital markets are efficient. Securities are always priced as they ought to be. After a trade, different circumstances will change the prices. But at a particular moment, the price, as a television show is prone to say, is right. Trying to beat the market doesn't work. Oh, you hear about people who've made a ton of money in the market. But check to see if this was only during a recent period. The person's record may have been dreadful for 20 years prior. As to those who've done well over longer periods, check to see if they didn't get wealthy investing *other* people's money. If you succeed in beating the market at first, you'll gain the impression that you can do it consistently. The chances are, you'll blow a lot of money trying to do it again.

As the technologies of communication improve, whipping the market becomes all the more difficult. Institutions and individuals

---

[1] I am indebted to Roger C. Gibson for the ideas expressed in his seminal book, *Asset Allocation*, 3rd Edition, 2000, McGraw-Hill.

are acquiring more information ever more quickly. As technology advances, trades can be executed faster, in bigger quantities, with fewer errors. These advances make it more likely that securities prices represent intrinsic values accurately. It becomes less likely that anyone can beat the market consistently in the long run. You are wise, therefore, to diversify among many asset classes, including the ones to which Americans give short shrift—international investments.

Some think it best to choose investments that mirror the proportions of actual worldwide investments. These total approximately $63.8 trillion—a nice piece of change. They are as follows:

World Capital Markets—2000 (preliminary)

U.S. Equity	22.6%
Dollar Bonds	19.9%
Other Equity	16.6%
Other Bonds	13.7%
Japan Bonds	8.0%
Japan Equity	5.3%
U.S. Real Estate	4.8%
Cash Equivalents	4.8%
Emerging Bond Markets	1.9%
Emerging Equity Markets	1.2%
High-Yield Bonds	1.0%
Venture Capital	0.2%
Total	100.0%[2]

Many investment managers purport to outperform the averages in one of two ways. Indeed, some use both:

- *Market Timing:* Some money managers endeavor to time markets so as to be out or partially out when prices fall, and in when they rise. If a bear market is anticipated in stocks, for example, market timers would sell at least some of their

[2] Printed by permission of Brinson Partners, a member of UBS Asset Management. Brinson excludes from the list those asset classes that are not readily accessible to institutional investors. Most real estate in foreign nations, for example, is unavailable for purchase by U.S. pension plans.

equities and beef up their cash holdings. Investment institutions tend not to engage in this activity, at least not as an intentional policy. But individual investors do make this effort, generally with poor results.

- *Picking Stocks:* Within a particular asset class, many investment managers try to select individual issues that are expected to outpace the class as a whole. They endeavor to choose stocks, for example, that will beat the S&P 500 Index. Institutional investors do indeed engage in this activity. Enormous amounts of money are spent trying to divine those stocks that will outstrip the others.

Many clients expect investment advisers to succeed at both market timing and security selection. When an adviser purports to do both, persuading the prospect to open an account may be a cinch. But keeping the account is quite another matter, because few managers successfully time the market or select outperforming securities. None do both consistently. Those who succeed for a few years in a row may proclaim that it was their skill that counted. In truth, they were given a gentle touch by Lady Luck.

Many individual investors put considerable efforts into timing the market. Mutual funds organizations are troubled by the number of people that shuffle money back and forth between stock funds and money market funds. Remarkably few people succeed at it. On the contrary, market timers tend to be loaded with cash when prices are low and laden with stocks when prices are high. Buying stocks high and selling low leads to an unfulfilling retirement.

Academics assert that, after taking into account transaction costs, those who try to time the stock market must be correct roughly three times out of four merely to match the performance of those who buy and hold. You don't expect to be right three times out of four, do you? Far more likely, you'll be wrong three out of four times and end up far behind.

The superior returns from common stocks can be traced to relatively few periods of strength, many of which occur when investors are pessimistic. For example, during the summer of 1932, when unemployment was about 25 percent, most people would rather have drunk from an oft-used spittoon than to buy stocks. Yet from

July to November of 1932, the Dow Average doubled from 42 to 84—the most rapid rise of stocks in U.S. history. The Dow being below 100 seems piddling in comparison to today's five-figured levels. Even so, a double is a double. This is by no means the only example of extremely rapid appreciation. Time and time again, stock prices begin spirited advances when investors feel most comfortable in cash.

Many money managers engage in market timing more than they think they do. Recently, at a time when stock prices were considerably lower than they had been two years prior, I asked a senior officer of a Registered Investment Advisor whether the firm engaged in market timing.

"No," he replied. "We generally hold about 5-percent cash. Right now, the cash is up to about 15 percent."

This is market timing gone awry. Being 95-percent invested most of the time but 85-percent invested when prices are low isn't exactly an ideal approach.

I asked the fellow, "Why hold 5-percent cash in normal times? Why not 1-percent cash?"

He answered, "The amount of cash partly depends on whether the account is making regular payouts. But our clients generally feel more comfortable with some level of cash."

Ah, there's the key: The clients are more comfortable with cash. And the clients are comfortable with even more cash, no doubt, when the market and economic news is unfavorable. The firm can hardly be blamed. For fear of losing business, it cannot help but give way to its clients' natural inclinations.

The inclinations are wrong. Stock prices are low when market and economic news is most worrisome. These are the very times when the exposure to stocks should be increased, not reduced. But alas, such apparent daring goes against the grain. Competition and the danger of losing business force the firm to engage in a faulty investment policy.

You are well advised to use exchange-traded funds, which hold no cash. You are well advised, also, to hold no cash yourself for investment purposes. For family purposes, of course you need cash. But as to funds you're setting aside for use many years in the future, hold nothing back; put it all to work. The best time to invest all available funds in an asset allocation program with a predominance of stocks is always when the money becomes available.

Although most investment advisors do not engage (or think they don't engage) in market timing, a great many advisors do indeed endeavor to select securities they expect to outperform the industrial sector of which they're a part. This, too, is easy to proclaim but hard to fulfill. Some succeed—for a while. They become the darlings of the industry and are called upon to share their supposed wisdom on television. But then, as suddenly as it came, the wisdom inexplicably departs, and they slink back to the pack.

Nearly everyone in the investment profession benefits from trading, especially by their customers. If you're a trader, your broker will consider you the cat's meow. Many money managers obtain business by implying that they can whip the averages. (They only imply it. Saying so outright causes their feet to end up all too often in their mouths.) Indeed, many money managers are evaluated on their short-term records. Their pay is dependent on how well their portfolios performed last *quarter!* This is ridiculous.

Newspapers and magazines must fill their pages, and television programs must fill their time. They all have to keep writing and talking. About what? Well, they strive to keep you up-to-date with the latest information. This is appropriate, of course, but as far as investments are concerned, there's always the implication that if you but learn the latest facts, you can whip other investors. Most people who supply investment services or investment information have a vested financial interest in your being a short-term trader. It is essential to resist this pressure.

A few money managers, probably the best ones, do not time the market or pick outperforming stocks. They engage in asset allocation. Such managers are unlikely to be interviewed on television. Despite marvelous long-term results, their approach is considered to be, and is in fact, boring. These managers attain excellent results in relation to the modest risks they bear. They diversify in two respects: First, they spread their funds among many asset classes. Secondly, within a single asset class, they diversify widely. We discuss each of these factors in more detail.

Diversification Among Investment Classes: A wide range of asset classes is available for diversification, as follows:

Short-Term Debt Instruments
   Money market funds

CDs
Fixed annuities
Guaranteed interest contracts
Short-term bonds

Longer-Term Bonds

Federal government bonds   Each of these five categories
Corporate bonds   can have intermediate or
Municipal bonds   long-term maturities. They
International bonds   can also vary in quality.
Emerging market bonds

Hybrids (crosses between stocks and bonds)

Preferred stocks
Convertible securities   Hybrids come in great
Other hybrids   variety.

Stocks

Domestic stocks   Each of these three categories
International stocks   can include large or small
Emerging market stocks   companies. They can also be
                                growth or value stocks.

Real Estate

REITs
Real estate partnerships
Real estate direct ownership

Commodities

Commodity mutual funds
Commodity-linked securities
Precious metal mining stocks
Precious metal bullion

Diversification pays. It's important to own asset classes whose fluctuations differ from one another. While one class, such as stocks, is falling in value, another, such as bonds or real estate, might be rising. The movements won't be exactly opposite, of course, but to the extent they're different at all, one offsets the other, and the volatility of the whole portfolio diminishes.

The first dollar you add to an investment class has more beneficial effect than the last dollar. For example, an increase in exposure from 0-percent stocks to 1-percent stocks has more beneficial effect than an increase from 99-percent stocks to 100-percent stocks.

The less the correlation between the cycles of two investment groups, the more likely that when the prices of one group fall, the prices of the other group will rise. Also, the less the correlation between the cycles, the more that the *first* dollar of a new group added to the mix has greater benefit than the *last* dollar. In other words, the more the cycles differ, the greater the benefits of diversification, and the more that a little diversification goes a long way.

Many of the preceding investment sectors are beyond the scope of this book. Nevertheless, a person can achieve a handsome return with relatively low risk from asset classes readily available with index funds and available for the most part with exchange-traded funds.

Without risk, you'll enjoy precious little gain. There's no such thing as a guaranteed security that returns high rates.

As a general rule, the higher the expected return from any particular asset class, the greater the volatility. Money market funds, for example, produce low volatility and low returns. Over extended periods, stocks produce high volatility and high returns.

Here are some of the basic asset classes. They are arranged so that, as you move down the list, the normal, long-term investment returns increase and so does the volatility:

Treasury Bills

Long-Term Treasury Bonds

Long-Term Corporate Bonds

Large Company Stocks

Small Company Stocks

Actually, as you proceed down the list, the volatility increases *more* than the returns. The difference between long-term corporate bonds and large company stocks is especially wide. The returns and volatility of large company stocks are significantly greater than the returns and volatility of long-term corporate bonds.

Diversification Within Investment Classes: Within a single asset class, it's important to diversify widely. Anyone who invests in stocks is subjected to market risk. As the market rises and falls, especially the bull and bear movements lasting months or years, it tends to pull most stocks with it. But when people invest in just one or two stocks, they are subject to "specific" risk in *addition* to market risk. Each individual stock has a fluctuation of its own, apart from other stocks. When just one or two stocks are acquired, the overall risks are particularly high.

But by diversifying to dozens or even hundreds of individual items within an asset class, specific risk disappears. The overall risk is greatly reduced. Exchange-traded funds are ideal vehicles for this purpose. One should be willing to put up with market risk. Without it, there is little gain. But specific risk is unnecessary and can in most cases be dissolved by the use of exchange-traded funds.

Academic studies have found that asset allocation has considerably greater beneficial effect on returns than either market timing or security selection. The best course is to own several sectors, with each one widely diversified. In 1999, for example, investors wouldn't touch value. In 2001, they shied away from growth. On both occasions, investors were on the wrong side. They would have been better off owning both sectors all along.

Those who engage in asset allocation generally believe that it's impossible to consistently time markets in any respect. I too believe this. From minute-to-minute, month-to-month, year-to-year, or five-years-to-five-years, market fluctuations cannot be anticipated. But as to market trends lasting 10 years or so, I part company with many of the rest. I think the character of the stock market over a period of a decade can indeed be anticipated. The key conditions that underlie stock markets are threefold. I place them here in the order of the reliability with which they can be predicted, as follows:

- ◆ The pace of technical innovation.
- ◆ The degree to which government is likely to help or hurt the economy.
- ◆ Monetary policy.

Technological Innovation: The current pace of technological invention is mind-boggling. New developments come pouring out of America's laboratories. For every person on earth there are over three million digital switches. A microprocessor installed in a robot's knee and containing one million transistors costs only two dollars. The Internet is spreading at high speed from China to Brazil. Perhaps most revolutionary of all are discoveries in biotech. Human conditions are improving and will continue to improve immeasurably. So will the resulting profits.

Better technology means higher productivity. Higher productivity causes supply to exceed demand and lessens inflation, thereby lowering interest rates. In the United Kingdom, interest rates generally fell for 82 years from 1815 to 1897. Interest rates have been falling in the United States for less than 25 years. To equal Great Britain's nineteenth-century feat, the U.S. has a long way to go.

Government: As mentioned earlier, it is right and proper, nay, essential, that government protect private property, enforce contracts, prevent citizens from directly harming other citizens by force or fraud, and defend the nation. U. S. governments have done these tasks reasonably well, enabling U.S. citizens to thrive. But all of the other functions taken on by U.S. governments have in the long run done more harm than good. In U.S. central cities and in certain rural areas, such as the Appalachians, the intrusions of federal and state governments have been overwhelming, causing poverty and unhappiness. As Professor Walter Williams put it several years ago: Since the 1960s, the amount of money poured by government into U.S. central cities equaled the value of all Fortune 500 companies plus the value of most U.S. farmland. Despite this (I think because of it), the problems have gotten worse.

Individual liberty is the highest form of civilization. Those governments that foster free markets and individual liberty minimize the gaps between rich and poor and create the most favorable conditions for economic growth.

Voters are catching on that big government causes more harm than good. They have not yet learned that big government hurts the poor more than the rich, but when they do, the gargantuan governmental edifice may come tumbling down. In the meantime, the trends are favorable. Elections throughout the world tend toward the antigovernment approach. Even Asian governments, for the first time, are coming to see the value of the free flow of information.

Since talk radio began in the United States in the early-1960s, callers have swung markedly toward antigovernment views. Rush Limbaugh's program reflects this trend. Liberal talk show hosts find it difficult to be hired, because their programs simply aren't popular enough to carry the day. Being a Libertarian, I disagree with Dr. Laura Schlesinger's opposition to abortion and homosexuality. But the popularity of her program isn't based on those views; it's based on her urging that people take personal responsibility for their moral behavior. This is a further indication of America's movement toward individual freedom.

Electronic equipment, such as computers, enable individuals to know more and do more than they ever could before. Thus empowered, individuals want government to reduce its intrusions. All of this indicates to me that the impact of government in the United States, over time, will lessen. This is highly positive, not only for the poor, but for the stock markets of the world.

On the infamous September 11, 2001, terrorism of course had disastrous effect. But I believe that the risk will be greatly reduced over the next several years. The war on terrorism, as our leadership has oft proclaimed, is a different kind of war. Television, the Internet, and other technologies are empowering individuals. This is a war against terrorist networks and, to some extent, the governments that support them. Wars are becoming less nation against nation, as in World War II. Technology empowers the individual, both bad and good. Warfare is coming to resemble ongoing international police work.

Even before September 11, 2001, the U.S. Congress was so delighted about the prospect of a federal surplus that it went whole hog on spending. Then came the war, making federal expenditures rise all the faster. The stock market performs poorly during periods when government expenditures are growing faster than the economy as a whole. To some extent, the bear market of 2000–2001 was a result.

Will government expenditures continue to rise faster than the economy? Yes, certainly they will, for a while. But the trend won't last. No way will the top income-tax rate increase to anything like 90 percent, where it stood in the 1950s. People are becoming too well informed to put up with that nonsense. Nations that attempt such confiscation will see their investment capital depart in the blink of an eye.

I believe the chances of massive inflation at any time in the next 20 years is so unlikely that any investor who plans for it is driving forward while looking at the rear view mirror. Inflation is a creation of big government. There will be no repeat of the rapid inflation that occurred in the United States in the late-1940s and the 1970s.

Monetary Policy: Monetary policy is largely controlled by the Federal Open Market Committee, whose members number only 12. The actions of so few people are difficult to predict. I can only say that monetary policy has improved in the last 20 years. No longer do we witness such disasters as Regulation Q, which placed a cap on the interest rates banks could pay for deposits. Unable to pay sufficient interest for deposits, banks were forced to pass out toasters and other tangibles. Citizens vacated the banking system in droves. (Some call it "disintermediation.") They circumvented the banking system, using other cash equivalents such as money market funds. All of this exacerbated the disastrous 1974 bear market.

In early-2000, Alan Greenspan said that the continued rapid growth of productivity would lower unit labor costs. This in turn would increase corporate profits, which would raise stock prices. Higher stock prices, he felt, would raise household net worth, which would make demand exceed supply. Finally, demand exceeding supply would bring higher inflation.

Jumping from the beginning to the end of this long line of reasoning, Greenspan in effect proclaimed that rising productivity would bring on inflation. As a result, the Federal Open Market Committee stepped on the monetary brakes, raised short-term interest rates up to 6.5 percent (nothing like the 14 percent of 1980), making the 2000–2001 bear market all the worse.

But Greenspan's reasoning contains a whopping disconnect. Rising productivity does not increase inflation. The effect is quite the opposite. Rising productivity makes supply *exceed* demand. Rising productivity causes the supply of goods to outstrip the supply of money, reducing inflation. The restriction of the money supply was therefore unnecessary. It would be helpful if the Federal Reserve Governors would stop trying to be so smart. The stupider government policymakers are, the less harm they do.

The Federal Reserve made another mistake in 1999–2000. It raised short-term rates slowly and let it be known that as long as the economy kept growing rapidly, the Fed would continue to raise rates. The actual result was opposite to the intended result. People felt the urgency to borrow and spend immediately, before the rates rose again. The Fed kept threatening to raise rates, and the economy kept growing. Finally, in the fall of 2000, the Fed said that rates would be raised no further. The economy then screeched to a halt. (Stock prices, of course, had already started down; stock prices always move first.)

As of this writing, the opposite has been occurring. The Fed is saying that as long as the slowdown continues, it will go on lowering rates. The result? People are postponing borrowing and buying in expectation of lower rates in the future. The Fed is threatening to lower rates, and the economy continues to stall.

These monetary policies are problems, certainly, but they are not the disasters that occurred in the 1970s. I consider it inevitable that, during the next decade or so, inflation will diminish. Eventually, I expect benign deflation, which means a reduction of the general price level. Long-term and short-term interest rates will fall. In 1943, the interest rate on 90-day Treasury Bills was 0.4 percent. I see no reason why this won't occur again, under far happier circumstances than World War II.

Since the end of 1925, inflation has at times been a serious problem. This is because, for extended periods, world governments grew far faster than the world economy. But the days of big, intrusive government are numbered. It's unwise to plan an asset allocation program on the assumption that inflation will be as much of a problem in the future as it has been in the past. It won't. The amount of money invested in short-term money markets and inflation hedges should therefore be minimized.

Most investment professionals disregard the machinations of politics. They should indeed be disregarded in the short term, just as should short-term changes in stock prices. But government has coercive power, and the private sector doesn't. Government provides, and certainly should provide, the framework within which the economy may thrive. Long-term trends in politics point the way toward poverty or prosperity. Investment professionals who disregard such trends deprive themselves unduly.

THE PROPER MIX

In an era of economic growth and diminishing inflation, one should minimize investments in short-term cash equivalents and commodities. As inflation retreats, the returns from those investments will diminish. Concentrate most heavily on common stocks.

The greater the expected returns of an investment, the more one should expect the fluctuation of those returns. Treasury Bills promise low returns, and their year-to-year fluctuations are modest. Big-capitalization stocks have considerably higher returns and much greater fluctuations. Small-capitalization stocks have even bigger returns and greater fluctuations still.

Many money managers believe that the two most important investment risks are:

+ Inflation, which is most damaging to interest-bearing investments
+ Volatility, which most affects equities, that is, stock investments

If you remove serious inflation from consideration as a significant risk for the next decade, as I do, short-term debt becomes unattractive. Except for those funds needed in the near term, forget about money market funds and other cash equivalents. If you're a newcomer to the investment world, get over your fears of volatility. A negative return for a year or two is not permanent. I'm not saying this is an easy adjustment. In the long run, stocks return about 7.4 percent more than Treasury Bills. This is the "equity risk premium," that is, the reward for contending with the volatility. But the 7.4-percent equity risk premium seems small when measured against the fluctuation of stocks by 30 percent or more.

All I can say is, learn to live with volatility. Besides, if my prognostications are correct, the equity risk premium will increase. As government policies throughout the world cause less and less harm, the returns from stocks will grow and short-term interest rates will diminish. The volatility will tend to be more consistently on the upside than it has been (although certainly not always). The reward for putting up with the volatility, as opposed to buying Treasury Bills, will grow.

Here are the four classes of investments that are essential for a successful asset allocation program:

STOCKS IN GENERAL

Stocks in general produce relatively high annual returns. They're a greater risk than bonds, but in the long run, the risk is well worthwhile. Be sure to diversify among the big and small, growth and value, domestic and foreign. The more the diversification, the better. By owning all types of stocks from throughout the world, you're riding on the backs of hundreds of millions of workers, all endeavoring to help their employers preserve and enhance their jobs.

During periods of high inflation, stocks perform poorly. During 1973 and 1974, the record was especially bad. In the next 10 years or so, the stock market will of course endure bear markets, as it did in 2000 and 2001. But I don't expect bear markets of the severity of 1973-1974 to reoccur for at least 15 years, if then.

If and when the double-taxation of dividends is relieved, dividend yields will no doubt increase. When this will occur I do not know, but I do expect it to occur. Corporations will pay out more to shareholders and have less cash to reinvest in the business. It will be a good thing to receive more of the returns in cash and less from those always-uncertain capital gains.

INTERNATIONAL STOCKS

I recommend that exposure to international investments be substantial. During the years when so many nations of the world were ruled by dictators, most people were poverty stricken. Western European nations were democracies, but their policies weren't all that great either. U.S. economic policies were bad enough, but they were so much better than the others that the U. S. economy dominated the world. Many Americans think that, as far as investments are concerned, the world ends at our shores.

Such an attitude is no longer fruitful. Now that most people are released from the shackles of dictatorship, they have nowhere to go but up—way up. Other nations can be as prosperous as America. I hope they will. It helps them, of course, and the more prosperous they become, the more of our products they can acquire.

You have every reason to participate in the growth of foreign economies. Some nations have economic growth rates twice that of the United States. Oh sure, the political situations in the emerging nations are volatile. Both Indonesia and the Philippines, for example, recently cast off incompetent presidents, causing equity prices in both nations to plummet. But how marvelous it is that both nations accomplished this by constitutional procedures, not by military takeovers! John Adams, author of the world's first constitution—that of Massachusetts—is smiling so broadly his face hurts.

In the midst of such political uncertainty, you don't suppose that the price-earnings ratios of stocks in Indonesia and the Philippines were sky high, do you? Of course they weren't. They were at rock-bottom lows. (The unrest was, and remains, greater in Indonesia than in the Philippines.)

The whole idea, I remind you, is to buy low and sell high. Better yet, buy low and hold. Just diversify your funds to many nations and take delight as the panoply of progress unfolds to marvelous effect. For the 15 years from 1980 to 1994, the MSCI EAFE (Europe, Asia, and Far East) Index, valued in U.S. dollars, outperformed the S&P 500 Index in every single year. I'll grant you that the MSCI EAFE Index underperformed the S&P 500 Index from 1995 to 2000. But you don't suppose that foreign stocks will never outperform U.S. stocks again, do you? Of course they will. Besides, the up-and-down cycles of foreign stocks differ from those of U.S. stocks. Diversification pays.

REAL ESTATE

Real estate, in the form of REITs, is suitable for an asset allocation portfolio, for three reasons:

Real estate cycles do not match those of stocks. The disparity serves as a form of diversification. As one class of assets falls, another may be rising.

Real property is an essential ingredient of the economy. People and businesses need roofs over their heads.

Real estate prices rise with inflation. My views about political trends may be wrong. Inflation might increase after all. A modest amount of real estate serves admirably as a hedge.

BONDS

In modest amounts, long-term bonds are highly appropriate for an asset allocation program. They appreciate in price as interest rates decline. More generally, the cycles of long-term bonds differ from those of stocks. The price trends of one sector offset another, reducing the volatility of the whole.

During periods of high inflation, interest tends to rise, to compensate for the loss of buying power of the future income. When the rates rise, the prices of bonds decline. But the opposite prevails as well. When inflation declines, as I expect it to continue doing, interest rates on bonds fall and principal values rise. The increase in principal values outweighs any reduction of interest, making bonds especially attractive during periods of declining inflation.

From 1970 to 1985, the United States suffered unusually high inflation. As inflation rose, so did interest rates. And as interest rates rose, the value of bonds went down. They fell so much that, in the late 1970s, the total annual returns from bonds were negative. But when the turnaround came and interest rates went down rapidly from 1982 on, bond the returns became very positive.

The prices of bonds were unusually volatile from 1970 to 1985. The returns from stocks were volatile also, as they always are. But during those years of unusual economic disruption, the bond cycles and stock cycles differed to an unusual degree. Therefore, the beneficial effect from adding the first dollar of stocks to a portfolio of bonds was unusually great. A little bit of stocks added to the mix of bonds went a long way. During the next 10 years or so, I expect stock prices generally to advance and interest rates generally to decline. As the political environment for business gradually improves, I expect less economic volatility than the United States experienced during the 1970s and 1980s. The cycles of stocks and bonds should differ to a lesser extent than they did from 1970 to 1985. The beneficial effect of diversification from one group to the other will be less. Therefore, funds should be allocated primarily to stocks during the next 10 or 20 years. I do favor the addition of bonds to the mix. But the addition of bonds should be relatively small, on the order of 20 percent.

A RECOMMENDED ASSET ALLOCATION PROGRAM

Before setting up a long-term asset allocation program, isolate significant funds you'll need within the next few years into certificates of deposit, short-term bonds, or money market funds. Short-term liabilities should be matched by short-term assets. If a big expense comes due in four years, buy a corporate bond or a Treasury due in four years.

For your long-term investments, here's a simple asset allocation portfolio that nicely balances reward and risk. I suggest 60 percent in common stocks, split equally between U.S. stocks and foreign stocks. I also suggest 20 percent in REITs and 20 percent in long-term bonds.

Now let's paint with a narrower brush.

As to the 30 percent in U.S. stocks, you have the opportunity to divide the funds between big stocks, small stocks, growth stocks, and value stocks. The Russell 3000 Index represents approximately 98 percent of the market capitalization of all publicly traded U.S. stocks. We'll take this as the universe of domestic stocks.

The economies of most nations are top-heavy. The largest 1000 stocks included in the Russell 3000 represent approximately 90 percent of the market capitalization of the Russell 3000. The Russell 2000 Index represents approximately 10 percent of the market capitalization of the Russell 3000. These proportions would call for dividing up the 30-percent segment into 27 percent for the big stocks and 3 percent for the small stocks.

This seems too lopsided to me. After all, small stocks outperform the biggies over time (although, to be sure, they're more volatile). I feel more comfortable realigning the proportions to 20 percent for the big stocks and 10 percent for the small ones. But even these segments you can split into growth and value portions.

Here, then, are my detailed recommendations for a suitable asset allocation program:

10 percent: iShares Russell 1000 Growth Index Fund, representing large U.S. stocks with relatively high price-to-book ratios.

10 percent: iShares Russell 1000 Value Index Fund, representing large U.S. stocks with relatively low price-to-book ratios.

5 percent: iShares Russell 2000 Growth Index Fund, representing small U.S. stocks with relatively high price-to-book ratios.

5 percent: iShares Russell 2000 Value Index Fund, representing small U.S. stocks with relatively low price-to-book ratios.

30 percent: iShares MSCI EAFE Index Fund, which at this writing contains a significant number of stocks, 793, from Europe, Australasia, and the Far East. Look to see, after the publication of this book, whether an exchange-traded fund has been developed that covers foreign stocks from all regions, including those of emerging markets. If so, by all means use it. Perhaps Vanguard will fill the bill with an International Viper. If you'd prefer a more inclusive investment from the beginning, use Vanguard's Total International Stock Market Index Fund. This mutual fund contains approximately 1500 foreign stocks, including not only Europe, Australasia, and the Far East, but also emerging nations.

20 percent: streetTRACKS Wilshire REIT Index Fund. Since REITs throw off relatively high, taxable income, place your REIT investment in a retirement program if you can.

20 percent: For long-term bonds, use the Vanguard Long-Term Bond Index Fund. With all bond investments in an asset allocation program, the overall volatility is reduced. When stocks are falling, bonds may be rising. (Read about Nuveen and Ryan Lab investments in the appendix. I consider the Nuveen offerings too risky and the Ryan Lab offerings not risky enough. But both are intriguing.)

If you have a minimum of funds, use just four investments. For domestic stocks, place 30 percent of your funds into the iShares Russell 3000 Index Fund. The foreign stocks, REITs, and bonds would remain the same.

To take an intermediate position, use five investments. Divide the domestic funds into 20 percent iShares Russell 1000 Index Fund and 10 percent iShares Russell 2000 Index Fund. The other three would remain the same.

To make your life far more complicated, you might omit the iShares MSCI EAFE Index Fund (or the Vanguard Total International Index Fund, as the case may be) and replace it with ETFs of foreign nations on an individual basis. Do not acquire these selections in equal amounts. You would purchase more of the iShares Europe 350 Index Fund, for example, simply because the European economy is larger than the others:

iShares S&P Europe 350 Index Fund

iShares S&P/TSE 60 Index Fund

iShares S&P Latin America 40 Index Fund

iShares S&P TOPIX 150 Index Fund

iShares MSCI Pacific ex-Japan Index

The greater the diversity, the greater the beneficial effect of the rebalancing described below.

If you can't stomach much in the way of stocks, increase your bond portfolio and cut down the others proportionately. But do not do this because you happen to be pessimistic about stocks at the very moment you're setting up your asset allocation program, only to increase your exposure to stocks later on when stock prices are soaring. Twenty percent in bonds seems sufficient to me.

Stocks are the main ingredient. The short term is always unpredictable. But the long term is indeed predictable. In the long run, prices rise. The right time to invest in stocks is always when you get the money.

REBALANCING

The values of the various sectors will not remain at their original percentages. As time passes, they will fluctuate in relation to each other. Therefore, set ranges within which they may fluctuate without interference. The permissible ranges can be fairly wide. I suggest you permit fluctuations of 30 percent each way.

For example, the iShares Russell 1000 Growth Index Fund is set at 10 percent:

30 percent less than 10 percent is 7 percent.

30 percent greater than 10 percent is 13 percent.

This means that, in relation to the entire portfolio, when the large domestic value stocks range from 7 to 13 percent, leave them be. But when they fall below 7 percent of the value of the total portfolio, add money to them, returning them to 10 percent. When they rise above 13 percent, sell some and return them to 10 percent.

Here are the permissible ranges I would choose for all of the investments:

(10%) Large domestic growth stocks: 7% to 13%

(10%) Large domestic value stocks: 7% to 13%

(5%) Small domestic growth stocks: 3.5% to 6.5%

(5%) Small domestic value stocks: 3.5% to 6.5%

(30%) International stocks: 21% to 39%

(20%) Bonds: 14% to 26%

(20%) REITs: 14% to 26%

Sell those sectors that, as a percentage of the total portfolio, exceed their permissible range. With the proceeds, add to those sectors that have underperformed. Such an automatic system causes you to sell high and buy low, which of course is the desirable way to go about it.

Do not make these adjustments frequently. Time your rebalancing to occur at intervals 13 months apart, so that any sales made outside of your retirement plans are always subject to favorable tax rates of long-term gains. If you begin in a January, rebalance in February, 13 months hence; then in March of the following year, and etc. In 12 years, you'll be back to January again. During each 13-month hiatus, you may be better off paying no attention whatever to your investments, except to dispose of dividends and to pay taxes. The more you take interest in your investments, the more you'll be inclined to take action. Other than rebalancing, you need take no action. Let the millions, if not billions, of people throughout the world do the work.

If you wish (and if you have sufficient funds), add additional diversification. You might select separate investments for gold stocks, hybrid stocks, hybrid bonds, intermediate bonds, foreign bonds, junk bonds, or any other sector you come across. If you want commodities, the Oppenheimer Real Asset Fund should satisfy you. I myself prefer a simpler life.

If you own real estate for investment purposes, you should cut down on your REIT investment. But your residence doesn't count as an investment; it serves your emotional well-being.

Without rebalancing, even if you do nothing, you'll be wrong at every market turn. If U.S. stocks perform unusually well, that portion of your total portfolio will be overinvested for any subsequent downturn. The failure to rebalance is similar to buying high and selling low.

Rebalancing is key. It forces you to sell high and buy low. When a segment of your portfolio outstrips your prechosen range, you slim it down and acquire a segment that's at the low end of its range.

IF INCOME IS NEEDED

If you require regular income from your portfolio, do not structure the portfolio differently to achieve it. Do not buy more bonds or REITs, for example, than is appropriate for maximum return. Unless you're dealing with a trust, whose income goes to one party and whose principal goes to another, treat the portfolio as a whole. To a great extent, the returns are derived from price appreciation. If you learned as a child never to spend principal, you were misled. Acquire a mix of investments that seems likely, over the long run, to maximize your total return with a minimum of volatility. Buy them, and, if need be, draw from them the income you need.

If income is needed, dividends may supply it. Your 13-month rebalancing also provides an opportunity to remove cash. Set aside from rebalancing the amount you need to spend during the coming year. If none of the sectors exceeds your permissible ranges, but you need income, rebalance anyway, bringing all the sectors closer to the original percentages.

To preserve your capital indefinitely, restrict your income withdrawals to 5–6 percent of the entire portfolio. The higher the income, the sooner the exhaustion. If you withdraw higher than 6 percent on an ongoing basis, be prepared to use up your capital. It might run out, for example, after you reach the century mark. By that time, you may feel a little used up yourself and not mind disappearing along with your capital. In any event, the money exists to serve you, not the other way around.

At the very beginning of your retirement, when you're especially active, you might withdraw a little more than 6 percent per year. Later on, when your lifestyle simmers down, cut the withdrawals to 5 percent or less. Your principal value should continue to appreciate handsomely.

Allocate your investments in proportion to your total investment assets, including your IRAs, 401(k) plans, and other retirement programs. To the extent the retirement plans lack a certain asset class, fill in with outside funds. If your IRA holds all the bonds you need, for example, you need none outside of the IRA. If you have a 401(k) plan whose investment you do not control, try to find out what it holds. If the plan contains nothing but large U.S. stocks, for example, your own investments should favor small and international stocks. Allocate your funds according to the complete picture.

Do not assume that IRA investments are for the long term and place only "aggressive growth" stocks therein. *All* of your long-term investments should be for the long term. Instead, take advantage of the tax shelter afforded by the IRAs. With traditional IRAs, the taxes on interest, dividends, and appreciation are deferred. With Roth IRAs, the funds are never taxed, even upon withdrawal.

Therefore, place in your IRAs those investments, such as corporate bonds and REITs, that generate relatively high, taxable income. Low-dividend-paying stock investments, however, should be held outright, apart from a retirement plan, so that you may gain the benefit of long-term capital gains rates.

For an asset allocation program, no skill is required—well, almost no skill. It's helpful if you can count higher than ten and can handle the dot in percentages. But market judgment is unnecessary; let the allocation and the rebalancing do the work. Despite the relative simplicity, you are likely to leave most other investors sputtering behind you in the dust. Successful and consistent timing of markets and choosing of stocks that outdo the indexes require tremendous skill—more skill, in my opinion, than is possessed by anyone. The chances are all too high that attempts to time markets and choose outperforming stocks will fail, especially after paying transaction costs. As a short-termer, you play a zero-sum game. You're fighting against the forces of the market.

To the extent they're available, exchange-traded funds are fine vehicles for asset allocation. Even though ETFs were designed for trading, do not use them in such a way. Just buy and rebalance.

There's a serious problem with asset allocation, although not an investment problem. Assume that small stocks become all the rage. Their prices are rising. Your friends are buying them and urging you to do so. But small stocks have exceeded the top of your permissible range, and according to your rebalancing standards, they're candidates for sale. What to do? Should you follow your friends or follow the plan?

Follow the plan, by all means. Sell some of the asset class your friends are buying. You may find this easier said than done. Going against the crowd is a lonely business. It's best to stay quiet about your investments. If you cannot avoid the derision they unload upon you, be assured that those miscreants will eventually get their comeuppance and fall behind your more reasoned approach.

Let diversification, rebalancing, and time make you a winner.

CHAPTER 12

A Brief on IRAs and Variable Annuities

CHARACTERISTICS OF ALL IRAS

Think of Individual Retirement Arrangements (IRAs) as umbrellas. They provide tax advantages for the investments you choose to hold within their shelter.

If you acquire an IRA from an organization that provides investments of its own—a mutual fund family, an insurance company, or a bank—the company will insist on your using the investments it offers. But a Self-Directed IRA, which you may acquire from a brokerage firm, enables you to acquire almost any investment you want—exchange-traded funds, for example.

There are nine kinds of IRAs altogether. The two most common ones for individuals are traditional IRAs and Roth IRAs. Here are the essential tax rules :

You may set up an IRA at any time during the year and until April 15 of the following year. On April 15, for example, you may make a contribution for both the current year and the prior year.

As long as the money remains within the IRA, the interest, dividends, and capital gains are not currently taxable. If you're foolish enough to try trading, this tax-free environment is a perfect vehicle for it.

If you've accumulated $10,000 or $20,000 in a mutual fund IRA, establish a self-directed IRA with an online brokerage firm. Direct that your mutual fund IRA be liquidated and the funds transferred to the brokerage firm. This is a nontaxable transfer; the funds pass from one tax umbrella to another.

The money you place in a traditional IRA is that which you've earned from your employment. It is not taxed in the year it is earned, because the IRA contribution for that year is deductible from your return. The taxable portion of your employment income is reduced by the contribution amounts. The government takes no part of your employment earnings when they go into the traditional IRA. But when money is later distributed out of the IRA, the government taxes it then, as ordinary income. The IRS requires that distributions begin by a certain age, so that it need not wait too long before taking its share. The tax rates on those distributions can rise all the way up to the highest brackets, just as would apply to the income from your salary.

(As an aside, this is a Libertarian approach to taxation. Americans are a caring people; they provide more in voluntary gifts than any people in world history. If I want some of your money and don't want to work for it, I have to persuade you to make a gift. If I force the issue, it's called stealing. When the government forces you to give it some of your money, it's called taxation. Why shouldn't the moral standards be the same? Why shouldn't all government revenues be voluntary gifts? The government could advertise and solicit, but exercise no coercion in collecting revenues. It would receive plenty of money for the things it should do and little money for the things it should not do. The change would help the poor more than the rich.)

Okay, back to business. With the Roth IRA, you contribute the money you earned to the Roth IRA *after* it has been taxed. Contributions are not deductible. If and when the money is distributed from the IRA, it comes out without being taxed. Since the government has already received its money, it imposes no requirements as to when the distributions begin. You don't have to remove any money from a Roth IRA during your life.

I favor Roth IRAs. The uninterrupted compounding within a tax-free environment, with the right to withdraw the money without tax—it's a beautiful thing.

You may contribute $3000 a year to a traditional or Roth IRA. This applies if you're less than 50 years old. If you're 50 or older, you can contribute an extra $500, totalling $3500 a year.

TRADITIONAL IRAS

With a traditional IRA, you begin to lose the deduction if your "modified AGI" (see next paragraph) exceeds $54,000 for married persons filing jointly. You lose it altogether when your modified AGI hits $64,000.

AGI stands for *adjusted gross income*, which is complicated enough; it's the number at the bottom of page 1 of IRS Form 1040. But the *modified* AGI is complicated to the point of absurdity. It's your adjusted gross income, plus your:

- Traditional IRA deduction
- Student loan interest deduction
- Foreign earned income exclusion
- Foreign housing deduction
- Qualified interest on U.S. Savings Bonds used for higher education
- Exclusion of employer-paid adoption expenses

By adding back these tax advantages to your income, your modified AGI becomes larger than the unmodified AGI. This makes it less likely that you can contribute to an IRA, because you're more likely to hit the $54,000-$64,000 limits. This is an example of the Congress creating tax benefits in one place (the six advantages above), but pulling them back in another (less chance of using IRAs). All this brings up one of my pet peeves about taxes: their complexity. In 2001, the cost of complying with federal income taxes reached about $140 billion. That's just the cost of compliance, mind you, not the taxes paid. The complexity enables the members of Congress to talk out of both sides of their mouths. They can say to one group, "See, we're helping you over here." But to a group with an opposing interest, they can say, "See, we're helping you over there." The costs, however, are borne by everyone.

Where was I? Oh yes, traditional IRAs. If you withdraw money from a traditional IRA prior to age 59½, the money is subject to ordinary income tax. But there's an additional *nondeductible* penalty of 10 percent if the distribution is attributable to anything other than the following:

- ◆ Death.
- ◆ Disability.
- ◆ Unreimbursed medical expenses exceeding 7.5% of adjusted gross income.
- ◆ Medical premiums after receiving unemployment insurance for at least 12 weeks.
- ◆ Higher education for you, your spouse, or you or your spouse's children or grandchildren.
- ◆ The purchase, up to $10,000, of a first home for you, your spouse, or you or your spouse's children, grandchildren, parent or other ancestor.
- ◆ The annuitization of distributions. That is, payments are made from the IRA in substantially equal amounts for life or for the joint lives of you and someone else.

After age 59½, all of these limitations come off. You may then withdraw money from a traditional IRA for any reason.

When you reach 70½, contributions *must* be discontinued, even if you're' still working. Annual distributions out of the IRA then become mandatory. They must be made by December 31 of each year, although the distributions for that first year, the year you reach 70½, may be delayed until April 1 of the following year. That's April 1, mind you, not April 15. (The IRS likes to keep you on your toes.) Therefore, if you wait until the year after you attain 70½, you must make your first distribution by April 1 and your second distribution by December 31 of that second year.

Got it? Aren't taxes fun?

The required annual distributions are based on an IRS table of life expectancy, which assumes that the distributions are paid jointly to you and to someone 10 years younger than you. Even though the payments may actually go to you alone, the assumption of a joint beneficiary being younger extends the payout period. The distributions are therefore less, and so is the tax. The same lower payout level prevails no matter who receives the payments. You may of course distribute more than the required amounts.

If distributions paid during the year from a traditional IRA are less than the total required, a penalty tax of 50 percent of the shortfall is assessed. This is a whopper! Make sure to withdraw enough.

An individual with several IRAs may withdraw from only one of them the distributions that meet the requirements of all of the IRAs owned by that person.

There's a serious problem with traditional IRAs: Investments made therein do not attain a stepped-up basis at death. The cost bases for tax purposes are not adjusted to the date-of-death value. The beneficiaries pay high, ordinary income-tax rates on the entire amount. The combination of these rates *plus* estate taxes can decimate the values.

ROTH IRAS

You may contribute up to $3000 (or $3500) of earned income to a Roth IRA each year, even after age 70½. Such contributions are permissible whether or not you're covered by a retirement plan at work. The maximum annual contributions to Roth IRAs are phased out when your modified adjusted gross income falls between $150,000 and $160,000 for joint taxpayers and between $95,000 and $110,000 for single taxpayers. For a single year, no more than $3000 ($3500) may be contributed to both a Roth IRA and a traditional IRA.

Contributions to Roth IRAs are *not* deductible. Only after-tax money goes into a Roth IRA.

As to withdrawals, let's start with the good news Again, age 59½ is key: If money has remained in the Roth IRA for five years and you have attained age 59½, you may withdraw money without tax or penalty for any purpose.

If the money has remained in the Roth IRA for five years and you have *not* attained age 59½, you may withdraw money from the IRA without tax or penalty, providing the following conditions are met:

- ♦ Death.
- ♦ Disability.
- ♦ The purchase of a first home for yourself, your spouse, or you or your spouse's children, grandchildren, parent or other ancestor (up to a $10,000 lifetime limit).

If money has remained in the IRA for five years and you have not attained age 59½, withdrawals over and above your contributions, taken out for purposes other than the above, are subject to income tax upon withdrawal. But the 10-percent non-deductible penalty is avoided, providing the withdrawal is for one of the following purposes:

- Unreimbursed medical expenses exceeding 7.5% of adjusted gross income.
- Medical premiums after receiving unemployment insurance for at least 12 weeks.
- Higher education for you, your spouse, or you or your spouse's children or grandchildren.
- The annuitization of distributions, that is, payments are made from the IRA in substantially equal amounts for life or for joint lives.

As to withdrawals subject to income taxes, there's a mitigating factor: The aggregate of your contributions, having already been taxed before the contributions were made, are not taxed again when they emerge from the Roth IRA. Only the earnings are subject to tax and penalty.

You have all this down cold, don't you? Taxes are a laugh-and-a-half.

A five-year period, by the way, begins with the first year in which a Roth IRA contribution was made. A separate five-year period begins with each rollover from a traditional IRA.

Once money is removed from a Roth IRA, subsequent earnings on funds invested outside of the Roth are subject to tax. Remove from the Roth IRA only what you need, therefore, and leave the rest inside.

If your modified AGI is $100,000 or less, you may convert a traditional IRA or a portion thereof to a Roth IRA. The entire amount then becomes subject to ordinary income tax in the year of conversion.

Lump-sum distributions from qualified retirement plans may not be converted directly to a Roth IRA. Such distributions must first be rolled over to a traditional IRA and thereafter to a Roth IRA. I guess this is because the IRS loves paperwork.

Do not, I pray you, acquire annuities or municipal bonds within an IRA. Each of those investments offers tax advantages of its own, but they generally come with higher costs or lower returns than investments that have no built-in tax advantages. Doubling the tax advantage gains no additional benefit. Besides, municipal bonds earn fairly high commissions for the salesperson, and annuities earn very high commissions. There's no sense in paying higher costs or earning lower returns when regular investments that have low costs and higher returns can be acquired within an IRA which itself prevents the income from being currently taxed. A single layer of tax advantages is quite enough, and IRAs are the cheapest way to obtain them. IRAs, after all, are not themselves investments; they are tax umbrellas within which to place investments.

Outside of a traditional IRA, trading produces high ordinary income-tax rates. Within a traditional IRA, the tax is at least postponed. Within a Roth IRA, income tax is never assessed at all. If you find trading irresistible, join Gamblers Anonymous, er, I mean, do your trading within an IRA.

Acquire taxable bonds and REITs within IRAs. But if you're a buy-and-hold investor with stocks, own them for long-term gains outside of the IRA. The IRA converts capital gains into ordinary income, which is a no-no. It's better to pay 18 or 20-percent rates outside of an IRA (and enjoy a stepped-up basis) than to pay high ordinary rates later, when the proceeds are withdrawn from the IRA.

Consider rolling over a traditional IRA to a Roth IRA. Tax is incurred on all of the funds rolled over. If you can pay the tax from funds other than the money being rolled over, the rollover is worthwhile. If you cannot pay the tax from other funds, rolling over the money makes no difference whatever.

If you have a traditional IRA, let's hope that by the time you need the money, government policies will have improved to the point that income taxes have been repealed altogether. It's a possibility, but I wouldn't hold my breath.

For further information about IRAs, consult IRS Publication 590. Go to www.irs.gov. At the bottom of the Web page, click on Forms & Publications.

VARIABLE ANNUITIES

As of this writing, variable annuities do not permit the purchase of exchange-traded funds within the policy. But insurance companies hate to see a popular financial concept pass by without hitching a ride. It's entirely possible that insurance companies will add ETFs to their variable-annuity repertoire.

Annuities in which the money is invested in bonds are called *fixed annuities*. Annuities in which the money is invested in stocks are called *variable annuities*. As a general rule, variable annuities are bum deals. Do not use them as vehicles for exchange-traded funds or anything else. The reason has to do with the very nature of annuities.

An annuity is an insurance policy—the opposite of life insurance. Unless a life insurance policy is stripped of its cash value, it pays out *after* death. An annuity policy pays out *until* death.

Annuities have two periods. The first is the accumulation period, when money is paid in, all at once or on a gradual basis. Like an IRA, the earnings compound tax free within the policy. The money can be withdrawn at any time.

To the extent the money is not withdrawn, the policy switches to the second period: the annuity payment period. The owner can make the switch at any time, but if she doesn't, the insurance company insists on switching the policy when she reaches an advanced age. It's called annuitizing the policy.

After annuitization, the insurance company begins paying out funds according to one of many payment formulas selected by the owner. A common formula is Joint Life Annuity with Ten Years Certain. According to this, a married couple would recceive regular income for their joint lives. If they both die within 10 years, payments would continue to the beneficiaries named in the policy. (There are choices as to the number of years.)

The reason annuity policies are always under the provenance of insurance companies is because they are the only ones who are willing to bet their own money on their estimates of longevity. (Once the payout formula is chosen, it cannot be changed, since the mortality factors are built into the payments. Many annuity policies are terminated prior to being annuitized. The balances are withdrawn, with the accumulated earnings then becoming subject to income tax.

Fixed annuities are invested in bonds at the insurance company's risk. Variable annuities are invested in one or more mutual funds of stocks or bonds chosen by you, mostly at your risk. While the funds remain within the annuity, the gains are nontaxable.

All of the earnings and gains coming out of a variable annuity are taxed as ordinary income. (The money contributed to an annuity has already been taxed; it's not taxed again on the way out.) The lower tax rates available for long-term capital gains on investments outside of the annuity are forfeited. If you buy stocks within a variable annuity, the annuity converts capital gains into ordinary income. The tax rates on ordinary income are higher than those on capital gains—an excellent reason to avoid variable annuities.

Like traditional IRAs, the tax bases of the investments within an annuity do not step up to the date-of-death values—another good reason to avoid variable annuities.

If you need an investment you cannot outlive, fine, an annuity is for you. Buy a policy and annuitize it immediately. Such policies are in fact called immediately annuities. But if you're accumulating money for the future, an annuity—even a variable annuity—isn't the right place. If you're buying exchange-traded funds and other investments in an asset allocation program, for example, you're better off doing so in your own name. Asset allocation generates low tax rates from long-term capital gains. Distributions from a variable annuity, however, are subject to ordinary income-tax rates.

Moreover, funds invested in your own name become subject to a stepped-up basis at death. Funds within a variable annuity, as mentioned, do not.

Insurance companies make variable annuities sound enticing. They guarantee that if you die, the insurance company will pay to the beneficiaries no less than your costs. This seems more beneficial than it actually is. Let's say that you invest $50,000 in a variable annuity and acquire stock mutual funds within it that decline to, say, $40,000. You then die. The insurance company will chip in $10,000 and pay your beneficiaries 50 grand.

Sounds like a good deal, right? Wrong. Insurance companies don't make guarantees for nothing. The annual costs of all of the policyholders are increased to pay for them. It's profitable for the insurance company, because the chances of the company having to make good on the guarantee are small. Here's why: You have to buy the policy, the market then has to go down, and *at that point*, you have to die.

About two-thirds of the time, the market doesn't go down; it goes up. The chances of it going down right after you buy the policy are less than 50 percent. Moreover, unless you're already on your last legs, the chances of your dying soon after you buy the policy are very small. These are two independent variables. One is unlikely, and the other is very unlikely. The chance of their both occurring at the same time, soon after you buy the policy, is extremely unlikely.

Unless both events occur with the proper timing, the guarantee will be unnecessary. Let's say, you buy a $50,000 variable policy. The market rises over time, and the policy is worth $80,000. A bear market then occurs, and the value declines to $60,000. You then die. Sorry, the annuity is worth more than the $50,000 you invested. The guarantee is inapplicable. Some insurance companies sweeten their guarantees by protecting values higher than the original costs in the event of death. But those guarantees are more expensive. Insurance companies charge hefty costs for guarantees, because the word "guarantee" means so much to customers, most of whom, not having read this book, are naïve. But the guarantee is unlikely to be used. It's a terrific deal—for the company.

CHAPTER 13

Hedging Risk

If mutual fund managers with multimillion-dollar portfolios feel a decline in prices coming on, they might sell a few dozen S&P 500 futures contracts. If the value of the contracts they sell equals the value of their portfolios, they're fully hedged, no matter what the market may do.

But for the rest of us, there's a little problem with hedging in the futures market. At this writing, a single S&P 500 futures contract is worth $289,800. You can't sell one-tenth of a contract to hedge a portfolio of $30,000; one futures contract is the minimum. All futures contracts run into big money. The S&P 500 minifutures contract is worth $57,900; the Dow futures contract $101,300; the Nasdaq 100 futures contract $161,300.

With exchange-traded funds, it's quite a different story. Spiders cost $116.06 a share; Diamonds $101.49; Nasdaq100 $40.01. I don't recommend buying or selling as little as a single share, of course, because the commissions outweigh any possible benefit. But you can acquire just the right number of shares. You can calibrate the amount needed to hedge any risk you please. There are no restrictions, remember, on short sales of ETFs. If you own shares in the Vanguard S&P 500 Index Fund and you turn pessimistic about the market, you can easily sell Spiders short. As the index fund goes, so go the Spiders, offsetting the risk. Until the hedge is lifted, the value of your total portfolio remains fixed.

Many hedgers feel more comfortable, furthermore, using exchange-traded funds as hedges rather than options. Most puts and calls expire within a relatively few months. But ETFs have no expirations. A hedger is likely to prefer selling short Spiders, for example, than to sell a call or buy a put on the S&P 500 Index.

Don't get carried away with hedging risk, however. You'll carry away your gains as well. When you get the feeling that the market will decline, the market is just as likely to rise as fall. In fact, the stronger your feeling that the market will decline, the more likely it will rise. As I've said elsewhere in this book, the market, in the short term, must make the majority wrong most of the time. If it didn't, everyone would throw all of their money into stocks and come out zillionaires. This is impossible, because there isn't sufficient real wealth to go around. To attain long-term gains, you must bear short-term risk. There's no way around it. Better to just buy stocks and, except for occasional rebalancing, forget about them.

You might say to yourself, "I want long-term gains, but I just want to reduce the risk during this brief period of uncertainty."

The trouble is, there's never any lack of short-term uncertainties. The market is always uncertain. It's always funny. The uncertainty you wanted to get past will eventually get resolved. But before it does, another uncertainty will appear that's every bit as worrisome. After the September 11 terrorist attack, for example, you might have said to yourself, "I'll just stay out of the market until the possibility of another attack disappears." But by that time, a recession hits. So you stay out a little longer. Finally, when the coast seems clear of those problems and you return to the market, the stock prices are probably higher than when you came out.

Besides, when everyone knows about a short-term uncertainty, prices are usually down. The best time to own stocks is when prices are down.

If all the short-term uncertainties ride off over the horizon and columns of divine light shine upon the world's stock markets, prices would immediately rise. If the light is bright enough, prices would be up by 30 percent or more right at the opening. After you see the light with your own eyes, any orders you enter would be too late; the prices would already have risen. If you complete your orders anyway, there you are, owning stocks at high prices, perched to fall when uncertainties once again appear and the light goes off. If you're a long-term investor, hedging risk is foolish. A good time to own stocks is all the time. The best time to own stocks is when the risks are especially apparent and other investors are especially apprehensive.

DIVERSIFYING SPECIFIC RISK

Let's say a fellow I'll call Fletcher is a long-time employee of Microsoft and has accumulated $10 million of Microsoft stock. He likes the company's prospects, and he'd rather not sell the stock. But having his entire financial future hinging on a single company is too much risk. If Microsoft falters, he might be laid off—there goes a high-paying job. And when the price of the stock falls, there goes his retirement income. It's too much of a double whammy. Financially, he'd be almost back at the starting gate. The risk is worth hedging. What to do?

The simplest approach is to sell the stock, pay the tax, and reinvest the net proceeds in an asset allocation program. If he'd held the stock for more than five years, the federal tax is only 18 percent. Even after paying the state tax, he would still have $7.5 to $8 million, which should get him by.

Another approach is to place the stock in a margin account, borrow $5 million against it, and invest the $5 million in an asset allocation program. Not a good idea. Fletcher would still have the specific risk of owning the Microsoft stock, and he would also have market risk from his investments. If Microsoft runs into trouble and the market falls significantly, his goose could be cooked.

A third approach is to arrange for what's called a "zero-cost collar." These are highly sophisticated arrangements that are undertaken only by major investment houses, such as Morgan Stanley or Goldman Sachs. The fees are significant, and the minimums are high. If you have a lousy $1 million of stock, a zero-cost collar probably wouldn't be worthwhile for them. But since you've worked your way almost to the end of this book, I have every confidence that you will someday attain the upper reaches.

Every collar is different. They're designed with the needs of the particular individual in mind. I explain how they work in general terms. Zero-cost collars can also be set up for stocks that are less liquid, but those are too complicated to describe here.

Collars involve options. Not everyday options like those traded on exchanges, you understand. These are long-term options contracts that last for, say, two years and cannot be exercised except at maturity. Fletcher would be one party to the contracts. Goldman Sachs, using its own money, might accept a position as the opposing party. Alternatively, it might find another institution willing to fill the bill. We'll assume that Goldman Sachs does the deed.

Here goes. Let's say Microsoft (MSFT) is selling at $67.50. Fletcher buys a two-year put with a strike price at $65. The put is out-of-the-money by $2.50. If the stock is priced below $65 two years hence, Fletcher would probably exercise his right to sell the stock at $65. The put provides Fletcher with protection against a big decline. If MSFT is selling for only $40 two years hence, Fletcher can nevertheless sell for $65.

Fletcher prefers not to sell the stock now. He hopes it rises in price. But if it's significantly lower two years from now, he can sell for only slightly less than the current price.

When Fletcher buys the put, he also writes a two-year call on MSFT at $75. If the stock is selling at $75 or higher two years hence, the stock would be called, and Fletcher would be required to sell at $75. If the price has risen to $100 by then, whoops, sorry, Fletcher sells for only $75.

Hence the term "collar." Microsoft currently stands at $67.50. If the price, two years hence, is higher than $65 or lower than $75, neither option is exercised, and Fletcher keeps his stock. But if the price then stands below $65, Fletcher could choose to sell. If it stands above $75, he would be required to sell.

I selected the strike prices of $65 and $75 because they're nice, half-round numbers. In actuality, the price of the put is set first. The premium of this Fletcher must pay. The strike price on the call is then selected at such a level that the premium Fletcher receives on the call is equal to the premium he pays on the put. Hence the term "zero-cost" collar. Naturally, if Fletcher is willing to pay more than he receives, the collar could be widened.

The zero-cost collar limits Fletcher's risk tightly on the downside, which is desirable. It also limits Fletcher's potential return, which, from his point of view, is not desirable. But this limitation he must contend with. After all, Goldman Sachs is protecting Fletcher against most of his downside risk. If MSFT falls to $40, Goldman Sachs must pay Fletcher $65 for the stock. Assuming that Fletcher has 148,000 shares (148,000 x $67.5 = $10,000,000) and assuming that

Goldman Sachs buys the stock for $65 and immediately sells it at $40, the firm would lose $3,700,000. Goldman Sachs doesn't like to lose money any more than anyone else. Therefore, the firm wants to gain the benefit if Microsoft should run away on the upside. For example, if MSFT should stand at $100 two years hence, Goldman Sachs could acquire Fletcher's stock at $65 and sell it for $100, for a profit of $5,200,000. Nice work if you can get it.

Here's the payoff for Fletcher. With his downside risk limited, he is entirely justified in borrowing against the stock, to invest in a broad-based asset allocation program. Goldman Sachs might be willing to lend him up to 90 percent of the strike price on the put. 148,000 shares times $65 is $9,620,000. Ninety percent of this is $8,600,000. Fletcher must pay interest on the margin, of course, but he limits his specific risk and takes on market risk, which is altogether desirable. If his portfolio goes up faster than Microsoft, the arrangement is especially advantageous.

The arrangement can be rolled over, enabling Fletcher to postpone, and possibly avoid, selling his Microsoft stock. This might be costly, however. If Microsoft stock stands at $80 two years hence, the call would be in-the-money by $15 ($80–$65). Fletcher would have to pay Goldman Sachs $2,220,000. If Fletcher's pockets aren't deep enough to handle this, or he refuses to borrow such a large amount, he would simply allow the call to be exercised.

Fletcher doesn't have to do any of this, of course. But let's say he doesn't hold Microsoft after all. Instead, he's the founder of a relatively new, high-tech company that's had a successful IPO. His stock is worth $100 million. It's restricted stock, meaning that he can't sell a penny of it for, say, two years. Under these circumstances, a zero-cost option might be very much in his interest.

CHAPTER 14

Final Comparisons, Suggestions, and Summary

HOW MUTUAL FUNDS ARE SUPERIOR TO EXCHANGE-TRADED FUNDS

- No-load funds incur no commissions. To some degree, ETFs always incur commissions.
- Most mutual funds cannot be traded rapidly. They force investors to hold. If the shareholder tries to buy and sell more often than the fund wishes, the fund imposes extra costs or prevents the trading altogether. Once out, the miscreant may be prevented from getting back in. The restrictions are entirely reasonable. The trading of mutual fund shares generates extra transaction costs and extra tax costs, which are borne by all of the shareholders, even the ones who wish to buy and hold. Going in and out of a mutual fund almost always results in poor long-term performance.
- Open-end mutual funds reinvest dividends and capital gains. Exchange-traded funds don't. With mutual funds, there's no dividend drag. The dividends are reinvested immediately into the purchase of additional shares of the fund from which they came.

HOW EXCHANGE-TRADED FUNDS ARE SUPERIOR TO MUTUAL FUNDS

- Exchange-traded funds can be traded at any time during the trading day. Most mutual funds can be traded only after the close.
- The minimums are lower. Many mutual funds insist on minimum initial investments of $2000. With exchange-traded funds, you can acquire a single share. If the price is $60, so be it. (Brokerage commissions on just a few shares decimate the profit potential.)
- ETFs generally have lower operating costs. In comparison to managed mutual funds, ETF costs are considerably lower.
- ETFs can be traded with any kind of order—limit, stop, market-if-touched—whatever. Mutual funds can be bought or sold only at market.
- Unlike mutual funds, exchange-traded funds rarely have embedded capital gains. ETFs continually pass out their low-cost securities, minimizing capital gains when sales by the trust must be made.
- ETFs rarely generate capital gains except when the owner sells. Mutual funds are much more likely to distribute capital gains even though the shareholder made no sale.
- Since the underlying trust of an ETF is not itself traded by the public, it is normal for the trust to hold little or no cash. Virtually all of the assets are invested, to match the performance of the index being tracked. Open-end mutual funds are traded by the public and must therefore hold at least some cash to honor withdrawals. Actively managed mutual funds may hold additional cash in the effort—a usually mistaken effort—to time the market.
- Exchange-traded funds have less paperwork than mutual funds.
- As long as the shareholder uses only a single broker, all of his holdings of ETFs are accounted for in one statement, including the current values. The percentage share of each ETF is readily apparent. To compare the values of mutual funds, one must refer to the values shown in each mutual fund statement and compare them in a separate statement of one's own.

- Rebalancing an asset allocation program among ETFs is easier than rebalancing among mutual funds.
- The distribution of dividends and capital gains by ETFs render unnecessary the upward adjustment of tax costs. The computation of the taxes generated by mutual funds is more complicated.
- The more trading other people do in an ETF, the more efficient it becomes for you. Increased trading provides arbitrageurs with a greater opportunity to narrow the gap between the ETF price and the net asset value per share of the underlying securities, all without creating capital gains for the ETF shareholders. Increased trading also narrows the spread. For mutual funds, the opposite is true; the more trading other people do in the fund, the less efficient it becomes. The fund must match the buying or selling with equivalent purchases or sales of the underlying securities. This widens spreads and creates more short-term capital gains for all of the shareholders.
- ETFs can be sold short with no restrictions. Open-end mutual funds and unit investment trusts cannot be sold short at all. ETFs can therefore be used as hedges; mutual funds cannot.

HOW ETFS AND MUTURAL FUNDS ARE SUPERIOR TO INDIVIDUAL STOCKS

- Diversification reduces risk and usually increases returns. Both ETFs and mutual funds provide diversification. Individual stocks don't, unless the shareholder has enough funds to choose a great many of them. Over the long run, one is unlikely to pick stocks that outdo the market. The less often such judgment is exercised, the better.
- ETFs and index funds provide suitable diversification at low cost. They don't choose the stocks. The stocks are chosen by whoever owns and operates the index.

HOW ETFS ALONE ARE SUPERIOR TO INDIVIDUAL STOCKS

- The purchases and sales of ETFs do not immediately move the market.

FIGURE 14-1

Comparison of ETFs, Stocks, and Mutual Funds

	ETFs	Stocks	Managed mutual funds	Index mutual funds
Participates in a portfolio of securities	yes	no	yes	yes
Can be bought & sold whenever the market is open	yes	yes	no	no
Limits consequences of redemptions by other shareholders	yes	—	no	no
Minimizes taxes	yes	yes	varies	yes
Cost-effective	yes	yes	varies	yes
Dividends reinvested immediately	no	no	optional	optional
Underlying investments are known	yes	—	no	yes

Adopted from materials of Barclays Global Investors. Used with permission.

SUGGESTIONS FOR EXCHANGE-TRADED FUNDS IN THE FUTURE

In Chapter 11, as an alternative to iShares MSCI EAFE Index Fund, I recommend the purchase of Vanguard's Total International Stock Index Fund. This fund makes no stock investments of its own. The funds are placed in three other Vanguard funds, as follows:

- European Stock Index Fund
- Pacific Stock Index Fund
- Emerging Markets Stock Index Fund

The Total International Stock Index Fund does not place its funds equally in the three funds above. The European Fund has the greatest participation, with the Pacific second and the Emerging Market last, all in proportion to the market capitalization of the stocks in the three regions. Overall, the Total International Stock Index Fund has approximately 1500 stocks spread among 30 or more countries.

No exchange-traded fund equivalent to the Vanguard Total International Stock Index Fund exists. There should be such a fund. I hope that Vanguard eventually fills that bill with an International Viper. By means of an ETF, investors should have the opportunity to place their funds across the entire panoply of foreign stocks in proportion to their relative capitalization. Oh, there are ETFs for individual countries and individual regions. The areas that have high political risk and limited potential for earnings growth are priced low. The areas that have low political risk and favorable potential for earnings growth are priced high. Trying to guess which regions the market has mispriced requires more vision and skill than most fallible human beings possess. Instead, investors should have the opportunity to place part of their financial future on the success of companies of all foreign nations, with the assumption that the stocks of all of them are priced properly.

The S&P Global 1200 Index is a possibility for a worldwide ETF. This index includes 1200 stocks in 29 countries. But unfortunately, it includes all 500 of the S&P 500 stocks, giving the U.S. 60 percent of the total capitalization of the Global 1200. I would prefer an ETF based on the Vanguard Total International Stock Index Fund, which contains non-U.S. stocks only, and in greater numbers.

I look forward to a day when, among ETFs of foreign nations, investors can isolate big stocks, small stocks, growth stocks, and value stocks. All this can be done now with U. S. stocks. The opportunity should be made available to the public with foreign stocks, too.

As mentioned in the appendix, it is high time for exchange-traded funds of bonds to be developed. Ryan Labs is creating intriguing ETFs based on Treasuries and later on corporate bonds, in which the risk of price change is removed. But additional ETFs that include price risk are also needed. Indexes of Treasury bonds, corporate bonds, and high-yield corporates might serve as models to track.

I suppose we shall have to put up with exchange-traded funds based on *managed* mutual funds. They're coming. As hotshot, million-dollar managers buy and sell, the parasite ETFs follow along behind. Traders of such ETFs are invited to guess whether the managers are going to be a little better or a little worse than they ought to be in the next few minutes or hours or weeks. This seems dicey. Maybe I'm missing something.

We are faced with altogether too many managed mutual funds. With their high expenses, high turnover, and resulting high taxes, most of them are long-term losers in comparison to indexes. Most of the investment and business media communities depend for their livelihood on fostering the fiction that if we can just be a tiny bit smarter and more informed, we can beat the indexes. We can't. Index funds may be tortoises, but they beat the managed-fund hares time after time. It's a delight to see a large, new class of investments—exchange-traded funds—that promote the concept of indexing.

SUMMARY

Exchange-traded funds are wonderful vehicles for the long-term holding of diversified portfolios. The operating costs are low. With even a moderately sized portfolio and low commissions from the online execution of trades, total costs are minimized. The rapid turnover of ETF shares by *other* people serves your interest. It provides maximum liquidity, which helps the arbitrageurs to minimize the gap between the ETF price and the underlying trading value per share. Despite this, the dynamics of exchange-traded funds minimizes capital gains. Most of the time, capital gains are realized only when you sell your shares. The gains can continue compounding for years without some of the funds being siphoned off in taxes to the government. If you feel compelled to *trade* indexes, exchange-traded funds are the only way to go about it. But the chances of long-term success are minuscule.

ETFs are entirely suitable for asset allocation programs. Each ETF is highly diversified. Spotting the relative values on a single statement is simple, and rebalancing among the various asset classes is especially convenient.

To the multitude of securities already available, exchange-traded funds are remarkable additions. Designed for traders, they nevertheless work marvelously as profitable, long-term investments. In your use of them, I wish you well.

Reference Information on Each Exchange-Traded Fund

INTRODUCTION

This Appendix explains salient features of each of the exchange-traded funds. Since ETFs continue to be created, you may well come across funds not mentioned here.

You can obtain prospectuses yourself, of course, but since you're not required to, I provide information from prospectuses, as well as other sources. You might dwell on the general discussion about each sponsor. But to the extent there's more here than you want to know, by all means ripple through these pages as rapidly as you please.

Most ETFs are structured about the same as Spiders, with which you're already familiar. VIPERS, HOLDRs, and fixed-income ETFs are structured differently than the others. They're also structured differently from each other. I therefore discuss each of those in some detail. You might find helpful the brief discussion of investment returns in the section about VIPERS. If you're a citizen of a nation other than the United States, you would take interest in the ETFs offered in foreign nations.

The sponsor of one group of exchange-traded funds may disclose different data about its offerings than the sponsor of another. To some extent, the information provided here varies from one group to another.

The number of shares held by the funds are frequently in flux in a modest way. Do not assume that something is wrong if an S&P 100 Index Fund, for example, is said to contain 101 or 102 stocks.

Data is available on:

www.amex.com
www.amextrader.com
www.streettracks.com
www.spdrindex.com
www.ishares.net
www.units.net

To a lesser extent, I obtained information also from the relevant organizations.

For the most part, exchange-traded funds come in broad groups:

Broad-based market funds
Industrial sector funds
Foreign market funds for purchase by Americans
Foreign market funds for purchase by foreigners
Funds that follow a specific mutual fund (so far, only one—VIPERS)
Quasi-ETFs, in particular, HOLDRs.
Fixed-income funds

This Appendix groups the ETFs by their sponsors, as follows:

- Nasdaq: The Nasdaq-100 Trust
- The American Stock Exchange: Spiders, Diamonds, and S&P MidCap
- Barclays Global Investors: iShares
- State Street Global Advisors: streetTRACKS and SPDR Selects
- The Vanguard Group: VIPERS
- Merrill Lynch: HOLDRs
- Nuveen Investments: Municipal Bonds
- Ryan Labs: Treasury and Corporate Bonds
- Barclays Global Investors: Foreign ETFs offered for purchase in foreign nations

NASDAQ

Nasdaq-100 Index

Qubes   Symbol QQQ

Such a weird name, Nasdaq. Perhaps you know that NASD stands for the National Association of Security Dealers, an association of broker-dealers that trade over-the-counter (unlisted) stocks. Add "aq," and you get National Association of Security Dealers Automated Quotation system.

The Nasdaq-100 Index Tracking Stock consists of the 100 largest stocks traded on Nasdaq, ranked in proportion to their capitalization. To be eligible for inclusion in the Index, a security must meet the following criteria:

- It must be traded on Nasdaq.
- The company must be nonfinancial.
- Only one class of security per issuer is allowed.
- The company must not be bankrupt.
- The security must have average daily trading volume of at least 100,000 shares.
- If the company's capitalization is in the top 25 percent of those in the Index, the security must have been "seasoned" by trading for at least a year on Nasdaq or other recognized market. If the company's capitalization is not in the top 25 percent, it must have been seasoned for at least two years. The history of any spin-off is taken into consideration.
- If the security is of a foreign issuer, the company must have a worldwide market value of at least $10 billion, a U.S. market value of at least $4 billion, and average trading volume on Nasdaq of at least 200,000 shares a day. The foreign security must also be eligible for listed options trading.
- The issuer must not have entered into an arrangement that would result in the security being delisted from Nasdaq within the next six months.

The average percentage weight of the 100 stocks in the Index is 1 percent. The Index securities are categorized as "Large Stocks" or "Small Stocks," depending on whether they rank higher or lower than 1 percent. Quarterly, the rankings of the components of the Index are adjusted to meet Securities and Exchange Commission requirements. The SEC doesn't want a portfolio purporting to be diversified to be too heavily concentrated in just a few stocks. Hence, the following changes are made:

- If the current weight of the single largest stock exceeds 24 percent, then the weights of all Large Stocks are scaled down proportionately towards 1 percent by enough to cause the adjusted weight of the single largest Index security to be set to 20 percent.
- If those securities whose individual weights are at least 4.5 percent have a collective weight exceeding 48 percent (I'll call these "the collectives), then the weights of all Large Stocks are further scaled down by enough to bring the weight of the collectives down to 40 percent. The weights of the "Small Stocks" are thereby increased, according to rules I won't review here for fear of your falling sleep and striking your nose on a hard object. In general, the SEC wants the biggest stocks and the pretty big stocks brought down to size, to give the little guys a change to show their stuff.

Except under extraordinary circumstances, the Index is reviewed annually as to the eligibility of its components. As a result, investors that use the Nasdaq 100 as a benchmark, including the Qubes, are generally required to rebalance (and possibly incur capital gains taxes) only once a year.

But changes in the number of shares outstanding of the components of the Index are monitored every day. Such changes might arise from secondary offerings, stock repurchases, conversions, or other corporate actions.

The symbol of the Nasdaq-100 Index Tracking Stock is QQQ. The security, as mentioned, is referred to as Qubes. At this writing, they're traded in nine U.S. markets. The trading volume of this exchange-traded fund is the largest of any security in the world.

Qubes are organized as a unit investment trust. The trustee is The Bank of New York, which, by the way, was founded by Alexander Hamilton, progenitor of America's financial system.

The expense ratio is 0.18 percent. Creation units consist of 50,000 shares. The ETF trades at approximately 1/40th of the value of the Nasdaq 100 Index.

On September 28, 2001, the major industry groups covered in the Index were as follows:

Technology	68.91%
Healthcare	14.29%
Consumer Cyclicals	5.55%
Consumer Staples	5.04%
Communication Services	3.25%

The fund includes 100 stocks. The five largest were:

Microsoft	11.97%
Intel	6.08%
Qualcomm	5.51%
Cisco	4.02%
Oracle	3.70%

What Do These Terms Mean?

Spin-Off: A company engages in a spin-off when it sells an affiliate it owns to investors. The investors receive what is for them a new company, and the parent company receives cash. Many years ago, AT&T bought NCR Corporation from the public. (This was not a spin-off. AT&T received the stock, and the public received either cash or AT&T stock—I don't remember which.) Subsequently, AT&T decided it didn't want to own NCR after all. It therefore spinned off the company to the public. Investors received NCR stock, which was large enough to be listed immediately on the New York Stock Exchange, and AT&T received cash. If a company spun off from another is large enough to be included in the Nasdaq 100, rebalancing might be called for immediately. The new company would be added to the Index. But since the Index is fixed at 100 securities, another company, presumably smaller, would be removed.

The following terms do not cause the company's capitalization ranking in the index to change.

Secondary Offering: A corporation engages in an initial public offering, or IPO, when it first sells its stock to the public. When the corporation later sells *another* issue of stock to the public, usually to finance the further growth of its business, this is called a "secondary offering."

Stock Repurchase: A company engages in a stock repurchase when it buys back some of its stock from public investors in the open marketplace. This causes subsequent earnings to be stretched among a lesser number of shares outstanding, causing the earnings *per share* to rise.

Conversion: A company may raise funds to finance its growth from the sale of a convertible preferred stock or a convertible bond. Under specified conditions in the future, these securities may be converted into the company's common stock. When such conversions occur, the total number of common shares of the company increases.

THE AMERICAN STOCK EXCHANGE

Standard & Poor's 500 Index—Spiders

SPDR   Symbol SPY

Spiders track the Standard & Poor's 500 Index, which is composed of 500 selected common stocks listed on the NYSE, AMEX, or Nasdaq. The companies represent approximately 78 percent of the market value of all domestic stocks. Spiders are discussed at length in Chapters 4, 5, and 6.

As of September 28, 2001, the five largest industry segments comprising the S&P 500 Index were:

Financial	17.77%
Technology	15.24%
Healthcare	15.02%
Consumer Staples	13.45%
Consumer Cyclicals	8.63%

The fund is organized as a unit investment trust. It's priced at approximately 1/10th the value of the index. Creation Units are 50,000 shares or multiples thereof. Dividends are distributed quarterly. The expense ratio is 0.12 percent.

The five largest stocks were:

General Electric	3.90%
Microsoft	2.91%
Exxon Mobil	2.87%
Pfizer	2.67%
Wal-Mart	2.34%

Dow Jones Industrial Average

Diamonds   Symbol DIA

The American Stock Exchange sponsors an exchange-traded fund called Diamonds, which tracks the Dow Jones Industrial Averages, the oldest and most famous market indicator. Next to Qubes and Spiders, Diamonds have the third largest trading volume of all ETFs.

Diamonds are organized as a unit investment trust. State Street Bank and Trust is trustee. Creation units are 50,000 shares or multiples thereof. Dividends are paid monthly. The expense ratio is 0.18 percent.

In Chapter 2, you'll find an explanation of how the Dow Jones Industrial Average (DJIA) is calculated. Unlike the S&P 500 and most other indexes, the Dow is not based on the capitalization of each stock. For indexes, the number of shares of each stock is greater or less, in proportion to the company's capitalization. Not so for Diamonds. Here, the number of shares is exactly the same for each of the 30 stocks. The higher the price, the higher the value and therefore the greater the stock's impact on Diamonds.

If one of the Dow stocks has a stock split, the number of shares of that stock owned by the trust increases. This renders the number of shares of all 30 stocks unequal. Some of the extra stock received from the stock split is therefore sold. The proceeds are used to purchase additional shares of the other 29 stocks, causing the number of shares of each stock once again to be as equal as possible.

Dow Jones occasionally changes the components of the Dow Industrials. It does so, I presume, when it feels that new components more accurately represent the current stock market than the old. The last change in the components became effective on November 1, 1999.

The companies removed were:

Union Carbide, which had been in the DJIA since 1928

Goodyear Tire & Rubber, which had been in the DJIA since 1930

Sears Roebuck, which had been in the DJIA since 1924

Chevron, which had been in the DJIA since 1930.

The companies added were:

Home Depot

Intel

Microsoft

SBC Communications

Intel and Microsoft were the first companies added to the Dow that did not trade on the New York Stock Exchange. Both of them trade on Nasdaq.

Following the acquisition of J.P. Morgan & Co. by Chase Manhattan Corp. and effective on January 1, 2001, J. P. Morgan was removed from the DJIA and replaced by J. P. Morgan Chase & Co. Perhaps in deference to the intimidating old J.P. himself, Chase placed the Morgan name in front of its own.

On September 28, 2001, the top five industrial groups in the Dow Jones Industrial Average were as follows:

Capital Goods	22.35%
Consumer Staples	16.65%
Technology	16.56%
Consumer Cyclicals	10.19%
Healthcare	9.51%

Since the Dow is so historic, and relatively short, all 30 of its components are shown here, arranged by price. On September 28, 2001, Diamonds held 1,963,886 shares of each Dow stock. Those with higher prices had a greater impact on the total value. Minnesota Mining & Mfg, with a price of 98.5 comprised 7.67 percent of the total. Hewlett Packard, with a price of 16.1 comprised only 1.25 percent of the total. The stocks were as follows:

Minnesota Mining & Mfg	7.67%
IBM	7.19%
Proctor & Gamble	5.67%
Merck	5.19%
Johnson & Johnson	4.32%
Microsoft	3.99%
WalMart	3.86%
Philip Morris	3.76%
SBC Communications	3.67%
Coca Cola	3.65%
United Technologies	3.62%
Caterpillar	3.49%

General Motors	3.34%
Citigroup	3.16%
Exxon Mobil	3.07%
Home Depot	2.99%
DuPont	2.92%
General Electric	2.90%
International Paper	2.71%
J. P. Morgan Chase	2.66%
Boeing	2.61%
Eastman Kodak	2.54%
Alcoa	2.42%
American Express	2.26%
McDonalds	2.12%
Honeywell	2.06%
Intel	1.59%
AT&T	1.50%
Disney	1.45%
Hewlett Packard	1.25%

If you're uncomfortable with anything except blue chips, Diamonds are for you. For many people, the Dow is the market. (Market professionals tend to favor the S&P 500 Index.) If you own Diamonds and you learn how the Dow is doing, that's how you're doing, except for those minuscule 0.18-percent annual expenses. You pay commissions, of course, but if you buy and hold, as you should, they become immaterial.

MidCap SPDRs   Symbol MDY

The MidCap SPDRs track the Standard & Poor's MidCap 400 Index. The Index is composed of 400 selected common stocks, all listed on the NYSE, AMEX, or Nasdaq. The S&P 400 is not a subset of the S&P 500. The S&P 400 represents approximately 6 percent of the market value of all domestic publicly held common stocks.

The fund is organized as a unit investment trust. The trustee is The Bank of New York. The fund is priced at approximately 1/5th the value of the index. Creation Units are 25,000 shares or multiples thereof. Dividends are distributed quarterly. The expense ratio is 0.25 percent.

At this writing, the five largest industry segments comprising the S&P MidCap 400 Index were:

Financials	19.49%
Technology	16.92%
Healthcare	13.71%
Consumer Cyclicals	12.67%
Utilities	8.45%

As of October 31, 2001, the five largest stocks were:

Genzyme	1.36%
IDEC Pharmaceuticals	1.17%
Electronic Arts	0.89%
Sungard Data Systems	0.88%
M&T Bank	0.83%

BARCLAYS GLOBAL INVESTORS: iSHARES

Barclays Global Investors, N.A. has created more exchange-traded funds than any other organization. The firm has incurred considerable expense to market these products. This has not only generated active trading in iShares, it has also caused increased volumes in all ETFs. The other companies are grateful, I'm sure.

Barclays Global Investors manages more than $800 billion in assets and bills itself as the world's largest institutional investment manager. It is a subsidiary of Barclays Bank, PLC, one of the United Kingdom's largest companies. The name of every Barclays ETF begins with "iShares." Barclays says that the "i" stands for "index." But it probably hasn't escaped the company's attention that the word places an unusual emphasis on the first person singular. I'm sure that Barclays would not object if the title's eccentric character induces you to say to yourself, "I'd like to buy some of those iShares, yes I would."

There are 76 domestic iShares, all but two of which trade on the American Stock Exchange. The two that don't are:

- iShares S&P Global 100 Index Fund, which trades on the New York Stock Exchange
- iShares S&P 100 Index Fund, which trades on the Chicago Board of Options

Although the AMEX started the ball rolling with exchange-traded funds, the popularity of ETFs has imbued other exchanges to get in on the act. Exchanges thrive on volume. Where trading action can be found, they hate to miss out. The iShares S&P Global 100 Index Fund is in fact the first security ever traded on the New York Stock Exchange that the Exchange has not listed. For the most part, this means that the item can trade without Barclays having to pay the Exchange a listing fee.

Except for the iShares MSCI EAFE Index Fund, 50,000 is the minimum number of shares permitted for creation and redemption, or multiples thereof. (For the iShares MSCI EAFE Index Fund, a whopping 200,000 shares are required.)

Some iShares replicate the underlying index as closely as possible, just as Spiders do. But for others, Barclays uses "representative sampling," in which the fund does not stick quite so closely to the securities of the underlying portfolio. It may substitute stocks that have similar investment profiles in terms of the following characteristics:

- Capitalization
- Industry weightings
- Return variability
- Earnings valuation
- Yield
- Liquidity

iShares that use representative sampling generally do not hold all of the securities that are included in the relevant underlying index. Such funds may not track the index as closely as those that use the replication method.

iShares are not organized as unit investment trusts, as are Spiders. They are organized as index mutual funds. This makes no difference to the individual investor, but it does enable the Securities and Exchange Commission to determine how to impose its regulations.

Additional information about iShares may be found on the Web at www.iShares.com.

S&PTHE iSHARES S&P SERIES

Barclays offers 20 funds based on indexes created by Standard & Poor's. They are as follows.

iShares S&P 100 Index Fund   Symbol OEF

Known by its ticker symbol OEX, the S&P 100 Index is a subset of
the S&P 500 Index and tracks the performance of the 100 largest
stocks in the S&P 500. These "blue chips," all of which have options
traded on them, represent approximately 45 percent of the market
capitalization of the U.S. equity market.

The iShares S&P 100 Index Fund trades on the Chicago Board
of Options. The fund is not an option, of course, but apparently the
CBOE is spreading its wings. In addition to picking up additional
volume, the exchange has good reason to do so. Options are derivatives; their values are based on the values found in another market, in this case, stocks. Options are used, in part, to hedge risk.
Exchange-traded funds are derivatives too, and they are also used
to hedge risk. The CBOE is expanding its repertoire of hedges.

On July 31, 2001, the iShares S&P 100 Index Fund contained
101 stocks. As of November 30, 2001, the five largest were:

General Electric	6.34%
Microsoft	5.73%
Pfizer	4.53%
ExxonMobil	4.28%
Wal-Mart	4.09%

The fund uses the replication strategy. Its expense ratio is 0.20
percent.

iShares S&P 500 Index Fund   Symbol IVV

Call this fund Son of Spiders. It tracks the very same S&P 500
Index. But as to operating costs, the iShares S&P 500 Index Fund
does Spiders one better. Its annual costs are only 0.09 percent, versus a still-low 0.12 percent for Spiders. It is remarkable that the
costs of these funds can be so low, especially those of the iShares.
Maybe they're both loss leaders. Isn't capitalism wonderful?

The S&P 500 represents approximately 79 percent of the market capitalization of all publicly traded U.S. equities. On July 31,
2001, the iShares S&P 500 Index Fund contained 501 stocks. As of
November 30, 2001, the five largest stocks were:

General Electric	3.75%
Microsoft	3.25%
Exxon Mobil	2.82%

Pfizer	2.75%
WalMart	2.39%

The fund uses the replication strategy. Its expense ratio, as mentioned, is 0.09 percent.

iShares S&P 500/BARRA Growth Index Fund Symbol IVW

Barra, Inc. advises investment professionals about risk management strategies. It splits the S&P 500 Index into growth and value segments, each having approximately half the market capitalization of the entire index. The division is based on price-to-book ratios. The stocks having the higher ratios are placed in the growth index.

As of July 31, 2001, the iShares S&P 500/BARRA Growth Index Fund contained 155 stocks. As of October 31, 2001, the five largest were:

General Electric	7.12%
Microsoft	6.16%
Pfizer	5.21%
WalMart	4.53%
IBM	3.70%

The fund uses the replication strategy. Its expense ratio is 0.18 percent.

iShares S&P 500/BARRA Value Index Fund Symbol IVE

The S&P 500/BARRA Value Index contains the other half of the split of the S&P 500 stocks into growth and value. On July 31, 2001, the iShares S&P 500/BARRA Value Index Fund contained 347 stocks. As of October 31, 2001, the five largest were:

Exxon Mobil	5.97%
Citigroup	5.02%
American International Group	4.52%
AOL Time Warner	3.03%
Verizon Communications	2.96%

The growth and value funds have approximately the same total market values. Since the average growth stock has a greater market value than the average value stock, the growth fund has fewer stocks.

The fund uses the replication strategy. Its expense ratio is 0.18 percent.

iShares S&P MidCap 400 Index Fund   Symbol IJH

The S&P MidCap 400 Index tracks the performance of the midcapitalization sector of U.S. equities; as mentioned above, it is not a subset of the S&P 500 Index. The S&P 400 represents approximately 6 percent of the market capitalization of the U.S. equity market. The market capitalizations range from $1 billion to $5 billion and are selected for liquidity and industry group.

On July 31, 2001, the iShares S&P MidCap 400 Index Fund contained 401 stocks. As of October 31, 2001, the five largest were:

Genzyme	1.36%
IDEC Pharmaceuticals	1.17%
Electronic Arts	0.89%
Sungard Data Systems	0.88%
M&T Bank	0.83%

The fund uses representative sampling. Its expense ratio is 0.20 percent.

iShares S&P MidCap 400/BARRA Growth Index Fund   Symbol IJK

This index consists of companies with the highest price-to-book ratios in the S&P 400 Index. The stocks within it represent approximately 50 percent of the market capitalization of the S&P 400 Index.

On July 31, 2001, the iShares S&P MidCap 400/BARRA Growth Index Fund contained 152 stocks. As of October 31, 2001, the five largest were:

Genzyme	2.81%
IDEC Pharmaceuticals	2.40%
Electronic Arts	1.84%
Sungard Data Systems	1.82%
Quest Diagnostics	1.65%

The fund uses a replication strategy. Its expense ratio is 0.25 percent.

iShares S&P MidCap 400/BARRA Value Index Fund   Symbol IJJ

This value portion is the other half of the capitalization of the S&P 400 Index, consisting of those companies with the lowest price-to-book ratios.

On July 31, 2001, the iShares S&P MidCap 400/BARRA Value Index Fund contained 250 stocks. As of October 31, 2001, the five largest were:

M&T Bank	1.61%
Marshall & Ilsley	1.53%
RJ Reynolds	1.43%
Telephone & Data Systems	1.30%
American Water Works	1.02%

The fund uses a replication strategy. Its expense ratio is 0.25 percent.

iShares S&P SmallCap 600 Index Fund   Symbol IJR

The S&P SmallCap 600 Index tracks the performance of the small-capitalization sector of stocks. The securities constitute approximately 3 percent of the market capitalization of all U.S. equities. All of the stocks:

- Have been trading for at least six months;
- Have a price greater than $1 on any three or more business days during a 12-month period;
- Have an annualized turnover exceeding 20 percent of the outstanding shares, with not more than 50 percent of the shares owned by a single shareholder;
- Have a bid-asked spread of 5 percent or less.

On July 31, 2001, the iShares S&P SmallCap 600 Index Fund contained 602 stocks. As of October 31, 2001, the five largest were:

Cephalon	0.94%
Advancepcs	0.76%
Universal Health Services, Cl. B	0.73%
Commerce Bancorp	0.71%
Smithfield Foods	0.68%

The fund uses representative sampling. Its expense ratio is 0.20 percent.

iShares S&P SmallCap 600/BARRA Growth Index Fund   Symbol IJT

This index consists of companies with the highest price-to-book ratios in the S&P SmallCap 600 Index, representing approximately 50 percent of the market capitalization of that Index.

On July 31, 2001, the iShares S&P SmallCap 600/BARRA Growth Index Fund contained 219 stocks. As of October 31, 2001, the five largest were:

Cephalon	1.92%
Advancepcs	1.55%
Universal Health Services, Cl. B	1.49%
Commerce Bancorp	1.45%
Varian Medical Systems	1.37%

The fund uses a replication strategy. Its expense ratio is 0.25 percent.

iShares S&P SmallCap 600/BARRA Value Index Fund   Symbol IJS

This value portion is the other half of the capitalization of the S&P SmallCap 600 Index, consisting of those companies with the lowest price-to-book ratios.

On July 31, 2001, the iShares S&P SmallCap 600/BARRA Value Index Fund contained 383 stocks. As of October 31, 2001, the five largest were:

Smithfield Foods	1.33%
Dr. Horton	1.01%
Michaels Stores	0.98%
Newfield Exploration	0.93%
Massey Energy	0.90%

Unlike the growth portion of SmallCaps, this fund uses representative sampling. Its expense ratio is 0.25 percent.

iShares S&P Global 100 Index Fund   Symbol IOO

This index tracks the performance of large transnational companies of major importance in global markets. It is a subset of the S&P

Global 1200 Index and contains approximately 100 stocks, screened for sector representation, liquidity, and size. The market capitalizations are adjusted to reflect only those shares that are available to foreign investors.

As of May 31, 2001, the Index was composed of stocks of companies in Australia, Belgium, Canada, Finland, France, Germany, Great Britain, Italy, Japan, Korea, Mexico, the Netherlands, Spain, Sweden, Switzerland, and the United States.

On July 31, 2001, the iShares S&P Global 100 Index Fund contained 98 stocks. As of November 30, 2001, the five largest were:

General Electric	6.34%
Microsoft	5.73%
Pfizer	4.53%
ExxonMobil	4.28%
Citigroup	4.00%

The fund uses representative sampling. Its expense ratio is 0.40 percent.

iShares S&P Global Energy Sector Index Fund
Symbol IXC

This index tracks the performance of companies deemed to be part of the energy sector. It is a subset of the S&P Global 1200 Index. Component companies include:

- Oil equipment and services
- Oil exploration and production
- Oil refineries.

As of May 31, 2001, the Index was composed of stocks of companies in Argentina, Australia, Austria, Brazil, Canada, France, Great Britain, Italy, Japan, the Netherlands, Norway, Spain, and the United States.

As of October 31, 2001, the five largest stocks were:

Exxon Mobil	24.26%
BP Plc	16.67%
Royal Dutch Petroleum	9.53%
Totalfinaelf	8.88%
Shell Transport & Trading	6.55%

The fund uses representative sampling. Its expense ratio is 0.65 percent.

iShares S&P Global Financials Sector Index Fund Symbol IXG

This index tracks the performance of companies deemed to be part of the financial sector. It is a subset of the S&P Global 1200 Index. Component companies include:

- Major banks
- Diversified financial companies
- Insurance companies
- Real estate companies
- Savings & loan associations
- Securities brokers

As of May 31, 2001, the Index was composed of stocks of companies in Argentina, Australia, Belgium, Brazil, Canada, Denmark, France, Germany, Great Britain, Hong Kong, Ireland, Italy, Japan, Korea, Malaysia, Mexico, the Netherlands, Portugal, Singapore, Spain, Sweden, Switzerland, Taiwan, and the United States.

As of October 31, 2001, the five largest stocks were:

American Int'l Group	6.20%
Citigroup	6.18%
HSBC Holdings	2.99%
Bank of America	2.84%
Fannie Mae	2.43%

The fund uses representative sampling. Its expense ratio is 0.65 percent.

iShares S&P Global Healthcare Sector Index Fund Symbol IXJ

This index tracks the performance of companies deemed to be part of the healthcare sector. It is a subset of the S&P Global 1200 Index. Component companies include:

- Healthcare providers
- Biotechnology

- Manufacturers of medical supplies, advanced medical devices, and pharmaceuticals

Currently, the index is composed of the stocks of companies from Australia, Belgium, Canada, Denmark, France, Germany, Great Britain, Ireland, Japan, Switzerland, and the United States.

As of October 31, 2001, the five largest stocks were:

Pfizer	11.97%
GlaxoSmithKline	8.32%
Johnson & Johnson	7.94%
Merck & Co.	7.22%
Novartis	5.33%

The fund uses representative sampling. Its expense ratio is 0.65 percent.

iShares S&P Global Technology Sector Index Fund   Symbol IXN

This index tracks the performance of companies deemed to be part of the information technology sector. It is a subset of the S&P Global 1200 Index. Component companies are involved in the development and production of technology products, including:

- Computer hardware and software
- Telecommunications equipment
- Microcomputer components
- Integrated computer circuits
- Office equipment utilizing technology

Currently, the index is composed of the stocks of companies from Canada, Finland, France, Germany, Great Britain, Japan, Korea, the Netherlands, Singapore, Spain, Sweden, Taiwan, and the United States.

As of October 31, 2001, the five largest stocks were:

Microsoft	15.75%
IBM	9.17%
Intel	7.86%
Cisco	5.10%
Nokia	4.41%

The fund uses representative sampling. Its expense ratio is 0.65 percent.

iShares S&P Global Telecommunications Sector Index Fund   Symbol IXP

This index tracks the performance of companies deemed to be part of the telecommunications sector. It is a subset of the S&P Global 1200 Index. Component companies include:

- Diversified communication carriers
- Wireless communications companies

Currently, the index is composed of the stocks of companies from Argentina, Australia, Brazil, Canada, Denmark, Finland, France, Germany, Great Britain, Hong Kong, Italy, Japan, Korea, Mexico, the Netherlands, Portugal, Singapore, Spain, Sweden, Switzerland, and the United States.

As of October 31, 2001, the five largest stocks were:

SBC Communications	13.09%
Vodafone Group	12.36%
Verizon Communications	12.07%
Bellsouth	6.42%
AT&T	5.49%

The fund uses representative sampling. Its expense ratio is 0.65 percent.

iShares S&P Europe 350 Index Fund   Symbol IEV

This Index tracks the performance of leading companies in Austria, Belgium, Denmark, Finland, France, Germany, Ireland, Italy, the Netherlands, Norway, Portugal, Spain, Sweden, Switzerland, and the United Kingdom.

The stocks are chosen for:

- Market size
- Liquidity
- Industry group representation
- Geographic diversity

The market capitalizations are adjusted to reflect only those stocks that are available to all investors, not just to the citizens of the country in which the company is domiciled.

The largest industrial groups were:

- Financial
- Consumer Non-Cyclical
- Communications
- Energy
- Industrial

On July 31, 2001, the iShares S&P Europe 350 Index Fund contained 340 stocks. As of October 31, 2001, the five largest were:

BP Amoco	4.19%
GlaxoSmithKline	3.91%
Vodafone Group (Great Britain)	3.60%
Novartis	2.46%
Total SA, Series B	2.38%

The fund uses representative sampling. Its expense ratio is 0.60 percent.

iShares S&P/TSE 60 Index Fund   Symbol IEV

The S&P/TSE 60 Index tracks the performance of Canada's largest publicly traded stocks. The index is maintained by representatives of Standard & Poor's and the Toronto Stock Exchange. The stocks are chosen for:

- Market size
- Liquidity
- Industry group representation

On July 31, 2001, the iShares S&P/TSE 60 Index Fund contained 60 stocks. As of October 31, 2001, the five largest were:

Royal Bank of Canada	6.51%
BCE	6.06%
Nortel Networks	5.84%
Toronto-Dominion Bank	5.14%
Bank of Nova Scotia	4.91%

The fund uses representative sampling. Its expense ratio is 0.50 percent.

iShares S&P Latin America 40 Index Fund
Symbol ILF

The S&P Latin America 40 Index Fund tracks high-capitalization stocks in the Mexican and South American equity markets.

The largest industrial groups were:

- Communications
- Financial
- Industrial
- Energy
- Consumer Non-Cyclical

The five largest stocks were:

Telefonos De Mexico	17.47%
Cemex	9.00%
Petroleo Brasileiro ADR	8.52%
America Movil	7.64%
Companhia De Bebidas ADR	5.04%

The fund uses representative sampling. Its expense ratio is 0.50 percent.

iShares S&P/TOPIX 150 Index Fund
Symbol ITF

The S&P/TOPIX 150 Index Fund tracks the S&P/Tokyo Stock Price 150 Index, which includes 150 highly liquid securities selected from each major sector of the Tokyo market. It represents 70 percent of the market value of the Japanese equity market.

The largest industrial groups were:

- Consumer Cyclical
- Industrial
- Financial
- Consumer Non-Cyclical
- Communications

As of October 31, 2001, the five largest stocks were:

Toyota	5.73%
NTT Docomo	4.39%
Nippon Telegraph & Telephone	3.29%
Takeda Chemical	3.05%
Sony	2.96%

The fund uses representative sampling. Its expense ratio is 0.50 percent.

iSHARES DOW JONES U.S. INDEX FUNDS

iShares Dow Jones U.S. Total Market Index Fund Symbol IYY

The Dow Jones U.S. Total Market Index is comprised of all the companies in the Dow Jones Large-Cap Index, the Dow Jones Mid-Cap Index, and the Dow Jones Small-Cap Index. It represents approximately 95 percent of the market capitalization of all publicly held U.S. equities.

As of July 31, 2001, the Dow Jones U.S. Total Market Index Fund contained 1770 stocks. As of October 31, 2001, the five largest were:

General Electric	3.43%
Exxon Mobil	2.60%
Microsoft	2.54%
Pfizer	2.52%
Citigroup	2.23%

The fund uses a replication strategy. Its expense ratio is 0.20 percent.

iShares Dow Jones U.S. Basic Materials Sector Index Fund   Symbol IYM

The Dow Jones U.S. Basic Materials Sector Index tracks the performance of U.S. companies involved in the production of:

- Aluminum
- Chemicals
- Commodities

- Chemical specialities
- Forest products
- Non-ferrous mining products
- Paper products
- Precious metals
- Steel

As of May 31, 2001, 55.82 percent of the Index, by market capitalization, was concentrated in chemicals.

On July 31, 2001, the iShares Dow Jones U.S. Basic Materials Sector Index Fund contained 68 stocks. As of October 31, 2001, the five largest were:

Dupont de Nemours	17.03%
Dow Chemical	12.77%
Alcoa	11.96%
International Paper	7.37%
Weyerhaeuser	4.58%

The fund uses representative sampling. Its expense ratio is 0.60 percent.

iShares Dow Jones U.S. Consumer Cyclical Sector Index Fund   Symbol IYC

The Dow Jones U.S. Consumer Cyclical Sector Index tracks the performance of U.S. companies involved in the following components:

- Airlines
- Auto manufacturers
- Tire and rubber manufacturers
- Auto parts
- Casinos
- Toy manufacturers
- Restaurant chains
- Home construction
- Lodging chains
- Broadline retailers
- Specialty retailers
- Footwear and clothing/fabric manufacturers

♦ Media companies, including advertising companies, entertainment and leisure companies, consumer electronics companies, broadcasters, and publishers

On July 31, 2001, the iShares Dow Jones U.S. Consumer Cyclical Sector Index Fund contained 273 stocks. As of October 31, 2001, the five largest were:

Wal-Mart	10.58%
AOL Time Warner	9.92%
Home Depot	6.62%
Viacom, Cl. B	4.19%
Disney	2.89%

The fund uses representative sampling. Its expense ratio is 0.60 percent.

iShares Dow Jones U.S. Consumer Non-Cyclical Sector Index Fund   Symbol IYC

The Dow Jones U.S. Consumer Non-Cyclical Sector Index tracks the performance of U.S. companies involved in the following components:

♦ Distillers and brewers
♦ Soft drink producers
♦ Consumer service companies
♦ Durable and nondurable household product manufacturers
♦ Cosmetic companies
♦ Food retailers
♦ Other food companies, tobacco and agricultural companies

As of May 31, 2001, 42.18 percent of the Index was concentrated in food and beverage, with 17.70 percent concentrated in household products.

On July 31, 2001, the iShares Dow Jones U.S. Consumer Non-Cyclical Sector Index Fund contained 106 stocks. As of October 31, 2001, the five largest were:

Coca-Cola	12.82%
Philip Morris	12.08%
Proctor & Gamble	11.26%

Pepsico   10.08%
Anheuser-Busch   4.42%

The fund uses representative sampling. Its expense ratio is 0.60 percent.

iShares Dow Jones U.S. Energy Sector Index Fund   Symbol IYE

The Dow Jones U.S. Energy Sector Index tracks companies involved in:

- Oil equipment and services
- Major oil companies
- Secondary oil companies
- Pipelines

As of May 31, 2001, 99.78 percent of the Index was concentrated in oil and gas.

On July 31, 2001, the iShares Dow Jones U.S. Energy Sector Fund contained 64 stocks. As of October 31, 2001, the five largest were:

Exxon Mobil   24.35%
ChevronTexaco   19.86%
Schlumberger   5.01%
Phillips Petroleum   4.25%
Conoco   4.14%

The fund uses representative sampling. Its expense ratio is 0.60 percent.

iShares Dow Jones U.S. Financial Sector Index Fund   Symbol IYF

The Dow Jones U.S. Financial Sector Index includes the following components:

- Major banks
- Regional banks
- Diversified financial companies
- Insurance companies
- Real estate companies

+ Savings and loan associations
+ Securities brokers

As of May 31, 2001, 40.10 percent of the Index was concentrated in specialty finance and 35.71 percent in banks.

On July 31, 2001, the iShares Dow Jones U.S. Financial Sector Index Fund contained 295 stocks. As of October 31, 2001, the five largest were:

Citigroup	11.69%
American Internation Group	10.19%
Bank of America	4.72%
Federal National Mortgage Assoc.	4.11%
J. P. Morgan Chase	3.49%

The fund uses representative sampling. Its expense ratio is 0.60 percent.

iShares Dow Jones U.S. Healthcare Sector Index Fund ·Symbol IYH

The Dow Jones U.S. Healthcare Sector Index includes the following components:

+ Healthcare providers
+ Biotechnology companies
+ Manufacturers of medical supplies
+ Manufacturers of advanced medical devices
+ Pharmaceuticals

As of May 31, 2001, 77.55 percent of the Index was concentrated in pharmaceuticals and biotechnology.

On July 31, 2001, the iShares Dow Jones U.S. Healthcare Sector Index Fund contained 189 stocks. As of October 31, 2001, the five largest were:

Pfizer	16.53%
Johnson & Johnson	10.90%
Merck & Co.	9.18%
Bristol-Myers Squibb	6.52%
Abbott Laboratories	4.80%

The fund uses representative sampling. Its expense ratio is 0.60 percent.

iShares Dow Jones U.S. Industrial Sector Index Fund   Symbol IYJ

The Dow Jones U.S. Industrial Sector Index includes the following components:

+ Aerospace and defense companies
+ Advanced industrial companies
+ Equipment manufacturers
+ Air freight companies
+ Building materials manufacturers
+ Packaging companies,
+ Electrical components and equipment
+ Heavy construction companies
+ Heavy machinery manufacturers
+ Industrial services companies
+ Industrial companies,
+ Marine transportation companies
+ Railroads
+ Shipbuilders
+ Trucking companies

As of May 31, 2001, 51.20 percent of the Index was "concentrated in industrial diversified," which provides plenty of leeway as to the degree of concentration.

On July 31, 2001, the iShares Dow Jones U.S. Industrial Sector Index Fund contained 233 stocks. As of October 31, 2001, the five largest were:

General Electric	24.52%
Tyco International	8.02%
Minnesota Mining & Manufacturing	4.16%
Automatic Data Processing	2.98%
Boeing	2.58%

The fund uses representative sampling. Its expense ratio is 0.60 percent.

iShares Dow Jones U.S. Technology Sector Index Fund　Symbol IYW

The Dow Jones U.S. Technology Sector Index includes companies involved in the development and production of technology products, including:

- Computer hardware and software
- Telecommunications equipment
- Microcomputer components
- Integrated computer circuits
- Office equipment utilizing technology

As of May 31, 2001, 70.03 percent of the Index was concentrated in hardware and equipment and 29.97 percent was concentrated in software.

On July 31, 2001, the iShares Dow Jones U.S. Technology Sector Index Fund contained 324 stocks. As of October 31, 2001, the five largest were:

Microsoft	16.23%
IBM	11.42%
Intel	9.96%
Cisco Systems	7.46%
Oracle	3.51%

The fund uses representative sampling. Its expense ratio is 0.60 percent.

iShares Dow Jones U.S. Telecommunications Sector Index Fund　Symbol IYZ

The Dow Jones U.S. Telecommunications Sector Index includes the following components:

- Fixed line communications
- Wireless communications

As of May 31, 2001, 91.38 percent of the Index was concentrated in fixed line communications.

On July 31, 2001, the iShares Dow Jones U.S. Telecommunications Sector Index Fund contained 43 stocks. As of October 31, 2001, the five largest were:

Verizon Communications   20.49%

SBC Communications   14.68%

AT&T   6.56%

Bellsouth   5.34%

Alltel   5.29%

The fund uses representative sampling. Its expense ratio is 0.60 percent.

iShares Dow Jones U.S. Utilities Sector Index Fund   Symbol IYU

The Dow Jones U.S. Utilities Sector Index includes:

+ Electric utilities
+ Gas utilities
+ Water utilities

As of May 31, 2001, 95.70 percent of the Index was concentrated in the electric industry.

On July 31, 2001, the iShares Dow Jones U.S. Utilities Sector Index Fund contained 83 stocks. As of October 31, 2001, the five largest were:

Duke Power   8.36%

Southern Co   4.66%

Dominion Resources   4.31%

American Electric Power   3.84%

Exelon Corporation   3.82%

The fund uses representative sampling. Its expense ratio is 0.60 percent.

iShares Dow Jones U.S. Chemicals Index Fund Symbol IYD

The Dow Jones U.S. Chemicals Index is a subset of the Dow Jones U.S. Basic Materials Sector Index. It includes:

+ Chemicals
+ Household products & wares
+ Commercial services
+ Miscellaneous manufacture

- Environmental control
- Pharmaceuticals
- Diversified metals

As of May 31, 2001, 100 percent of the Index was concentrated in chemicals.

On July 31, 2001, the iShares Dow Jones U.S. Chemicals Index Fund contained 33 stocks. As of October 31, 2001, the five largest were:

Dupont de Nemours	24.10%
Dow Chemical	17.95%
Air Products & Chemicals	5.92%
Praxair	4.91%
Avery Dennison	3.97%

The fund uses representative sampling. Its expense ratio is 0.60 percent.

iShares Dow Jones U.S. Financial Services Index Fund   Symbol IYG

The Dow Jones U.S. Financial Services Index is a subset of the Dow Jones U.S. Financial Sector Index. It includes the following components:

- Banks
- Savings and loan associations
- Specialty financial firms
- Other financial services firms

As of May 31, 2001, 53.31 percent of the Index was concentrated in specialty finance and 46.70 percent in banks.

On July 31, 2001, the iShares Dow Jones U.S. Financial Services Index Fund contained 165 stocks. As of October 31, 2001, the five largest were:

Citigroup	16.13%
Bank of America	6.51%
Federal National Mortgage Assoc.	5.67%
J. P. Morgan Chase	4.82%
Wells Fargo	4.63%

The fund uses representative sampling. Its expense ratio is 0.60 percent.

iShares Dow Jones U.S. Internet Index Fund Symbol IYV

The Dow Jones U.S. Internet Index includes the following components:

- ◆ Internet Commerce: companies that derive the majority of their revenues from providing goods and/or services through an open network, such as a web site.
- ◆ Internet Services: companies that derive the majority of their revenues from providing access to the Internet or providing services that enable people to use it.

As of May 31, 2001, 48.40 percent of the Index was concentrated in software and 22.44 percent in consumer services.

On July 31, 2001, the iShares Dow Jones U.S. Internet Index Fund contained 41 stocks. As of October 31, 2001, the five largest were:

Check Point Software	10.15%
eBay	9.96%
BEA Systems	9.68%
Verisign	8.27%
Yahoo!	7.84%

The fund uses representative sampling. Its expense ratio is 0.60 percent.

iShares Dow Jones U.S. Real Estate Index Fund Symbol IYR

The Dow Jones U.S. Real Estate Index is a subset of the Dow Jones U.S. Financial Sector Index. It includes the following components:

- ◆ Hotel companies
- ◆ Resort companies
- ◆ Real estate investment trusts that invest in apartments, office and retail properties

On July 31, 2001, the iShares Dow Jones U.S. Real Estate Index Fund contained 72 stocks. As of October 31, 2001, the five largest were:

Equity Office Properties REIT   10.43%
Equity Residential Properties REIT   6.18%
Plum Creek Timber   4.39%
Archstone-Smith REIT   3.57%
Simon Property Group REIT   3.44%

The fund uses representative sampling. Its expense ratio is 0.60 percent.

iSHARES RUSSELL INDEX FUNDS

All of the Russell indexes are based on the Russell 3000 Index, which is owned and operated by the Frank Russell Company. It consists of 3000 of the largest public companies domiciled in the United States and its territories, weighted by capitalization. The companies represent approximately 98 percent of the market capitalization of all publicly held U.S. equities. The Russell 3000 Index is adjusted for free floats. Here's an explanation:

Not all of the shares issued by a company are available to regular investors. Shares held by company founders, directors, and employee ownership plans, for example, are usually unavailable for public trading. This is especially true of smaller companies, whose closely held stocks and cross-holdings can make up 50-to-80 percent of the stock. Companies that were recently issued are especially likely to have restricted stock held by insiders and venture capitalists. To better represent the shares actually available for general purchase, Russell adjusts its 3000 Index by removing from the capitalization of each component company the stock generally unavailable for public trading. Russell wants the index to reflect only the stocks available to the public, called the "free float." If the free float of a stock is small, the impact of the price changes of that stock on the Russell 3000 Index is thereby reduced. It makes the Index more "microconsistent," which is a fancy way of saying that it's more realistic. Since all of the Russell indexes are based in one way or another on the 3000 Index, they are all thus affected.

If a relatively large company is created by a spin-off, and that company properly belongs in a Russell index, it may be added to the index right away. But most index changes, as might be caused by mergers, acquisitions, delistings, and other corporate events, are undertaken only once a year. A "snapshot" of conditions is taken as of May 31, and the index, thus reconstituted, becomes effective on

July 1. The reconstitutions are kept infrequent to reduce the costs of those institutions that utilize the indexes.

iShares Russell 3000 Index Fund   Symbol IWV

The Russell 3000 Index, as mentioned, consists of 3000 of the largest public companies domiciled in the United States and its territories, weighted by capitalization. The companies represent approximately 98 percent of the market capitalization of all publicly held U.S. equities.

On July 31, 2001, the iShares Russell 3000 Index Fund contained 2,988 stocks. On October 31, 2001, the five largest were:

General Electric	3.45%
Exxon Mobil	2.60%
Pfizer	2.53%
Microsoft	2.43%
Citigroup	2.27%

The fund uses a replication strategy. Its expense ratio is 0.20 percent.

iShares Russell 3000 Growth Index Fund
Symbol IWZ

The Russell 3000 Growth Index represents approximately half of the market capitalization of the Russell 3000 Index. It tracks the performance of those Russell 3000 Index companies that have higher price-to-book ratios and higher forecasted growth.

On July 31, 2001, the iShares Russell 3000 Growth Index Fund contained 1482 stocks. As of October 31, 2001, the five largest were:

General Electric	6.93%
Pfizer	5.07%
Microsoft	4.88%
Intel	3.15%
Wal-Mart	2.72%

The fund uses a replication strategy. Its expense ratio is 0.25 percent.

iShares Russell 3000 Value Index Fund   Symbol IWW

The Russell 3000 Value Index represents approximately half of the market capitalization of the Russell 3000 Index. It tracks the performance of those Russell 3000 Index companies that have lower price-to-book ratios and lower forecasted growth.

On July 31, 2001, the iShares Russell 3000 Value Index Fund contained 1865 stocks. As of October 31, 2001, the five largest were:

Exxon Mobil	5.17%
Citigroup	4.04%
Verizon Communications	2.56%
SBC Communications	1.89%
Bank of America	1.80%

Unlike the growth segment, the value fund uses representative sampling. Its expense ratio is 0.25 percent.

Barclays rebalances once a year. With the growth and value segments each consisting of half the capitalization of the parent, you can imagine that price changes would cause some of the stocks to bounce back and forth between the two. To counterbalance this, Barclays uses a weighted approach, whereby some of the stocks in the Russell 3000 are included in both segments. A certain percentage of a stock might be in the growth side, with the balance of the stock in the value side.

iShares Russell 2000 Index Fund   Symbol IWM

The Russell 2000 Index tracks the performance of the 2000 smallest companies in the Russell 3000 Index. Their capitalization represents approximately 8 percent of the capitalization of the Russell 3000 Index.

On July 31, 2001, the iShares Russell 2000 Index Fund contained 1996 stocks. As of October 31, 2001, the five largest were:

Triquint Semiconductor	0.32%
New York Community Bancorp	0.29%
Tyco International	0.28%
Alliant Techsystems	0.26%
Ball Corp	0.24%

The fund uses representative sampling. Its expense ratio is 0.20 percent.

iShares Russell 2000 Growth Index Fund
Symbol IWO

The Russell 2000 Growth Index represents approximately half of the market capitalization of the Russell 2000 Index. It tracks the performance of those Russell 2000 Index companies that have higher price-to-book ratios and higher forecasted growth.

On July 31, 2001, the iShares Russell 2000 Growth Index Fund contained 1287 stocks. As of October 31, 2001, the five largest were:

Triquint Semiconductor	0.68%
New York Community Bancorp	0.47%
Renal Care Group	0.45%
Lee Enterprises	0.45%
The Titan Corp	0.43%

The fund uses a replication strategy. Its expense ratio is 0.25 percent.

iShares Russell 2000 Value Index Fund   Symbol IWN

The Russell 2000 Value Index represents approximately half of the market capitalization of the Russell 2000 Index. It tracks the performance of those Russell 2000 Index companies that have lower price-to-book ratios and lower forecasted growth.

On July 31, 2001, the iShares Russell 2000 Value Index Fund contained 1328 stocks. As of October 31, 2001, the five largest were:

Ball Corp	0.47%
Dean Foods	0.44%
Tyco International	0.40%
United Dominion REIT	0.39%
Independence Community Bank	0.39%

The fund uses representative sampling. Its expense ratio is 0.25 percent.

iShares Russell 1000 Index Fund   Symbol IWB

The Russell 1000 Index tracks the performance of the 1000 largest companies in the Russell 3000 Index. Their capitalization represents approximately 92 percent of the market capitalization of the Russell 3000 Index.

On July 31, 2001, the iShares Russell 1000 Index Fund contained 998 stocks. As of October 31, 2001, the five largest were:

General Electric	3.68%
Exxon Mobil	2.77%

Pfizer	2.69%
Microsoft	2.59%
Citigroup	2.42%

The fund uses a replication strategy. Its expense ratio is 0.15 percent.

iShares Russell 1000 Growth Index Fund
Symbol IWF

The Russell 1000 Growth Index represents approximately half of the market capitalization of the Russell 1000 Index. It tracks the performance of those Russell 1000 Index companies that have higher price-to-book ratios and higher forecasted growth.

As of July 31, 2001, the iShares Russell 1000 Growth Index Fund contained 551 stocks. As of October 31, 2001, the five largest were:

General Electric	7.42%
Pfizer	5.42%
Microsoft	5.22%
Intel	3.37%
Wal-Mart	2.93%

The fund uses a replication strategy. Its expense ratio is 0.20 percent.

iShares Russell 1000 Value Index Fund   Symbol IWD

The Russell 1000 Value Index represents approximately half of the market capitalization of the Russell 1000 Index. It tracks the performance of those Russell 1000 Index companies that have lower price-to-book ratios and lower forecasted growth.

As of July 31, 2001, the iShares Russell 1000 Value Index Fund contained 719 stocks. As of October 31, 2001, the five largest were:

Exxon Mobil	5.50%
Citigroup	4.31%
Verizon Communications	2.74%
SBC Communications	2.02%
ChevronTexaco	1.92%

The fund uses a replication strategy. Its expense ratio is 0.20 percent.

iShares Russell Midcap Index Fund   Symbol IWR

The Russell MidCap Index tracks the performance of 800 smallest companies in the Russell 1000 Index. These represent approximately 19 percent of the market capitalization of all U.S. equities.

On July 31, 2001, the iShares Russell MidCap Index Fund contained 798 stocks. As of October 31, 2001, the five largest were:

USA Education	0.58%
Albertson's	0.57%
Guidant	0.56%
Conagra	0.54%
Equity Office Properties REIT	0.52%

The fund uses representative sampling. Its expense ratio is 0.20 percent.

iShares Russell Midcap Growth Index Fund
Symbol IWP

The Russell MidCap Growth Index represents approximately half of the market capitalization of the Russell Midcap Index. It tracks the performance of those Russell Midcap Index companies that have higher price-to-book ratios and higher forecasted growth.

On July 31, 2001, the iShares Russell MidCap Growth Index Fund contained 423 stocks. As of October 31, 2001, the five largest were:

USA Education	1.59%
Guidant	1.53%
Genzyme Corp, General Division	1.28%
TJX Companies	1.12%
Best Buy	1.10%

The fund uses representative sampling. Its expense ratio is 0.25 percent.

iShares Russell Midcap Value Index Fund
Symbol IWS

The Russell MidCap Vaue Index represents approximately half of the market capitalization of the Russell Midcap Index. It tracks the performance of those Russell MidCap Index companies that have lower price-to-book ratios and lower forecasted growth.

On July 31, 2001, the iShares Russell MidCap Value Index Fund contained 579 stocks. As of October 31, 2001, the five largest were:

Albertson's	0.91%
Conagra	0.86%
Equity Office Properties REIT	0.83%
Raytheon	0.78%
Avon Products	0.73%

The fund uses representative sampling. Its expense ratio is 0.25 percent.

MISCELLANEOUS iSHARES FUNDS

iShares Cohen & Steers Realty Majors Index Fund Symbol ICF

The Cohen & Steers Realty Majors Index consists of relatively large and liquid Real Estate Investment Trusts (REITs) that may benefit from future consolidation and securitization of the U.S. real estate industry. The Index is weighted according to the total market value of the outstanding shares of each REIT and is adjusted quarterly. No REIT represents more than 8 percent of the Index.

As a general rule, commercial real estate produces a relatively high level of income and is heavily mortgaged. Real estate investment trusts are required to distribute most of the net cash inflow to shareholders. Because of large writeoffs for depreciation, which reduce taxable earnings, the cash outflow to investors may be larger than the earnings. A portion of the dividends from REITs may therefore be nontaxable.

The REITs are selected on the basis of:

- Management
- Portfolio quality
- Sector and geographic diversification
- Minimum market capitalization and liquidity requirements

On July 31, 2001, the iShares Cohen & Steers Realty Majors Index Fund contained 31 stocks. As of October 31, 2001, the five largest were:

Equity Office Properties REIT	7.94%
Equity Residential Properties REIT	7.71%

Simon Property Group REIT	6.77%
Public Storage REIT	5.62%
Vornado Realty REIT	4.83%

The fund uses representative sampling. Its expense ratio is 0.35 percent.

iShares Nasdaq Biotechnology Index Fund
Symbol IBB

The Nasdaq Biotechnology Index is one of the eight subindices of the Nasdaq Composite, which measures all common stocks listed on the Nasdaq Stock Market. The Index represents companies primarily engaged in biomedical research for the development of new treatments or cures for human disease.

In the past, Amgen Inc. has weighed heavily on this index. Since the IRS code requires investment companies to limit individual positions to no more than 25 percent of the assets at the end of each calendar quarter, Barclays' fund managers limited Amgen's weighting accordingly.

On July 31, 2001, the iShares Goldman Sachs Biotechnology Index Fund contained 66 stocks. As of October 31, 2001, the five largest were:

Amgen	16.27%
Immunex	3.97%
Genzyme Corp, General Division	3.97%
Chiron	3.54%
IDEC Pharmaceuticals	3.16%

The fund uses representative sampling. Its expense ratio is 0.50 percent. This is considerably less than the average biotech mutual fund, which charges approximately 1.6 percent per year.

iShares Goldman Sachs Technology Index Fund
Symbol IGM

The Goldman Sachs Technology Index is an equity benchmark for U.S.-traded technology stocks. It includes companies in the following categories:

- Producers of sophisticated computer-related devices
- Electronics networking and Internet services
- Producers of computer and Internet software

- Consultants for information technology
- Providers of computer services

On July 31, 2001, the iShares Goldman Sachs Technology Index Fund contained 228 stocks. As of October 31, 2001, the five largest were:

Microsoft	9.72%
IBM	9.45%
Intel	8.17%
AOL Time Warner	6.62%
Cisco	6.16%

The fund uses representative sampling. Its expense ratio is 0.50 percent.

iShares Goldman Sachs Networking Index Fund Symbol IGN

The Goldman Sachs Technology Index is an equity benchmark for U.S.-traded multimedia networking stocks. It includes companies in the following categories:

- Producers of telecom equipment
- Data networking
- Wireless equipment

On July 31, 2001, the iShares Goldman Sachs Networking Index Fund contained 34 stocks. As of October 31, 2001, the five largest were:

Motorola	16.10%
Cisco	11.86%
Lucent	11.21%
Qualcomm	6.06%
JDS Uniphase	5.17%

The fund uses representative sampling. Its expense ratio is 0.50 percent.

iShares Goldman Sachs Semiconductor Index Fund   Symbol IGW

The Goldman Sachs Semiconductor Index is an equity benchmark for U.S.-traded semiconductor stocks. It includes companies in the following categories:

- Producers of capital equipment
- Manufacturers of wafers and chips

On July 31, 2001, the iShares Goldman Sachs Semiconductor Index Fund contained 54 stocks. As of October 31, 2001, the five largest were:

Motorola	10.49%
Intel	9.47%
Texas Instruments	8.59%
Applied Materials	7.36%
ST Microelectronics	7.24%

The fund uses representative sampling. Its expense ratio is 0.50 percent.

iShares Goldman Sachs Software Index Fund Symbol IGV

The Goldman Sachs Software Index is an equity benchmark for U.S.-traded software-related stocks. It includes producers of client/server, enterprise software, Internet software, PC and entertainment software.

On July 31, 2001, the iShares Goldman Sachs Software Index Fund contained 56 stocks. As of October 31, 2001, the five largest were:

Microsoft	11.15%
Oracle	11.06%
Computer Associates International	8.96%
Veritas Software	5.33%
Peoplesoft	4.40%

The fund uses representative sampling. Its expense ratio is 0.50 percent.

iShares Goldman Sachs Natural Resources Index Fund   Symbol IGE

This fund tracks stocks related to U.S. natural resources. Industries represented were:

- Extractive industries
- Energy companies

- Owners & operators of timber tracts
- Forestry services
- Producers of pulp and paper
- Owners of plantations

The five largest stocks were:

ChevronTexaco	11.87%
BP Amoco ADR (Great Britain)	8.42%
Exxon Mobil	8.15%
Royal Dutch Petroleum	7.63%
Alcoa	3.51%

The fund's expense ratio is 0.50 percent.

iSHARES MSCI SERIES

The iShares MSCI Series consists of 23 exchange-traded funds, most of which track an index of a single foreign market. The indexes used to be known as "WEBS," an acronym for World Equity Baskets.

These indexes of foreign markets are operated by Morgan Stanley Capital International, Inc. (MSCI). They're widely utilized. In North America and Asia, over 90 percent of institutional international equity assets are benchmarked to MSCI indexes.

By May 31, 2002, MSCI expects to have completed a revision of its indexes, raising from 60 percent to 85 percent the portion of each nation's total market capitalization that will be captured by the country's index.

Also, by May 31, 2002, MSCI will have adjusted all of its indexes to reflect only those shares that are available in each component's "free float." To learn what this means, please refer to the beginning of the section about Russell indexes in this appendix.

Some of the MSCI indexes are identified, in parenthesis, as being "(Free)." This has a slightly different meaning from "free float," mentioned above. "(Free)" means that the stocks chosen for that index are available for foreigners to purchase. Stocks that the government of that particular nation prevents foreigners from purchasing are excluded from the index.

As a general rule, the iShares MSCI funds use representative sampling. They do, however, "reserve the right" to use the replication method. This covers both bases.

All of these MSCI funds are listed on the American Stock Exchange. Except for the iShares MSCI EAFE Index Fund, the shares required for a creation or redemption unit are 50,000.

Some of the iShares MSCI Series Funds hold relatively few stocks. At times, one of those stocks may catch the fancy of the world's investors. In 1999 and 2000, for example, Ericsson, of Sweden, and Nortel, of Canada, grew tremendously in value, to the point where the one stock made up more than 25 percent of the value of the index. This brought the fund face to face with an important rule of the Securities and Exchange Commission. The rule is, no fund may allow a single security to constitute more than 25 percent of the total portfolio value. All iShares made available in the U.S. are subject to SEC regulations. The fund was therefore required to reduce its holding of the runaway stock, so that its value became less than 25 percent of the value of the total fund. The sales were of sufficient volume as to generate capital gains for shareholders. Moreover, the reduction of the holding caused the net asset value of the fund to diverge from the value of the index. During the fiscal year ending August 31, 2000, the Sweden Fund had a maximum tracking error of 12.50 percent, and the Canada Fund had a maximum tracking error of 13.34 percent.

Additional information about MSCI may be found in www.msci.com.

iShares MSCI EAFE Index Fund   Symbol EFA

Morgan Stanley Capital International, Inc. (MSCI) developed this index as an equity benchmark for international stock performance. Here is the list of regions from which the fund draws its stocks. You may observe from this what the acronym EAFE stands for:

- ◆ Europe
- ◆ Australasia
- ◆ The Far East

The minimum number of shares of this fund for creation and redemption, unlike the others, is not 50,000. A monumental 200,000 shares are required, currently worth approximately $25 million, or multiples thereof. It's like holding up a sign that says to arbitrageurs, "Big-Time Players Only."

On August 24, 2001, iShares MSCI EAFE Index Fund contained 778 stocks. On October 31, 2001, the five largest were:

BP Amoco	3.04%
GlaxoSmithKline	2.79%
Vodafone Group (Great Britain)	2.63%
Royal Dutch Petroleum	1.84%
Novartis	1.83%

The fund uses representative sampling. Its expense ratio is 0.35 percent.

iShares MSCI Australia Index Fund   Symbol EWA

In 2001, the five largest industries represented were:

- ◆ Banks
- ◆ Metals & Mining
- ◆ Media
- ◆ Real Estate
- ◆ Insurance

On July 31, 2001, the iShares MSCI Australia Index Fund contained 72 stocks. As of October 31, 2001, the five largest were:

National Australia Bank	10.35%
New Corporation	8.91%
Commonwealth Bank of Australia	8.10%
BHP Billiton	7.23%
Westpac Banking Corp.	5.65%

The expense ratio is 0.84 percent.

iShares MSCI Austria Index Fund   Symbol EWO

The Index consists of stocks traded primarily on the Vienna Stock Exchange. Founded in 1771, the Vienna Stock Exchange is one of the oldest in the world. In 2001, the five largest industries represented in the index were:

- ◆ Oil & Gas
- ◆ Banks

- Diversified Telecommunication Services
- Metals & Mining
- Electric Utilities

On July 31, 2001, the iShares MSCI Austria Index Fund contained 17 stocks. As of October 31, 2001, the five largest were:

OMV	15.82%
Erste Bank Der Oesterreichischen Sparkassen	15.75%
Telekom Austria	15.53%
Oster Elek	7.24
Voest-alpine Stahl	6.64%

The expense ratio is 0.84 percent.

iShares MSCI Belgium Index Fund   Symbol EWK

The Brussels Stock Exchange was founded in 1801 by Napoleonic decree. In 2001, the five largest industries represented in the index were:

- Diversified Financials
- Banks
- Electric Utilities
- Food & Drug Retailing
- Beverages

On July 31, 2001, the iShares MSCI Belgium Index Fund contained 20 stocks. As of October 31, 2001, the five largest were:

Fortis B	21.73%
Dexia	18.67%
Electrabel Befords	9.93%
Interbrew	5.31%
Delhaize-le Lion	5.02%

The expense ratio is 0.84 percent.

iShares MSCI Brazil (Free) Index Fund   Symbol EWZ

Brazil has nine stock exchanges, but the Sao Paulo Exchange is by far the most important. In 2001, the five largest industries represented in the index were:

- ◆ Oil & Gas
- ◆ Banks
- ◆ Diversifed Telecommunication Services
- ◆ Electric Utilities
- ◆ Beverages

On July 31, 2001, the iShares MSCI Brazil Index Fund contained 34 stocks. As of October 31, 2001, the five largest were:

Petroleo Brasileiro	25.27%
Cia De Bebidas Das Americas	9.07%
Banco Itau	8.74%
Tele Norte Leste Participacoes	7.01%
Vale Do Rio Doce	6.03%

The expense ratio is 0.99 percent.

iShares MSCI Canada Index Fund   Symbol EWC

Canada has five stock exchanges, with the Toronto Stock Exchange the most important. In 2001, the five largest industries represented in the index were:

- ◆ Banks
- ◆ Oil & Gas
- ◆ Insurance
- ◆ Metals & Mining
- ◆ Communications Equipment

On July 31, 2001, the iShares MSCI Canada Index Fund contained 84 stocks. As of October 31, 2001, the five largest were:

Royal Bank of Canada	6.52%
Nortel Networks	6.02%
Bank of Nova Scotia	4.49%
Manulife Financial	3.82%
Canadian Imperial Bank of Commerce	3.71%

The expense ratio is 0.84 percent.

iShares MSCI EMU Index Fund   Symbol EZU

EMU stands for the European Economic and Monetary Union. The countries represented are Austria, Belgium, Finland, France,

Germany, Ireland, Italy, the Netherlands, Portugal, and Spain. The only member of the EMU whose stocks are not represented in the index is Luxembourg. In 2001, the five largest industries in the index were:

- Banks
- Oil & Gas
- Insurance
- Diversified Telecommunication Services
- Communications Equipment

On July 31, 2001, the iShares MSCI EMU Index Fund contained 270 stocks. As of October 31, 2001, the five largest were:

Royal Dutch/Shell Group	5.53%
Nokia	5.07%
TotalFinaelf	4.51%
Telefonica	2.62%
Aentis	2.53%

The expense ratio is 0.84 percent.

iShares MSCI France Index Fund   Symbol EWQ

France has seven stock exchanges, with the Paris Exchange by far the most important. In 2001, the five largest industries represented in the index were:

- Oil & Gas
- Pharmaceuticals
- Media
- Banks
- Insurance

On July 31, 2001, the iShares MSCI France Index Fund contained 54 stocks. As of October 31, 2001, the five largest were:

TotalFinaelf	15.71%
Aventis	8.72%
Vivendi	7.20%
BNP Paribas	5.88%
Axa	5.32%

The expense ratio is 0.84 percent.

iShares MSCI Germany Index Fund   Symbol EWG

There are eight stock exchanges in Germany, with Dusseldorf and Frankfurt the most important—especially Frankfurt, which has been a financial center since the early Middle Ages. In 2001, the five largest industries represented in the index were:

- Insurance
- Automobiles
- Industrial Conglomerates
- Banks
- Chemicals

On July 31, 2001, the iShares MSCI Germany Index Fund contained 44 stocks. As of October 31, 2001, the five largest were:

Siemans	10.51%
Allianz Ag	9.20%
Deutsche Telekom	7.73%
DaimlerChrysler	7.44%
Deutsche Bank	7.16%

The expense ratio is 0.84 percent.

iShares MSCI Hong Kong Index Fund   Symbol EWH

In 2001, the five largest industries represented were:

- Real Estate
- Industrial Conglomerates
- Banks
- Electric Utilities
- Diversified Financials

On July 31, 2001, the iShares MSCI Hong Kong Index Fund contained 29 stocks. As of October 31, 2001, the five largest were:

Hutchison Whampoa	17.63%
Cheung Kong Holdings	14.14%
Hang Seng Bank	8.55%
Sun Hung Kai Properties	8.20%
Hong Kong & China Gas	5.64%

The expense ratio is 0.84 percent.

iShares MSCI Italy Index Fund   Symbol EWI

In 2001, the five largest industries represented were:

- Banks
- Oil & Gas
- Insurance
- Diversified Telecommunication Services
- Wireless Telecommunication Services

On July 31, 2001, the iShares MSCI Italy Index Fund contained 40 stocks. As of October 31, 2001, the five largest were:

ENI	16.72
Telecom Italia	13.75%
Assicurazioni Generali	12.86%
Tim	9.61%
Unicreditor Italiano	4.80%

The expense ratio is 0.84 percent.

iShares MSCI Japan Index Fund   Symbol EWJ

Japan has eight stock exchanges, with the Tokyo Stock Exchange the most important. In 2001, the five largest industries represented in the index were:

- Household Durables
- Banks
- Pharmaceuticals
- Automobiles
- Diversified Financials

On July 31, 2001, the iShares MSCI Japan Index Fund contained 290 stocks. As of October 31, 2001, the five largest were:

Toyoto Motor	4.15%
NTT Docomo	3.77%
Takeda Chemical	2.89%
Sony	2.41%
Tokyo Electric Power	2.22%

The expense ratio is 0.84 percent.

iShares MSCI Malaysia (Free) Index Fund Symbol EWM

Kuala Lumpur and Singapore formed a single exchange in the early-1930s, but separated in 1973. In 2001, the five largest industries represented in Malaysia Index were:

- Banks
- Hotels, Restaurants & Leisure
- Electric Utilities
- Diversified Telecommunication Services
- Industrial Conglomerates

On July 31, 2001, the iShares MSCI Malaysia Index Fund contained 68 stocks. As of October 31, 2001, the five largest were:

Malayan Banking	11.04%
Telekom Malaysia	8.80%
Tenaga Nasional	7.36%
Sime Darby	5.73%
Genting Berhad	4.32%

The expense ratio is 0.84 percent.

iShares MSCI Mexico (Free) Index Fund   Symbol EWW

Mexico has only one stock exchange, established in 1894 in Mexico City. In 2001, the five largest industries represented in the index were:

- Diversified Telecommunications
- Wireless Telecommunications
- Beverages
- Construction Materials
- Multiline Retail

On July 31, 2001, the iShares MSCI Mexico Index Fund contained 24 stocks. As of October 31, 2001, the five largest were:

Telefonos de Mexico, Series L	27.09%
America Movil	15.32%
Cemex SA de Cv-series	9.03%
Wal-Mart Mexico	5.45%

Kimberly-Clark de Mexico SA
de Cv Series A   5.15%

The expense ratio is 0.84 percent.

iShares MSCI Netherlands Index Fund   Symbol EWN

The Netherlands claims the honor of having the oldest established stock exchange in existence. In 1611, it introduced to investors the United East India Company, the world's first company financed by an issue of shares. In 2001, the five largest industries represented in the index were:

- Oil & Gas
- Diversified Financials
- Insurance
- Food Products
- Media

On July 31, 2001, the iShares MSCI Netherlands Index Fund contained 25 stocks. As of October 31, 2001, the five largest were:

Royal Dutch	25.11%
ING Groep	15.01%
Aegon	7.36%
Philips Electronic	5.44%
Ahold	5.33%

The expense ratio is 0.84 percent.

iShares MSCI Pacific ex-Japan Index Fund Symbol EPP

This fund tracks stocks of Australia, Hong Kong, New Zealand, and Singapore. In 2001, the largest industrial groups were:

- Banks
- Real Estate
- Metals & Mining
- Media
- Industrial Conglomerates

As of October 31, 2001, the five largest stocks were:

National Australia Bank	6.46%
News Corporation	5.59%
Commonwealth Bank of Australia	5.06%
Hutchinson Whampoa	4.75%
BHP Billiton	4.52%

The expense ratio is 0.50 percent.

iShares MSCI Singapore (Free) Index Fund Symbol EWS

The Stock Exchange of Singapore was formed in 1973, after separation from a joint stock exchange with Malaysia. In 2001, the five largest industries represented in the index were:

- Banks
- Diversified Telecommunication Services
- Real Estate
- Aerospace & Defense
- Airlines

On July 31, 2001, the iShares MSCI Singapore Index Fund contained 34 stocks. As of October 31, 2001, the five largest were:

United Overseas Bank	14.03%
DBS Group Holdings	13.01%
Singapore Telecommunications	11.90%
Oversea-Chinese Banking	11.82%
Singapore Technologies Engineering	4.38%

The expense ratio is 0.84 percent.

iShares MSCI South Korea Index Fund   Symbol EWY

The predecessor of the South Korea Stock Exchange began in 1956. The market was opened to foreign investors only in 1992. In 2001, the five largest industries represented in the index were:

- Semiconductor Equipment & Products
- Wireless Telecommunication Services
- Banks

- Metals & Mining
- Diversified Financials

On July 31, 2001, the iShares MSCI South Korea Index Fund contained 78 stocks. As of October 31, 2001, the five largest were:

Samsung Electronics	23.32%
SK Telecom	10.61%
Pohang Iron & Steel	6.84%
Kookmin Bank	5.26%
Korea Electric Power	4.60%

The expense ratio is 0.99 percent.

iShares MSCI Spain Index Fund   Symbol EWP

Spain has four stock exchanges. In 2001, the five largest industries represented in the index were:

- Banks
- Diversified Telecommunication Services
- Electric Utilities
- Media
- Oil & Gas

On July 31, 2001, the iShares MSCI Spain Index Fund contained 34 stocks. As of October 31, 2001, the five largest were:

Telefonica	22.09%
Banco Bilbao Vizcaya	14.34%
Banco Santander Central Hispano	12.81%
Iberdrola	5.28%
Endesa	4.84%

The expense ratio is 0.84 percent.

iShares MSCI Sweden Index Fund   Symbol EWD

Organized trading of securities in Sweden can be traced back to 1776. In 1999, the Stockholm Stock Exchange and the Copenhagen Stock Exchange formed a common Nordic securities market. In 2001, the five largest industries represented in the index for Sweden were:

- Communication Equipment

- Banks
- Machinery
- Diversified Telecommunication Services
- Specialty Retail

On July 31, 2001, the iShares MSCI Sweden Index Fund contained 31 stocks. As of October 31, 2001, the five largest were:

Ericsson	25.06%
Nordea	8.87%
Hennes & Mauritz	6.37%
Svenska Handelsbanken	6.21%
Sandvik	4.84%

The expense ratio is 0.84 percent.

iShares MSCI Switzerland Index Fund   Symbol EWL

Sweden has three principal stock exchanges, with the largest in Zurich. In 2001, the five largest industries represented in the index were:

- Pharmaceuticals
- Banks
- Food products
- Chemicals
- Diversified Telecommunication Services

On July 31, 2001, the iShares MSCI Switzerland Index Fund contained 38 stocks. As of October 31, 2001, the five largest were:

Novartis	21.31%
Nestle	12.28%
UBS	10.82%
Roche Holding AG—Genussein	9.58%
Swiss Re	5.29%

The expense ratio is 0.84 percent.

iShares MSCI Taiwan Index Fund   Symbol EWT

The Taiwan Stock Exchange, in Taipei, is the only stock exchange in Taiwan. In 2001, the five largest industries represented in the index were:

- Semiconductor Equipment & Products
- Computers & Peripherals
- Banks
- Electronic Equipment & Instruments
- Chemicals

On July 31, 2001, the iShares MSCI Taiwan Index Fund contained 90 stocks. As of October 31, 2001, the five largest were:

Taiwan Semiconductor	17.97%
United Microelectronics	9.65%
Asustek Computer	5.35%
Hon Hai Precision Industry	4.83%
Cathay Life Insurance	3.61%

The expense ratio is 0.99 percent.

iShares MSCI United Kingdom Index Fund
Symbol EWU

In terms of aggregate market capitalization, the United Kingdom is Europe's largest equity market. In 2001, the five largest industries represented in the index were:

- Banks
- Oil & Gas
- Pharmaceuticals
- Wireless Telecommunication Services
- Insurance

On July 31, 2001, the iShares MSCI United Kingdom Index Fund contained 122 stocks. As of October 31, 2001, the five largest were:

BP	9.05%
GlaxoSmithKline	8.58%
Vodafone	8.49%
HSBC Holdings	5.05%
AstraZeneca	4.86%

The expense ratio is 0.84 percent.

Additional Funds

The iShares Board of Directors has authorized iShares MSCI index funds to be created for the following countries:

- Greece
- Indonesia (Free)
- Portugal
- South Africa
- Thailand (Free)
- Turkey
- USA Index Funds

STATE STREET GLOBAL ADVISORS
streetTRACKS^{SM}

State Street Global Advisors is the investment management arm of State Street Corporation. Both are affiliates of the State Street Bank & Trust Company. Having helped to create Spiders back in 1993, these organizations were in at the beginning of exchange-traded funds. State Street manages over $720 billion in investment assets. It also serves as custodian for over $6 trillion in investment assets, meaning that it holds the assets and furnishes statements on behalf of mutual funds and investment advisors.

More recently, State Street Global Advisors has created 10 exchange-traded funds of its own, called the streetTRACKS^{SM} Series Trust. The 10 ETFs share the following characteristics:

- They all trade on the American Stock Exchange.
- They're organized as mutual funds.
- Like Spiders, 50,000 is the minimum number of shares permitted for creation and redemption.
- All of the stocks included in these indexes trade on the New York Stock Exchange, the American Stock Exchange, or Nasdaq.

The capitalization of some of the indexes on which these 10 funds are based are float-adjusted. "Float" means the portion of a company's stock that is commonly available for sale. Stock unlikely to be sold by a major holder or institution is excluded from the float.

Capitalization, you may recall, is the company's total market value—the current price times the total number of shares outstanding. Float-adjusted capitalization is a smaller number. It is the current price times the number of shares generally available for sale. You can readily see that the more shares held by people or institutions that have no intention of selling in the foreseeable future, the lower the float-adjusted capitalization and the less impact that stock would have on the Index.

It seems realistic for an exchange-traded fund to be based on an index that reflects shares actually available for sale. If a company has a total capitalization that's very large, but only 10 percent of the stock is generally available for sale, the stock should not dominate the index unduly.

Bill Gates owns something like 40 percent of Microsoft. He sells some of his stock from time to time and gives other stock away. But these reductions merely nibble at the edges of the tens of billions of dollars his stock is worth. At least a portion of his holding might well be adjusted out of the company's float.

The separate StreetTRACK portfolios are as follows:

streetTRACKS Fortune 500 Index Fund   Symbol FFF

"Fortune 500" is an oft-used phrase representing the largest American companies. Created by Time, Inc., the list includes the 500 largest United States companies, ranked by revenues (another name for sales). Only domestic, publicly held companies that are not majority-owned by another company qualify for inclusion.

Beginning on December 31, 1999, Time created the Fortune 500 Index, consisting of 433 out of the 500 stocks included in the Fortune 500 List. Although the Fortune 500 includes 500 stocks, the index may exclude some of them as not qualified. To be included in the index, the stock, in addition to high revenues, must also qualify as follows:

- It must trade on the NYSE, AMEX, or Nasdaq.
- The stock price must remain at $5.00 a share or above for 25 consecutive trading days preceding initial inclusion.

- The average daily trading volume must remain at 100,000 shares or more for 25 consecutive trading days prior to initial inclusion.
- The total market capitalization must have a minimum market capital equal to or in excess of $100 million at the time of inclusion.

Prudential Insurance Company was for some time a member of the Fortune 500. But until its stock began publicly trading, it was excluded from the Index.

At $11.4 trillion, the market capitalization of the stocks in the Index represent approximately 70 percent of the market valuation of all shares listed on the New York Stock Exchange, the American Stock Exchange, and the Nasdaq National Market combined. The Index is capitalization-weighted.

The stocks included in the Index are biggies. As of March 31, 2001, the average capitalization was $106 billion. The largest was $414 billion and the smallest a piddling $230 hundred million. The 10 largest stocks made up about a quarter of the value of the Index. In other words, 2.5 percent of the issues made up about 25 percent of the total value.

The sector weightings were as follows:

Financials	18.81%
Information Technology	15.44
Consumer Discretionary	14.24
Healthcare	13.91
Industrials	11.05
Consumer Staples	8.81
Telecommunication Services	6.09
Energy	5.14
Utilities	4.34
Materials	2.17
	100.00%

"Beta" is a measure of the volatility of the rates of return between one index and another. A value of less than 1 indicates a lower risk than the benchmark. Higher than 1 indicates higher risk.

The Dow Jones U.S. Total Market Index includes large, mid, and small-cap stocks to represent approximately 95 percent of the overall capitalization of the U.S. market. Assuming that the beta of this Index is 1. The beta of the Fortune 500 Index is 0.83. It is generally less risky than the total market.

The fund that tracks the Fortune 500 Index was begun on October 4, 2000. As of June 19, 2000, the Index was comprised of 433 component companies. The average capitalization of the stocks was approximately $106 billion. On September 28, 2001, the five largest stocks were:

General Electric	4.20%
Microsoft	3.12%
Exxon Mobil	3.07%
Pfizer	2.88%
WalMart	2.51%

The expense ratio is 0.20 percent.

streetTRACKS Fortune e-50 Index Fund
Symbol FEF

The Fortune e-50 Index, created on December 31, 1999, tracks 50 companies selected from the following subsectors:

E-Companies[*]

Internet Communications

Internet Hardware

Internet Software and Services

To be included in the Index, a company must generate at least 10 percent of its total revenues from Internet activities. Foreign stocks are ordinarily excluded. In addition to revenues, the standards for inclusion of stocks in the index are the same as those applying to the Fortune 500 Index Fund above.

Assuming that the beta of the Dow Jones U.S. Total Market is 1, the beta of the Fortune e-50 Index is 2.01. It is approximately twice as risky as the entire U.S. market.

[*]E-companies engage in electronic commerce, meaning that they use computer and electronic communications in business transactions. E-commerce may include the use of electronic data interchange, electronic money exchange, Internet advertising, Web sites, online databases, computer networks, and point-of-sale computer systems.

The fund that tracks the Fortune e-50 Index holds 50 stocks. As of March 31, 2001, the average capitalization was $89 billion. On September 30, 2001, the five largest stocks were:

AOL Time Warner	7.96%
Microsoft	7.62%
Cisco Systems	7.21%
Oracle	6.80%
Intel	6.72%

In case you're wondering, Amazon is included in the Fortune e-50 Index Fund. It just isn't in the top 5, or even the top 10. The expense ratio of this fund is 0.20 percent.

streetTRACKS Dow Jones US Large Cap Value Index Fund   Symbol ELV

The Dow Jones U.S. Large Cap Value Index represents the large-cap value segment of the entire U.S. equity market. Started in 1997, Dow Jones & Co. each year selects the largest common stocks by float-adjusted market capitalization to represent approximately 70 percent of the total U.S. equity market. With the large-cap universe determined, the list is then split into value and growth segments. Dow Jones uses six factors in these determinations. Exactly how the factors come into play is not disclosed:

- Price/Earnings Ratios: Stocks with relatively low PEs would be in the value portion. Those with relatively high PEs would be in the growth portion.
- Projected Earnings Growth: The faster the growth, the more likely the stocks would show up in the growth index.
- Trailing Price-Earnings Ratios
- Trailing Earnings Growth
- Price/Book Ratios: Stocks with lower P/B ratios would appear in the value segment.
- Dividend Yield: The higher the dividend yield, the more likely the stock would appear in the value index.

The sector weightings are as follows:

Financial	32.32%
Healthcare	17.51
Telecom	11.40
Consumer Non-Cyclical	9.96
Energy	8.67
Consumer Cyclical	6.05
Industrial	5.70
Technology	3.91
Basic Materials	2.82
Utilities	<u>1.66</u>
	100.00%

The Large Cap Value Index includes 103 stocks, representing 30-to-40 percent of the market values of all U.S. common stocks. On September 30, 2001, the five largest stocks were:

Exxon Mobil	6.25%
Citigroup	4.77%
Johnson & Johnson	3.81%
IBM	3.66%
SBC Communications	3.64%

Measured by market value, the turnover rate of the Index is only 2.03%.

Assuming that the Dow Jones U.S. Total Market Index has a beta of 1, the beta of the Dow Jones U.S. Large Cap Value Index is only 0.70. The volatility of the Large Cap Value Index is less than that of the market as a whole.

The fund's expense ratio is 0.20 percent.

streetTRACKS Dow Jones U.S. Large Cap Growth Index Fund   Symbol ELG

The Dow Jones U.S. Large Cap Growth Index represents the large cap growth segment of the U.S. equity market. The previous section regarding the Dow Jones U.S. Large Cap Value Index describes that Dow Jones & Co. creates a float-adjusted index of large-cap stocks representing approximately 70 percent of the total U.S. equity market. From this universe, the company uses six factors to identify which are value and which are growth stocks. As explained more fully in the previous section, the six factors are P/E, projected earnings growth, trailing P/E, trailing earnings growth, P/B, and dividend yield. The average capitalization of the stocks in the Index is $159.7 billion.

The sector weightings are as follows:

Technology	32.42%
Consumer Staples	15.96%
Healthcare	15.22%
Capital Goods	13.75%
Consumer Cyclical	10.38%
Financials	8.38%
Communication Services	3.04%
Transportation	0.38%
Energy	0.31%
	99.84%

The fund has all 76 stocks included in the index. On September 30, 2001, the five largest were:

General Electric	13.75%
Pfizer	9.44%
Microsoft	8.77%
American International Group	7.57%
AOL Time Warner	5.25%

Measured by market value, the turnover rate of the Index is 3.79 percent.

Assuming that the Dow Jones U.S. Total Market Index has a beta of 1, the beta of the Dow Jones U.S. Large Cap Growth Index is 1.31. The volatility of the Large Cap Value Index is greater than that of the market as a whole.

The expense ratio is 0.20 percent.

streetTRACKS Dow Jones U.S. Small Cap Value Index Fund   Symbol DSV

The Small Cap Value Index represents the small cap value segment of the U.S. equity market. To create a small-cap universe, Dow Jones selects small U.S. publicly held stocks by float-adjusted market capitalization representing approximately 8–10 percent of the total U.S. equity market. It then uses a proprietary six-factor model to identify the value stocks with that universe. The six factors are as follows:

+ Price/Earnings Ratios: Stocks with relatively low PEs would be in the value portion. Those with relatively high PEs would be in the growth portion.
+ Projected Earnings Growth: The faster the growth, the more likely the stocks would show up in the growth index.
+ Trailing Price-Earnings Ratios
+ Trailing Earnings Growth
+ Price/Book Ratios: Stocks with lower P/B ratios would appear in the value segment.
+ Dividend Yield: The higher the dividend yield, the more likely the stock would appear in the value index.

The sector weightings are as follows:

Financial	42.65%
Industrial	15.34
Consumer Cyclical	12.85
Utilities	9.23
Basic Materials	6.33
Consumer Non-Cyclical	6.11
Energy	3.05
Healthcare	3.02
Technology	1.42
Telecom	0.00
	100.00%

The Small Cap Value Index contains 337 stocks, whose capitalizations range from $6.4 billion to $81.7 million. The fund holds all of them. On September 30, 2001, the five largest stocks were:

Old Republic International	0.95%
Astoria Financial	0.94%
Heller Financial	0.81%

Sovereign Bancorp   0.77%

Tyson Foods   0.75%

Measured by market value, the turnover rate of the Index is a relatively high 10.37 percent.

Assuming that the Dow Jones U.S. Total Market Index has a beta of 1, the beta of the Dow Jones U.S. Small Cap Value Index is 0.53. The volatility of the Small Cap Value Index is considerably less than that of the market as a whole.

The expense ratio is 0.25 percent, which is slightly higher than the expense ratio of the large cap funds. This is understandable, given numerous small stocks and a high turnover.

streetTRACKS Dow Jones U.S. Small Cap Growth Index   Symbol DSG

The Small Cap Growth Index represents the small cap growth segment of the U.S. equity market. To create a small-cap universe, Dow Jones selects small U.S. publicly held stocks by float-adjusted market capitalization representing approximately 8-to-10 percent of the total U.S. equity market. It then uses the proprietary six-factor model to identify the value stocks with that universe. The six factors are explained in the previous section concerning the Small Cap Value Index, namely P/E, projected earnings growth, trailing P/E, trailing earnings growth, P/B, and dividend yield.

The sector weightings are as follows:

Healthcare	21.67%
Consumer Cyclical	18.66
Technology	18.23
Industrial	16.51
Energy	7.98
Financial	6.67
Consumer Non-Cyclical	6.04
Telecom	3.29
Basic Materials	0.95
	100.00%

The capitalizations of the stocks in the Small Cap Growth Index range from $4.1 billion to $28.8 million. The fund contains all

432 of the stocks included in the index. On September 30, 2001, the five largest were:

Cytyc Corp	1.40%
Oxford Health Plans	1.28%
Expeditores Int'l Wash	1.12%
Trigon Healthcare	1.09%
Newport News Shipbuilding	1.08%

Measured by market value, the turnover rate of the Index is 8.11 percent.

Assuming that the Dow Jones U.S. Total Market Index has a beta of 1, the beta of the Dow Jones U.S. Small Cap Growth Index is 1.28. The volatility of the Small Cap Growth is only slightly greater than that of the market as a whole.

The expense ratio is 0.25 percent.

streetTRACKS Dow Jones Global Titans Index Fund   Symbol DGT

The Global Titans Index represents 50 of the world's largest global companies. To create the Global Titan universe, Dow Jones each year lists the world's largest stocks by market capitalization. It then uses a proprietary model based on capitalization, assets, book value, sales, and net profits to select 50 large multinationals—"the biggest of the big and the bluest of the blue."

The sector weightings are as follows:

Financial	20.46%
Technology	18.38
Telecom	14.84
Energy	13.21
Consumer Cyclical	9.58
Healthcare	8.52
Industrial	8.00
Consumer Non-Cyclical	7.02
	100.00%

The fund includes all 50 of the stock included in the index. On September 30, 2001, the five largest were:

General Electric	6.86%
Exxon Mobil	5.07%

Pfizer	4.71%
Microsoft	4.38%
Citigroup	3.88%

Measured by market value, the turnover rate of the Index is 7.00 percent.

Assuming that the Dow Jones U.S. Total Market Index has a beta of 1, the beta of the Dow Jones Global Titans Index is moderately less, 0.77. The average capitalization is $165.6 billion.

The expense ratio is 0.50 percent.

streetTRACKS Morgan Stanley High-Technology 35 Index Fund   Symbol MTK

The Morgan Stanley High-Tech 35 Index is composed of electronics-based technology companies, drawn from the following subsectors:

Internet & PC Software	19.46%
Semiconductors	16.95
Networking & Telecom Equipment	14.62
Server & Enterprise Hardware	12.11
Enterprise/Technical Software	11.88
PC Hardware & Data Storage	10.12
Computer & Business Services	7.75
Semiconductor Capital Equipment	4.40
Electronics Manufacturing Services	2.71
	100.00%

The fund holds all 35 of the stocks included in the index. On September 30, 2001, the five largest were:

Electronic Arts	6.77%
Electronic Data Systems, New	5.95%
Computer Associates	5.93%
IBM	5.90%
Microsoft	5.83%

Assuming that the Dow Jones U.S. Total Market Index has a beta of 1, the beta of the Morgan Stanley High-Tech 35 Index is considerably greater: 1.70. The average capitalization is $57.17 billion.

The expense ratio is 0.50 percent.

streetTRACKS Morgan Stanley Internet Index Fund (Symbol MII)

The Morgan Stanley Internet Index is composed of U.S. companies that are driving the growth of the Internet. The selection of companies is based on current leadership, business momentum, market share, and market capitalization. The sector weightings are as follows:

Internet Vertical Portals	21.86%
Internet Infrastructure	20.98
Internet Portals	14.24
Internet Infrastructure Services	13.52
Internet B2B Software*	12.34
Internet Commerce	7.07
Internet Consulting & Services	6.38
B2B Commerce	3.62
	100.00%

On September 28, 2001, the five largest stocks were:

Web MD	4.40%
Inktomi	4.19%
Worldcom, Inc./Worldcom Group	4.18%
Schwab Charles	4.16%
Oracle	4.02%

Assuming that the Dow Jones U.S. Total Market Index has a beta of 1, the beta of the Morgan Stanley Internet Index is more than twice as great: 2.28.

The expense ratio is 0.50 percent.

streetTRACKS Wilshire REIT Index Fund
Symbol RWR

Wilshire Associates has created a representation of the U.S. Real Estate Investment Trust market. The Index is comprised of companies whose charters are the equity ownership and operation of commercial real estate. In other words, no real estate developers. The stocks are selected for their market capitalization, source of revenue, and liquidity. Wilshire generally rebalances monthly.

---

* B2B means business-to-business.

The sector weightings are as follows:

Apartment	22.92%
Office	22.35
Diversified	13.53
Regional Retail	10.64
Local Retail	8.92
Industrial	8.19
Hotels	6.66
Storage	4.36
Manufactured Homes	1.71
Factory Outlets	0.72
	100.00%

On September 28, 2001, the five largest stocks were:

Equity Office Partnerships	10.72%
Equity Residential Partnerships	6.35%
Simon Partnership Group	3.73%
Public Storage	3.08%
Prologis Trust	2.98%

Assuming that the Dow Jones U.S. Total Market Index has a beta of 1, the beta of the Wilshire REIT Index is far less: 0.24.

The expense ratio is 0.25 percent.

Select Sector SPDRs

Nine exchange-traded funds track various sectors of the Standard & Poor's 500 Index. They were created by State Street Global Advisors, a division of the State Street Bank and Trust Company. Every company in each of the sectors is a component of the Standard & Poor's 500 Index. Taken together, the companies included in the nine sector indexes comprise all of the companies in the S&P 500.

As explained in Chapter 4, SPDRs, otherwise known as Spiders, track the entire S&P 500 Index. Sharing in the famous name, the various sectors of that Index are collectively referred to as Select Sector SPDR Funds.

With the consultation of Standard & Poor's, each stock in the S&P 500 Index is assigned to a sector by the Index Compilation Agent, this being Merrill Lynch & Company, Inc. The allocation is made on the basis of:

- The sales and earnings composition of each company
- The sensitivity of the stock price and business results to factors that affect other companies in each Select Sector Index

The composition of each Select Sector Index is then determined by the Index Services Group of the American Stock Exchange, using a methodology called modified market capitalization. This design ensures that the capitalization of each stock in an index is proportionate to the capitalization of all the stocks in the index. Under certain conditions, however, the number of shares of a component stock within its index may be adjusted to conform to Internal Revenue Code requirements.

For regulatory purposes, the funds are treated as index funds. All of them are traded on the American Stock Exchange. The minimum number of shares acceptable for creation or redemption is 50,000. The expense ratio of each fund is 0.28 percent.

The separate funds are as follows:

The Basic Industries Select Sector SPDR Fund Symbol XLB

The Basic Industries Select Sector Index includes:

- Integrated steel products
- Chemicals
- Fibers
- Paper
- Gold

As of September 30, 2001, the fund contained 41 stocks whose weight within the S&P 500 Index was approximately 2.66 percent. The five stocks largest were:

DuPont de Nemours	15.57%
Dow Chemical	11.70%
Alcoa	10.65%
International Paper	6.69%
Weyerhaeuser	4.17%

The Consumer Services Select Sector SPDR Fund   Symbol XLV

The Consumer Services Select Sector Index includes:

- Entertainment
- Publishing
- Prepared foods
- Medical services
- Lodging
- Gaming

As of September 30, 2001, the fund contained 44 stocks, whose weight in the S&P 500 Index was approximately 4.97 percent. The five largest stocks were:

Viacom	12.93%
Disney	8.19%
Comcast	5.90%
HCA	5.18%
Clear Channel Communications	5.03%

The Consumer Staples Select Sector SPDR Fund Symbol XLP

The Consumer Staples Select Sector Index includes:

- Cosmetics and personal care
- Pharmaceuticals
- Soft drinks
- Tobacco and food products

As of September 30, 2001, the fund contained 69 stocks whose weight within the S&P 500 Index was approximately 23.65 percent. The five largest stocks were:

Pfizer	11.32%
Johnson & Johnson	7.50%
Merck & Co.	6.83%
Coca Cola	5.21%
Bristol Myers Squibb	4.83%

The Cyclical/Transportation Select Sector SPDR Fund   Symbol XLY

The Cyclical/Transportation Select Sector Index includes:

- Building materials
- Retailers
- Appliances
- Housewares
- Air transportation
- Automotive manufacturing
- Shipping and trucking

As of September 30, 2001, the fund contained 66 stocks whose weight within the S&P 500 Index was approximately 7.79 percent. The five largest stocks were:

WalMart	22.45%
Home Depot	12.12%
Ford	4.34%
Target	3.97%
Lowes Cos	3.43%

The Energy Select Sector SPDR Fund Symbol XLE

The Energy Select Sector Index includes:

- Crude oil
- Natural gas
- Drilling
- Other energy-related services

As of September 30, 2001, the fund contained 30 stocks whose weight within the S&P 500 Index was approximately 7.45 percent. The five largest stocks were:

Exxon Mobil	23.25%
Royal Dutch Petroleum	15.85%
Chevon	8.25%

Texaco	4.56%
Schlumberger	4.30%

The Financial Select Sector SPDR Fund
Symbol XLF

The Financial Select Sector Index includes a wide array of diversified financial services whose business lines include:

- Investment management
- Commercial and business banking

As of September 30, 2001, the fund contained 70 stocks whose weight within the S&P 500 Index was approximately 18.29 percent. The five largest stocks were:

American International Group	11.81%
Citigroup	11.76%
Bank of America	5.41%
Federal National Mortgage Assoc.	4.63%
Wells Fargo	4.41%

The Industrial Select Sector SPDR Fund
Symbol XLI

The Industrial Select Sector Index includes companies involved in the development and production of industrial products, including:

- Electrical equipment
- Construction equipment
- Waste management services
- Industrial machinery

As of September 30, 2001, the fund contained 44 stocks whose weight within the S&P 500 Index was approximately 8.52 percent. The five stocks largest were:

General Electric	17.19%
Tyco International	11.86%
Minnesota Mining & Mfg	5.23%
Waste Management	4.59%
Emerson Electric	3.72%

The Technology Select Sector SPDR Fund Symbol XLK

The Technology Select Sector Index includes:

- Defense
- Telecommunications equipment
- Microcomputer components
- Integrated computer circuits
- Process monitoring systems

As of September 30, 2001, the fund contained 97 stocks whose weight within the S&P 500 Index was approximately 19.52 percent. The five stocks largest were:

Microsoft	14.87%
IBM	8.66%
AOL Time Warner	7.96%
Intel	7.42%
Cisco Systems	4.81%

The Utilities Select Sector SPDR Fund   Symbol XLU

The Utilities Select Sector Index includes:

- Communication services
- Electrical power providers
- Natural gas distributors

As of September 30, 2001, the fund contained 39 stocks whose weight within the S&P 500 Index was approximately 7.16 percent. The five stocks largest were:

SBC Communications	21.20%
Verizon Communications	19.55%
Duke Energy	4.51%
Bellsouth	3.61%
American Electric Power	2.79%

THE VANGUARD GROUP

VIPERS

Not to be outdone by those scary insects, SPIDERS, the Vanguard Group designed and operates an exchange-traded fund called Vanguard Index Participation Equity Receipts, whose acronym is even scarier: VIPERS.

VIPERS differ markedly from most other exchange-traded funds, in that they do not track an index. Instead, they track a particular index mutual fund, one of Vanguard's very own, in fact—the Vanguard Total Stock Market Index Fund. That fund, in turn, tracks the Wilshire 5000 Equity Index. The prospectus refers to this exchange-traded fund as "Vanguard Total Stock Market VIPERS, a class of shares issued by Vanguard Total Stock Market Index Fund."

Developed by Wilshire Associates, the Wilshire 5000 Index is capitalization based. It tracks all of the stocks regularly traded on the New York Stock Exchange, the American Stock Exchange, and the Nasdaq over-the-counter market. The Index may have started out tracking 5000 stocks. But as the U.S. stock market has grown, so has the number of issues included in the Index. The Wilshire 5000 Index now consists of something like 7000 stocks and represents approximately 98 percent of the market value of all publicly-held U.S. equities. It is the broadest index of U.S. stocks.

If the Vanguard Total Stock Market Index Fund bought every one of the 7000 stocks, this would be a whale of a portfolio. Thousands of small companies would be represented by relatively few shares, making the transaction costs prohibitive. (Vanguard can trade without commisions, but don't forget the spreads between the bid and asked prices. As a general rule, the smaller and less actively traded the stock, the wider the percentage spread.) Vanguard therefore uses a sampling technique to reduce the holdings in its fund to a little over 3000 stocks.

The sampling technique is nicely explained in the prospectus as follows:

Vanguard "uses a sophisticated computer program to select a representative sample of stocks from the Wilshire 5000 Index that resembles the Index in terms of industry weightings, market capitalization, price/earnings ratio, dividend yield, and other characteristics. For instance, if 10 percent of the Wilshire 5000 Index were made up of utility stocks, the Vanguard Total Stock Market Index Fund would invest about 10 percent of its assets in some—but not all—of those utility stocks. The particular utility stocks selected by the Fund, as a group, would have investment characteristics similar to those of the utility stocks in the Index."

The technique seems to have worked. Vanguard started its Total Stock Market Index Fund on April 27, 1992. From then until December 31, 2000, the average total return of the Wilshire 5000 Index was 16.01 percent per year. (Average annual returns are always higher than compounded annual returns. See the following sidebar.) The annual expense ratio of the Vanguard Total Stock Market Index Fund is 0.20 percent a year. One would expect that, from April 27, 1992 to December 31, 2000, the fund would achieve average annual returns of 15.81 percent (16.01 less 0.20). But the fund actually performed slightly better. Its average annual return was 15.83 percent a year, rather than 15.81 percent. Vanguard's sampling, and perhaps other techniques as well, seem imbued with magic.

Average Returns Versus Compounded Returns

Let's say a fund achieves the following returns:

Year 1	12%
Year 2	-2%
Year 3	20%

The *average* return (total the three returns and divide by 3) is 10 percent per year.

Okay, let's assume that you place $1000 in a fund and draw out nothing until the end of the third year. We disregard taxes:

For Each Year

	Beginning Balance	Percentage Return	Dollar Gain	Ending Balance
Year 1	1,000.00	+12%	120.00	1,120.00
Year 2	1,120.00*	-2%	-22.40	1,097.60
Year 3	1,097.60*	+20%	219.52	1,317.12

*Each year's beginning balance is the same as the previous year's ending balance.

You invest $1000. Exactly three years later, you draw out $1317.12. Based on those beginning and ending values over three years, your trusty calculator informs you that the compound return is 9.62 percent (9.616293953 percent, to be exact).

Here's how the investment would work if the annual returns were the same each year, with a constant return of 9.616293953 percent:

	The Year's Beginning Balance	The Year's Percentage Return	The Year's Dollar Gain	The Year's Ending Balance
Year 1	1,000.00	+9.62%	96.16	1,096.16
Year 2	1,096.16	+9.62%	105.41	1,201.57
Year 3	1,201.57	+9.62%	115.55	1,317.12

Note that the beginning and ending balances ($1000 and $1317.12) are the same as before. But because we converted varying annual returns into a single, constant return, all the other balances are different.

This contrived, constant return is in fact the compound return, 9.62 percent. It is lower than the 10.00-percent average return. (If you're a stickler for good grammar, you'd say "compounded return," but in this regard, we'll follow the crowd.)

Why is the compound return lower than the average return? Because compound returns are cumulative. Each year's return builds on that of the previous year. Average returns are not cumulative. They get less bang for the buck. Therefore, an average return must be higher to achieve the same final result.

The greater the variation in the returns, the more the average return exceeds the compound return. Likewise, the greater the number of years, the more the average return exceeds the compound return.

Banks generally quote compound returns on their deposits, probably because their returns vary relatively little from year to year. A moralist would say that mutual funds ought to quote compound returns because those are the more realistic. But mutual funds are hotly competitive. If a few quote average returns, the others feel called upon to do the same. The Securities and Exchange Commission does not insist on the use of compound returns. Maybe this is because it doesn't understand the issues as well as you do.)

VIPERS hold the very same 3000-plus stocks that the Vanguard Total Stock Market Index Fund holds. Jack Bogle, the widely respected founder and former Chief Executive of Vanguard, protested mightily about the company's development of VIPERS. Bogle is a buy-and-hold man. He feels moral indignation about creating investment vehicles that encourage people to trade and thereby lose their money. But he lost the battle. His successors in Vanguard's management are buy-and-hold people too. They want investors to buy and hold the Vanguard mutual funds, reducing the costs of those funds all the more. The creation of VIPERS, they felt, would draw the short-term traders away from Vanguard mutual funds and into one or more exchange-traded funds that are based on those mutual funds. With those, they could trade to their heart's content.

Vanguard was the first to base an ETF on a mutual fund. It will probably not be the last.

Secondary trading of VIPERS takes place on the American Stock Exchange. Creation Units for VIPERS consist of 50,000 shares or multiples thereof.

The expense ratio for the Vanguard Total Stock Market Index Fund, as mentioned, is 0.20 percent. This is marvelously low, in my opinion. But the expense ratio for VIPERS is even lower: 0.15 percent.

The five largest stocks are:

General Electric	3.22%
Microsoft	2.40%
Exxon Mobil	2.37%
Pfizer	2.20%
Wal-Mart	1.93%

MERRILL LYNCH & COMPANY

HOLDRs

Merrill Lynch & Co., Inc. offers a series of investments that go by the name of HOLDRs. As you can see, the word has a paucity of vowels. The derivation stems from **HOL**ding Company **D**epositary Receipt**S**, which is a stretch. Other ETFs, Spiders and VIPERS in particular, are given the names of intimidating and belligerent creatures. Merrill Lynch lost a splendid opportunity to differeniate itself. It could have displayed its soft, cuddly side by calling its ETFs PANDAS.

At the beginning of this book, I pointed out that 199 equity ETFs are being traded throughout the world, not counting 17 quasi-ETFs. The "quasi's" are HOLDRs. Whether they're exchange-traded funds or not, HOLDRs certainly are different, as follows:

1. They're not mutual funds. Instead, shareholders are treated as owners of the underlying securities.
2. HOLDRs do not track indexes.
3. They are never rebalanced.
4. Under some circumstances, the short sellers of HOLDRs are subject to the uptick rule.

We take up these differences in more detail:

1. Each of the 17 HOLDRs represents a specific industry. In each case, the shareholder is treated as owner of the underlying securities. If you own 100 Pharmaceutical HOLDRs, for example, you are treated as owner of all 18 of the pharmaceutical stocks it includes. You may vote the company shares at the annual meetings or by signing proxies. (Imagine trying to do this with the thousands of issues in the iShares Russell 3000 Index Fund!)

The minimum number of shares of HOLDRs required for creation and redemption is not 50,000 shares or more, as is true with other ETFs. With HOLDRs, a simple 100 shares will do. Even you and I can be arbitrageurs.

To acquire HOLDRs, you can provide the trustee with the underlying stocks and receive HOLDRs in exchange. Or you can buy HOLDRs in the secondary market. (Secondary trading of HOLDRs takes place on the American Stock Exchange.) To redeem HOLDRs, you can furnish the shares to the trustee and receive the underlying shares of stock in exchange. Or you can sell your HOLDRs in the secondary market. With 100 shares the minimum, you can do all this with relatively little money.

But in the secondary market, you may not buy or sell just one share of HOLDRs, as you can with other ETFs. You may trade only in round lots or multiples thereof. Whether you're creating, redeeming, or trading shares on the AMEX, 80 shares won't do; 1010 shares won't do. Only 100 shares, 30,800 shares, or any multiple of 100 are permitted.

To undertake the creation or redemption of HOLDR shares, the trustee charges $10 per round lot. If you present the proper number of underlying shares in exchange for 100 HOLDRs, you pay a fee of $10. If you present 1200 HOLDRs in exchange for underlying shares, you pay $120.

Being treated as owner of the underlying securities opens up a tax advantage that is unavailable to the owners of other ETFs. Let's say you own Pharmaceutical HOLDRs. Assume that each of the 18 stocks included therein are priced at $100 a share. Also assume that half of the shares subsequently rise to $150 a share and the other half fall to $50 a share. The HOLDRs price remains the same. But if you redeem the HOLDRs and take delivery of the underlying shares, you could sell the nine stocks that have fallen in price and take tax losses on those. This might improve your after-tax results.

With other ETFs, you are not treated as owner of the underlying stocks. Unless you're an Authorized Participant, you cannot take delivery of the underlying shares and sell just some of the issues. HOLDRs are unique.

Despite my admiration of Merrill Lynch for designing these intriguing products, I caution you to count all of the costs in connection with any investment approach that involves trading. To carry the above examples a few steps further, let's assume that you redeem 10 round lots of Pharmaceutical HOLDRs—1000 shares.

You pay trustee's fees of $100. You then sell the nine losing stocks at $50 commissions each, for a total of $450. (You need not make such trades through Merrill Lynch, but that firm's minimum commission is $50.) Let's say you're selling 900 shares, total, on which one-half of the bid-asked spread is $.10 a share. That's $90. The total cost ($100 + $450 + $90) comes to $640.

Now, if you need the tax losses, you must have made sales that realized gains during the same year. To come out to a nice round number, I reverse two of the numbers in the $640 costs above and assume that the transaction costs on these other sales total $460. The sum of $640 and $460 means you're paying $1100 in transaction costs you would have avoided had you sold neither the gains nor the losses. At 8 percent (the rate I presume to be after tax), $1100 compounds in 30 years to $11,000. Many trading accounts these days are set up with no commissions. But they do have extra fees, ranging from .8 percent to 1.5 percent. These fees, too, have deleterious effect in the long term.

Although any Merrill Lynch broker worth his salt would disagree, I stoutly maintain that the majority of short-term sales prove in the long term to be mistakes. The eventual loss of wealth stems from many causes: appreciation not attained because of having sold the securities too soon, commissions, spreads, and other transaction costs, taxes paid unnecessarily on premature sales, and the extra costs of preparing more-complicated tax returns. Over 30 years, the compounding of these costs, just from the two sets of trades I describe for that one year, could easily amount to tens of thousands of dollars. Most trading meets the broker's needs, not yours.

2. For most exchange-traded funds, the choice of stocks is determined by the index being followed—an index that is owned and operated by a company other than the company that's running the fund. An index created by the Frank Russell Company, for example, becomes the basis for several iShares ETFs set up by Barclays Global Investors. The operators of most indexes have standards for choosing and replacing the component stocks. For example, the stocks must be traded on an exchange or on Nasdaq, the price must be above a certain level, the company must not be in bankruptcy, etc. If a stock fails to meet the standards, it is removed from the index and replaced with another.

With HOLDRs, the component shares of stocks are selected, not by another company, but by Merrill Lynch itself. As a general rule, it chooses those stocks that have the largest market capitalization for the industry.

3. Except for unavoidable changes, such as mergers or bankruptcies, the portfolios remain fixed as to the choice of stocks and the number of shares. HOLDRs are not rebalanced, an approach that reduces turnover and possibly unfavorable tax consequences. The fortunes of the various companies change, of course. As some of them thrive, their prices rise. Since the number of shares remains fixed, the price increases cause those stocks to have greater impact on the HOLDR of which they're a part. As other companies falter, their prices fall, causing their impact to lessen.

4. With regard to short selling, the Securities and Exchange Commission generally exempts ETFs from the uptick rule (see Chapter 9 for an explanation). The SEC exempts HOLDRs from the rule, too, except when the number of securities in a particular HOLDR falls to 15 or below. Bankruptcy has in fact caused the number of securities in Internet HOLDRs to fall to 15. Unless you're functioning as an arbitrageur (arbitrage is never subject to the uptick rule), a short sale of Internet HOLDRs can be executed only on an uptick.

I now leave the differences between HOLDRs and other ETFs and take up an aspect of the HOLDRs prospectus that seemed, on the face of it, to be impractical. A verbal inquiry assured me, however, that the matter is being dealt with realistically. I share the issue with you in case you concern yourself with minutia.

If you struggle through a HOLDRs prospectus, you will find the following turgid prose:

> "In the event of a stock split, reverse stock split, or other distribution by the issuer of an underlying security that results in a fractional share becoming represented by a round-lot of . . . HOLDRs, the trust may require a minimum of more than one round-lot of . . . HOLDRs for an issuance so that the trust will always receive whole share amounts for issuance of . . . HOLDRs."

On October 4, 2001, the Internet Architecture HOLDRs, for example, had 21 stock components. As you will see in the listing of shares below, three of them were as follows:

Roxio	0.1646 shares
Veritas Software	0.893
McDATA Corporation	0.58891

To make all three of these fractional shares come out to whole shares, the minimum number of shares of the HOLDRs acceptable for creation or redemption would have to be increased by thousands and possibly millions of times. This of course is unrealistic. In practice, however, you may indeed create or redeem HOLDRs in 100-share lots even though the underlying stocks include fractional shares. The trustee simply adjusts the transaction by the payment or receipt of petty cash.

Here are the number of shares that stand behind a round lot for each HOLDRs:

Biotech HOLDRS   Fund Symbol BBH
This is the list of stocks as of October 4, 2001:

Name	No. of Shares
Affymetrix	4
Alkermes	4
Amgen	46
Applear Corp-Applied Celera Genomics Group	4

Name	No. of Shares
Applera Corp - Applied Biosystems Group	18
Biogen	13
Chiron	16
Enzon	3
Genentech	44
Genzyme	14
Gilead Science	8
Human Genome Sciences	8
ICOS	4
IDEC Pharmaceuticals	12
Immunex	42
MedImmune	15
Millennium Pharma	12
QLT	5
Sepracor	6
Shire Pharmaceuticals	6.8271

Broadband HOLDRS   Fund Symbol BDH

This is the list of stocks as of October 4, 2001:

Name	No. of Shares
Applied Micro Circuits	2
Broadcom	2
CIENA	2
Conexant Systems	2
Converse Technology	2
Copper Mountain Networks	1
Corning	9
JDS Uniphase	11.8
Lucent Technologies	29
Motorola	18
Next Level Communications	1
Nortel Networks	28
PMC-Sierra	1

Name	No. of Shares
QUALCOMM	8
RF Micro Devices	2
Scientific-Atlanta	2
Sycamore Networks	3
Tellabs	4
Terayon Communications	2

B2B Internet HOLDRS   Fund Symbol BHH

During the bear market of 2000 and 2001, this index was hit hard, as you can well imagine. This is the list of stocks as of November 8, 2001:

Name	No. of Shares
Agile Software	4
Ariba	14
CheckFree Corp.	4
Commerce One	12
FreeMarkets	3
ImageX.com	1
Internet Capital Group	15
Pegasus Solutions	2
PurchasePro	4
QRS Corp	1
Retek	3
Scient Corp.	6.2
SciQuest.com	3
Ventro Corp	2
VerticalNet	6

Europe 2001 HOLDRS   Fund Symbol EKH

This is the list of stocks as of October 4, 2001:

Name	No. of Shares
AEGON N.V.	5
Alcatel - ADS	3

Name	No. of Shares
Amdocs Ltd.	3
ARM Holdings ADR	8
ASM International	13
ASM Lithography Holding	7
AstraZeneca ADR	4
Autonomy Corp. ADR	6
Aventis S.A. ADR	2
AXA Financial ADR	6
Bookham Technology ADR	12
BP Amoco ADR	4
Business Objects ADR	4.5
Cable & Wireless ADR	4
DaimlerChrysler	4
Deutsche Telekom ADR	5
Diageo ADR	5
Elan Corp ADR	4
Ericsson L.M. ADR	16
GlaxoSmithKline ADR	6
Infineon Technologies ADR	5
ING Group ADR	4
IONA Technologies ADR	3
Jazztel ADR	11
KNPQuest ADR	8
Koninklijke Phlps Elc ADR	5
Millicom International Celluar	6
Nokia Corp. ADR	5
Novartis ADR	5
QIAGEN	6
Repsoi YPF ADR	11
Royal Dutch Petroleum	3
Ryanair Holdings ADR	4
SAP ADR	4
Scottish Power Group ADR	7

Name	No. of Shares
Serono ADR	9
Shire Pharmaceuticals ADR	4
Smartforce Public ADR	6
Sonera Group ADR	9
STMicroelectronics	4
Telefonica ADR	3.06
Terra Networks ADR	15
Total Fina Elf ADR	3
UBS	3
Unilever N.V. NY Shares	3
United Pan-Europe Comm ADR	13
Vivendi Univl S.A. Adr	3
Vodafone Airtouch ADR	6
WPP Group ADR	3

Internet HOLDRS   Fund Symbol HHH

This is the list of stocks as of October 31, 2001:

Name	No. of Shares
Amazon.com	18
Ameritrade Holding	9
AOL Time Warner	42
CMGI	10
CNET Networks	4
DoubleClick	4
E*Trade Group	12
EarthLink Network	6.23
eBay	12
Inktomi	6
Network Associates	7
Priceline.Com	7
RealNetworks	8
Yahoo	26

Internet Architecture HOLDRS   Fund Symbol IAH

This is the list of stocks as of October 4, 2001:

Name	No. of Shares
3Com Corp.	3
Adaptec	1
Apple Computer	2
CIENA Corp.	2
Cisco	26
Compaq Computer	13
Dell Computer	19
EMC	16
Extreme Networks	2
Foundry Networks	1
Gateway	2
Hewlett-Packard	14
IBM	13
Juniper Networks	2
McDATA Corp	0.58891
Network Appliance	2
Roxio	0.1646
Sun Microsystems	25
Sycamore Networks	2
Unisys Corp.	2
Veritas Software	0.893

Internet Infrastructure HOLDRS   Fund Symbol IIH

This is the list of stocks as of October 17, 2001:

Name	No. of Shares
Akamai Technologies	3
BEA Systems	10
BroadVision	9
E.piphany	1.5

Name	No. of Shares
InfoSpace.com	8
Inktomi Corp.	4
InterNAP Network Services	5
Kana Communications	2
NaviSite	2
Openwave Systems	3.221
Portal Software	6
RealNetworks	6
Usinternetworking	3
VeriSign	6.15
Vignette Corp.	6
Vitria Technology	4

Market 2000+HOLDRS   Fund Symbol MKH

This is the list of stocks as of November 19, 2001:

Name	No. of Shares
America Online (AOL)	6
American International Goup	2
Astrazeneca	4
AT&T Wireless Services	1.9308
AT&T	6
Avaya	0.3333
BellSouth	5
BP Amoco	3
Bristol-Meyers Squibb	3
BT Group	2
Cisco	3
Citigroup	3
Coca-Cola	3
Dell Computer	5
Deutsche Telekom	5
Eli Lilly	2
EMC	2

Name	No. of Shares
Exxon Mobil	4
France Telecom	2
General Electric	3
Glaxo Smith Kline	3
Hewlett-Packard	4
Home Depot	4
IBM	2
Intel	2
JDS Uniphase	2
Johnson & Johnson	4
LM Ericsson	9
Lucent Technologies	4
McDATA Corp.	0.073614
Merck & Co.	3
Microsoft	3
mmp2	2
Morgan Stanley Dean Witter	2
Nokia	4
Nortel Networks	2
Novartis	5
NTT Data	3
Oracle	4
Pfizer	4
Qwest Communications	4
Royal Dutch Petroleum	3
SBC Communications	4
Sony Corp	2
Sun Microsystems	4
Syngenta	1.038609
Texas Instruments	3
Total Fina Elf	2
Toyota Motor	2
Verizon Communications	4

Name	No. of Shares
Viacom	3
Vodafone Airtouch	5
Wal-Mart Stores	4
WorldCom – MCI Group	0.2
WorldCom	5

Oil Service HOLDRS   Fund Symbol OIH

This is the list of stocks as of November 26, 2001:

Name	No. of Shares
Baker Huges	21
BBJ Services	14
Cooper Cameron	4
Diamond Offshore Drilling	11
Ensco International	11
Global Santa Fe	19.975
Grant Prideco	9
Halliburton	22
Hanover Compressor	5
Nabors Industries	12
National-Oil Well	7
Noble Drilling	11
Rowan Cos	8
Schlumberger	11
Smith International	4
Tidewater	5
Transocean Sedco Forex	18
Weatherford Intl	9

Pharmaceutical HOLDRS   Fund Symbol PPH

This is the list of stocks as of October 4, 2001:

Name	No. of Shares
Abbot Laboratories	14
Allergan	1

Name	No. of Shares
American Home Products	12
Andrx Corp.	2
Biovail Corp. International	4
Bristol-Meyers Squibb	18
Eli Lilly	10
Forest Laboratories	2
ICN Pharmaceuticals	1
IVAX Corp.	1.875
Johnson & Johnson	26
King Pharmaceuticals	4.25
Merck & Co	22
Mylan Laboratories	1
Pfizer	58
Schering-Plough	14
Watson Pharmaceuticals	1
Zimmer Holdings	1.8

Regional Bank HOLDRS   Fund Symbol RKH

This is the list of stocks as of December 4, 2001:

Name	No. of Shares
AmSouth Bancorp	12
Bank One	33
BB&T Corp.	10
Comerica	5
Fifth Third Bancorp	13.5
FleetBoston Financial	25
KeyCorp	13
Marshall & Ilsley	3
Mellon Financial	14
National City	18
Northern Trust	7
PNC Financial Services	9
State Street Corp.	10
SunTrust Banks	9

Name	No. of Shares
Synovus Financial	8
U.S. Bancorp	56.83
Wachovia	41
Wells Fargo	24

Retail HOLDRS   Fund Symbol RTH
This is the list of stocks as of October 4, 2001:

Name	No. of Shares
Albertsons	8
Amazon.Com	7
Best Buy	4
Costco	8
CVS	7
Federated Departments Stores	4
GAP	16
Home Depot	40
Kohls	6
Kroger	15
Limited	8
Lowe's	14
May Departments Stores	6
Radioshack	3
Safeway	9
Sears Roebuck	6
Target	16
TJX Companies	5
Walgreen	19
Wal-Mart	36

Semiconductor HOLDRS   Fund Symbol SMH
This is the list of stocks as of October 4, 2001:

Name	No. of Shares
Advanced Micro Devices	4
Altera Corp	6

Name	No. of Shares
Amkor Technology	2
Analog Devices	6
Applied Materials	13
Atmel Corp.	8
Broadcom	2
Intel	30
KLA-Tencor	3
Linear Technology	5
LSI Logic	5
Maxim Integrated Products	5
Micron Technology	9
National Semiconductor	3
Novellus Systems	2
SanDisk Corp.	1
Teradyne	3
Texas Instruments	22
Vitesse Semiconductor	3
Xilinx	5

Software HOLDRS   Fund Symbol SWH

This is the list of stocks as of October 4, 2001:

Name	No. of Shares
12 Technologies	10
Adobe Systems	6
BMC Software	7
Check Point Software	6
Computer Associates	17
Intuit	6
Macromedia	1
Mercury Interactive	2
Micromuse	2
Microsoft	15
Nuance Communications	1
Openwave Systems	2

Name	No. of Shares
Oracle	24
PeopleSoft	8
Rational Software	5
SAP ADR	16
Sapient	3
Siebel Systems	8
Tibco Software	5
Veritas Software	7

Telecom HOLDRS   Fund Symbol TTH

This is the list of stocks as of October 4, 2001:

Name	No. of Shares
ALLTEL	2
AT&T Wireless	8.045
AT&T	25
BCE	5
BellSouth	15
Broadwing	2
Century Telephone	1
Global Crossing	6
Level 3 Communications	3
MCI	0.88
McLeodUSA	3
Nextel	6
NTL	1.25
Qwest Communications	12.9173
SBC Communications	27
Sprint Corp. (FON Group)	6
Sprint Corp. (PCS Group)	6
Telephone & Data Systems	1
Verizon Communications	21.76
WorldCom	22

Utilities HOLDRS   Fund Symbol UTH
This is the list of stocks as of October 4, 2001:

Name	No. of Shares
American Electric Power	14
Consolidated Edison	9
Dominion Resources	11
Duke Energy	30
Dynegy	12
Edison International	15
El Paso Energy	10
Enron	12
Entergy	10
Exelon	15
FirstEnergy	10
FPL Group	8
Mirant Corp.	11.5308
PG&E	17
Progress Energy	7
Public Services Enterprise	10
Reliant Energy	13
Southern Company	29
TXU Corp.	12
The Williams Companies	20

Wireless HOLDRS   Fund Symbol WMH
This is the list of stocks as of October 4, 2001:

Name	No. of Shares
Aether Systems	1
AT&T Wireless Group	40
Crown Castle International	4
Deutsche Telecom ADS	18.4841
LM Ericsson	74
Motorola	41

Name	No. of Shares
Netro Corp.	1
Nextel Communications	16
Nextel Partners	4
Nokia	23
Qualcomm	13
Research in Motion	2
RF Micro Devices	4
SK Telecom	17
Sprint Corp. (PCS Group)	21
Telesp Celular Participaceos	3
United States Cellular	1
Verizon	17
Vodafone Group	21
Western Wireless	2

NUVEEN INVESTMENTS

Bond ETFs

Exchange-traded funds came into being to enable people to trade aggregations of stocks. ETF sponsors have concentrated almost exclusively on stocks. In connection with trading, one thinks of stocks, not bonds. But the total value of fixed-income securities rivals the total value of stocks. On this score alone, it's inappropriate to leave bond ETFs out in the cold.

I do not expect bond ETFs to outnumber stock ETFs, of course. Bond prices tend to be homogeneous. The prices of individual issues of bonds do not generally go their own way, hither and yon, as do the prices of individual stocks. Therefore, the need for indexing—the idea of spreading risk among many issues—is less important for bonds than it is for stocks. But so far, there is not a single full-fledged exchange-traded bond fund—a noticeable omission.

Nuveen

The Chicago firm of Nuveen Investments has been offering the public municipal bond investments for more than a century.

The firm currently offers 79 municipal bond investments it refers to as "Closed-End Exchange-Traded Funds." In truth, the investments are more similar to closed-end funds than they are to ETFs. But they're close enough to ETFs to be included in this book.

The funds do not track indexes of bonds. Instead, each one purchases and manages an aggregation of bonds largely from a particular state, rendering most of the income federally and state tax free for the residents of that state. The investor does not acquire the bonds directly; he or she acquires common stock, preferred stock, or both.

The common stock represent shares of a closed-end fund, which, as mentioned, purchases long-term municipal bonds mostly from a particular state or the municipalities of that state. Some of the shares trade on the NYSE; others trade on the AMEX.

The preferred shares are cash-equivalent investments earning tax-free dividends whose interest rates are reset every seven days. The price per share is always $25,000. But the proceeds from the preferred share offerings are not actually used to acquire short-term, seven-day notes from municipalities. The proceeds are used to instead purchase long-term municipal bonds. (Bear with me; when we cross the finish line, all will be clear.)

The money for the long-term munis acquired by the preferred stock is borrowed. In particular, approximately half of the market value of the assets held in the common stock's portfolio is borrowed. The borrowed money is used to purchase additional long-term municipal bonds. If a fund's common stock portfolio is worth $10 million, for example, approximately $5 million in preferred shares would be created, making a combined portfolio of $15 million. The $5 million borrowed represents one-third of the $15 million combined total.

As mentioned, the preferred shares pay dividends tied to short-term interest rates, not long-term rates. Every seven days, the interest rate payable on the preferred shares is set in accordance with an auction among a group of dealers. At each auction, the prices of the preferred shares, as mentioned, remain constant at $25,000 a share. The auction determines the rate of interest to be earned on all such shares for the ensuing seven days. Rates on the preferred shares are competitively determined. They follow the overall trends of the short-term, tax-free interest rate market.

Usually, the interest earned on the long-term municipal bonds purchased with the borrowed money exceeds the seven-day interest payable on the preferred. In this case, the excess interest is added to the payouts received by the shareholders of the common stock.

If the yield curve inverts and the interest payable to preferred shareholders exceeds the interest earned on the long-term bonds, the amounts needed to fulfill the seven-day requirements reduce the amount that would otherwise be payable to the common shareholders. The preferred shares have priority. Any income available is first used to pay the preferred share dividends. Whatever's left goes to the common shareholders.

This means that the risk created by the borrowing is absorbed entirely by the common shares. The prices of the common shares therefore fluctuate more widely than the prices of municipal bonds in general. If long-term interest rates should rise, the price of the common would fall significantly. If long-term rates should fall, the price would rise significantly. The price of the preferred shares remain constant. All of the changes in value are absorbed by the common.

Under normal circumstances, the payouts to shareholders of the common stock are modestly higher than the rate an investor could obtain from purchasing a long-term municipal bond of his state. Not a third higher, however, as the one-third leverage might indicate. The interest paid on the borrowing and the modest fees charged by Nuveen draw down the net interest to something like 10 percent higher than the interest from an individually acquired, long-term bond.

At this writing, for example, one of the Nuveen offerings has a net asset value of $13.82. The common is selling at a premium—$15.17. A recent month's payout was $0.069 per share. Multiplying this number by 12 determines an estimated annual figure—$0.828 per share. Dividing that number by the current price of $15.17 determines a yield of 5.5 percent.

At the same time, the interest yield on individually acquired, long-term bonds is approximately 5.0 percent. The 5.5-percent yield on the common stock is higher than those of individual bonds, but only modestly so.

Holders of the common stock are given the option of reinvesting the income distributions. If the common is selling at a premium over the net asset value, Nuveen creates additional shares to meet the demand, just as would an open-end fund. But if the common is selling at a discount, additional shares are purchased in the secondary market, as is true of a closed-end fund. In either case, the price is pulled in the direction of the net asset value.

Although I am impressed with the inventiveness of these investments, I do not favor the preferred stocks. I believe that long-term investment money should be invested at risk and remain at risk, not parked in seven-day cash equivalents. The right time to invest long-term funds is always when you get the money. Money needed in the short-term should be invested in a short-term vehicle whose maturity matches the time when the money needs to be spent. If a tuition expense, for example, comes due in two years, buy a two-year bond. The interest thereof is likely to be higher than that of a seven-day security. Now if the yield curve happens to be inverted and seven-day interest is higher than long-term interest, by all means, use the shorter-term vehicle.

The common stocks of these Nuveen investments interest me more than the preferreds. The interest of approximately 5.5 percent, almost completely tax free, is attractive. But nevertheless, I cannot recommend these shares because I feel that the risk is too high.

I happen to believe that interest rates will continue down in the next decade or two. If I'm correct, the increase in the price of the common will add to the total return.

But the borrowing is disturbingly high. As explained, if the portfolio held by the common stock is $10 million, $5 million is borrowed, and $15 million of municipals becomes the aggregate holdings. The Nuveen prospectus emphasizes that the borrowing is only one-third of the aggregate, which is true. But the borrowing is one-half the original $10 million, and this is the material ratio. For example, if you place $10,000 into a margin account, you can borrow $5000—that's the maximum you're permitted to borrow for stock investments. You acquire $15,000 of stocks. Even though the borrowing is only a third of the aggregate, you are nevertheless borrowing half of your $10,000 equity. Your risk is increased by half.

I would expect the volatility of the Nuveen common shares to be about half again greater than that of unleveraged municipal bonds. But the increase in the interest rate is only about 10 percent higher than that of unleveraged municipal bonds. You're receiving about 10 percent more income to compensate for 50 percent more risk. If my expectations about generally lower interest rates turn out to be wrong, you'd lose considerably more than you'd gain.

If the increase in risk were only 25 or 30 percent, I could be persuaded. But 50 percent is too much.

I don't care for municipal bonds bought outright, either. Almost all of them can be called by the municipality 10 years after the bond is issued. The call price is generally 2 percent above par. If interest rates rise, the price of the bond is allowed to fall all it pleases. In such circumstances, the municipality would be foolish to call the bond because the money would have to be borrowed again at higher rates than the municipality is already paying.

But if interest rates fall, ahhh, the municipality sells a new issue of bonds at a lower rate and uses the proceeds to call the old bond, paying it off early. The called bond pays 2 percent more than it would at maturity, but the municipality saves considerably more than 2 percent in interest costs. When interest rates fall, everyone knows that the bond will be called in the tenth year. Therefore, the price of the bond doesn't rise much above the call price.

The bond price can fall all it wants. But any increase is limited. Heads, the municipality wins. Tails, you lose, or at least you don't gain much. My objection to municipal bond calls applies to the Nuveen common stock too. Tax-free interest is enticing. If you're in a very high bracket, individual municipal bond holdings may serve you well (although, to be sure, the interest is subject to the alternate minimum tax). But in general, most people are unaware of the unfavorable aspect of calls on municipal bonds.

For the 20-percent fixed-income share of your asset allocation portfolio, I would stick to the Vanguard Long-Term Bond Index Fund. If you possibly can, buy it within a tax-sheltered vehicle, preferably a Roth IRA.

RYAN LABS, INC.

Taxable Bonds

In the presentation of asset allocation in Chapter 11, I recommend that 20 percent of a portfolio be placed in an index fund of long-term bonds. I noted ruefully that no ETFs has been created for such securities.

Ryan Labs, a New York City quantitative research firm specializing in the mathematics of indexing, expects to rectify this situation. Early in 2002, the firm will offer exchange-traded funds of U. S. Treasuries. Called Fixed Income Trust Receipts, or FITRs, they will initially be offered in four maturities, 1, 2, 5, and 10 years in length. The maturities will be kept nearly constant. On the 5-year maturities, for example, the bonds will be rolled over every month so that the maturity remains within a month of the 5-year target. On the 10-year maturities, the bonds will be rolled over every three months. Nuveen would be the sponsor, with the Bank of New York as custodian.

On an individual bond, the interest payments remain fixed, but the price of the bond fluctuates. The longer the maturity, the greater the fluctuation of price. Nearly all of the risk of a bond stems from the changes in price.

With Ryan Labs' Fixed Income Trust Receipts (FITRs), the risk of price fluctuation is almost entirely removed. The principal value stays roughly the same.

With *individual* bonds, the interest payments remain constant. With FITRs, they do not. FITRs do not own a single bond until maturity; they own an aggregation of bonds. More importantly, every month or so, the bonds are sold and new ones of slightly longer maturity are acquired. This keeps the maturities roughly constant.

Let's say the date is September 1. The FITRs of 5-year maturity acquires Treasuries maturing on September 15, 5 years hence. The maturity is 5 years, 1/2 month. The interest yield is 4.3 percent.

A month later, on October 1, the maturity on these bonds has changed to 4 years, 11 1/2 months. The bonds are sold. New ones are acquired that come due on October 15, 5 years hence. The new bonds again have maturities of 5 years, 1/2 month.

But let's assume that, during the 1-month interim from September 1 to October 1, interest rates on 5-year Treasuries decline from 4.3 percent to 4.2 percent. The yield on the FITRs also declines by 10 basis points.

With individual bonds, the interest payments stay constant and the price fluctuates. FITRs are quite the opposite: The interest payments fluctuate, and the price remains roughly constant. With individual bonds, the total return from the interest and the fluctuations of principal vary quite considerably (although not as much as the variation of returns from stocks). When inflation increases and interest rates pick up, the total returns from bonds can fall substantially, even resulting in net losses for the year. When inflation diminishes and interest rates fall, the bond investors enjoy substantial returns. The total returns of Ryan Lab's FITRs fluctuate less than those of individual bonds.

After completing its Treasury offerings, Ryan expects to offer FITRs of corporate bonds, structured similarly.

Over the long term, the total returns from bonds are less than those of stocks. If risk were not a factor, there would be no reason to invest in bonds at all. Just jump on those bucking-bronco stocks and let 'em have their head. But for most people, risk is indeed a factor. To mitigate it, one acquires different types of investments whose return fluctuations differ in timing from one another. When the prices of one are falling, the prices of another might be rising. By diversifying to bonds, as well as to REITs, the long-term returns for the entire portfolio are almost the same, if not equal to, the returns from the stocks alone. But the fluctuations of returns are significantly reduced.

For the 20-percent portion of your asset allocation program, I continue to favor the Vanguard Long-Term Bond Index Fund. I have tremendous respect for the innovative work of Ryan Labs. But I believe that its Fixed Income Trust Receipts are not appropriate, for two reasons:

1. The longest maturity is only 10 years. I prefer 20-year bonds, whose yields are higher.

2. Most importantly, the FITRs are structured to minimize the fluctuation of total returns. As mentioned, most of the risk of holding individual bonds emanates from changes in the bond's price. FITRs remove most of that risk. But in an asset allocation program, I want the returns of bonds to fluctuate. As long as the timing of those fluctuations differ from those of stocks, the more fluctuation, the better.

BARCLAYS GLOBAL INVESTMENTS

Exchange-Traded Funds Offered in Other Nations

Like the British Empire of old, sponsors want the sun never to set on exchange-traded funds. They are busy setting up ETFs in other nations, with the goal of 24-hour global trading. But they can't just say to the investors of other nations, "Here are funds that trade in the United States, including the MSCI variety. Why don't you buy those?"

No, that won't do. Each nation has rules and regulators of its own. Governments are prone to restrict the purchase of foreign securities by their citizens. They also tend to restrict the purchase of the nation's securities by foreigners. Limitations are particularly likely on purchases of foreign securities within tax-advantaged retirement programs. (Such restrictions apply also in the United States.) All such restrictions are self-defeating. Thus far, my opinion on the matter has not be solicited.

More information about these ETFs may be found on www.ishares.net.

Canada

Barclays Global Investors offers 11 Canadian exchange-traded funds, all of which trade on the Toronto Stock Exchange. The first 8 involve Canadian stocks and are based on indexes created jointly by Standard & Poor's and the Toronto Stock Exchange:

- i60: Tracks an index of 60 large-cap Canadian stocks listed on the Toronto Stock Exchange. These stocks are included in the S&P Global 1200 Index. .――
- i60C: The same 60 stocks. But here, the capitalization of no single stock is permitted to exceed 10 percent of the entire portfolio.
- iEnergy
- iFinance
- iGold
- iIT: Canadian companies engaged in information technology.
- iMidCap

100 Percent RSP Eligible Foreign Equity

- i500R
- iIntR

"RSP" stands for Retirement Savings Plans, which are tax-advantaged. Canadian citizens may not acquire non-Canadian securities within Retirement Savings Plans. Yet both of these exchange-traded funds qualify for RSP purchase, even though they provide exposure to non-Canadian stocks. Tricky. Here's how the task is accomplished:

i500R places half of the money in S&P 500 *futures* contracts and the other half in Canadian money market funds. By acquiring futures contracts instead of direct investments in the U.S. stocks, the fund eases its way around the Canadian limitation.

Ordinarily, futures contracts are highly leveraged. You can, if you wish, place, say, $100,000 with a futures broker and acquire a S&P 500 futures contract that provides exposure to $1 million or more of risk. But you're not required to put down so little money. You can invest the entire $1 million if you like. This would provide one-to-one leverage, just as if you acquired a mutual fund or bought stocks in a nonmargined brokerage account. This is what Barclays does with its futures purchases—no leverage. But Barclays may not feel it can go whole-hog into S&P stocks. Putting half the money into Canadian money market funds assuages Canadian officials and perhaps Canadian investors as well.

iIntR places half the money into futures contracts based on the MSCI EAFE index (again, nonleveraged) and the other half into Canadian money market funds.

Fixed Income Exchange-Traded Funds

- iG5
- iG10

The iG5 acquires five-year Government of Canada bonds. Once a year, it sells its holdings, which by then are four-year bonds, and reinvests in five-year bonds. The ETF never matures. With only a modest fluctuation, the maturity of roughly five-years remains constant.

The iG10 does the same, except that it acquires 10-year Government of Canada bonds, not five, and rolls them over once a year. These investments are similar to those of Ryan Labs.

Additional information about Canadian iShares can be found at www.units.net.

iShares United Kingdom

The following offerings of Barclays Global Investors are available to British citizens and are traded on the London Stock Exchange:

- iShares iFTSE 100: The "Footsie 100," consisting of 100 stocks, is the most widely followed index of the London stock market.
- iShares iFTSE TMT: "TMT" stands for technology, media and telecoms.
- iShares FTSE Euro 100: This tracks 100 leading European stocks
- iShares iBloomberg Technology
- iShares iBloomberg Pharmas
- iShares iBloomberg Telecoms
- iShares iBloomberg Financials
- iShares iBloomberg Cyclicals
- iShares iBloomberg Resources
- iShares iBloomberg Industrials
- iShares iBloomberg Staples

iShares Holland

The following offerings are available to Dutch citizens and are traded on the Amsterdam Stock Exchange. The prospectus is written in Dutch:

- iShares iBloomberg Technology
- iShares iBloomberg Pharmas
- iShares iBloomberg Telecoms
- iShares iBloomberg Financials
- iShares iBloomberg Cyclicals
- iShares iBloomberg Resources
- iShares iBloomberg Industrials
- iShares iBloomberg Staples
- iShares FTSE Euro 100 (excludes UK stocks)
- iShares FTSE Eurotop 100 (includes UK stocks)

Hong Kong

State Street Global Advisors sponsors an exchange-traded fund that tracks the Hang Seng Index and trades on the Hong Kong Exchange. If you read Chinese, you'll find information about it in www.hkex.com.

Others to Follow

In September 2000, the Amsterdam, Brussels, and Paris stock exchanges merged to form Euronext. The American Stock Exchange will be Euronext's exclusive U.S. partner for cross-trading Euronext's recently launched exchange-traded funds.

In partnership with Euronext, the Directory of Lyxor Asset Management has created three exchange-traded funds, called Trackers, as follows:

- Master Share CAC 40: The CAC 40 is the principal index of the Paris Stock Exchange.
- Dow Jones STOXXSM 50.
- Dow Jones EURO STOXXSM 50.

Regarding the two Dow Jones indexes, "EURO" stands for the European Monetary Union, which excludes Denmark, Norway, Sweden, Switzerland, and the United Kingdom. STOXXSM is the broader index, and EURO STOXXSM is the narrower.

At this writing, the American Stock Exchange is setting up a joint venture to offer one or more ETFs to the citizens of Singapore.

INDEX

adjusted gross income (AGI) and IRA, 157
American Stock Exchange, 49, 50, 66, 71–72,
    119, 178, 182–186, 282
Ameritrade, 132
Amsterdam Stock Exchange, 282
analysis of market
    fundamental, 102–108
    technical, 108–111, 114
annuities, variable vs. fixed, 161–164
appreciation, stock, 7
arbitrage, 56–59
    HOLDRs and, 257
asset allocation, 133–154
at the money option, 126
AT&T, 19
Australia Index Fund, 221
Austria Index Fund, 221–222
authorized participants
    capital gains taxes and, 69–71
    spiders and, 48–49, 51–53, 55, 57
average returns vs. compounded returns,
    252–253
averages, 14–18

B2B Internet HOLDR, 260
banking, 143
Barclay Global Investments, 50, 178,
    186–187, 278–282
Barron's, 15
Basic Industries Select Sector SPDR Fund, 246
basis points, 60
bear markets, 25, 38, 75–76, 106, 129, 134–135
Belgium Index Fund, 222
Biggs, Barton, 106–107
Biotech HOLDR, 258–259
Biotechnology Index Fund, 216
Bloomberg electronic order system, 125
Bogle Financial Markets Research Center, 33
Bogle, John (Vanguard), 33, 111
bonds, 5, 6, 10–11, 137, 138, 139, 147–148, 178
    ETFs as, 272
    fixed income trust receipts (FITRs),
        277–278
    interest rate vs. interest payment in,
        10–11, 147–148
    maturity date of, 10

bonds (*Cont.*):
    taxable, 276–278
    unit investment trusts (UIT) and, 23
book value, 9
Boston Stock Exchange, 119
bottoms, 119
Brazil (Free) Index Fund, 222–223
Breeden, Richard, 50
broad U.S. stock market ETFs, 49
Broadband HOLDR, 250–260
brokerage accounts, 87–95
    brokers of, 88–89
    capital gains taxes and, 92–93
    cash on deposit in, 94
    clearing function for, 95
    dates (trade date, ex date, etc.), 94–95
    discount firms for, 88
    insurance for, 95
    online firms for, 88
    opening, 91–94, 91
    ownership of account (joint, right of
        survivorship, etc.), 92–93
    statements, 95
    traditional firms for, 88
    trust accounts in, 93–94
brokers, 88–89, 131
Brussels Stock Exchange, 282
bull markets, 38, 106, 129, 134–135
buy stop orders, 124
buying ETFs, 2, 87, 118–119

call rates, 97–98
calls, 99–100, 125–128
Canada ETFs, 279–280
Canada Index fund, 223
cancel former order (CFO), 124
cancel orders (CXL), 124
capital, making income from, 152–154
capital gains, 5, 68–70, 92–93
    in kind trading and, 69–71
    index funds and, 40, 41–42
    long- vs. short-term, 7–8
    mutual funds and, 27–28, 35–37
    mutual funds vs. ETFs, 172, 173
    spiders and, 51–53
    stepped up basis in, 92–93

ABOUT THE AUTHOR

Archie M. Richards Jr., CFP, was a stockbroker and financial planner for more than 25 years. The author of numerous articles on investing, he writes the nationally syndicated column, "Richards on Money Matters." His web site is www.ArchieRichards.com.